MOSES SHEPPARD

Quaker Philanthropist of Baltimore

Baltimore in 1850
"A brave, gay town, bustling and full of business."
Courtesy, The Cator Collection, Enoch Pratt Library, Baltimore.

Moses Sheppard

MOSES SHEPPARD

Quaker Philanthropist of Baltimore

BLISS FORBUSH, LL D
President, Sheppard and Enoch Pratt Hospital,
Headmaster Emeritus, Baltimore Friends
School

With a Foreword by

KENNETH O. WALKER, PhD
Professor and Chairman, Department of History,
Goucher College, Towson, Maryland

J. B. LIPPINCOTT COMPANY
Philadelphia & Toronto

TO
"Wendy"

Foreword

THIS BIOGRAPHY of Moses Sheppard materially enriches our knowledge of American history in the first half of the nineteenth century. It constitutes the first full-length study of an important but little known Baltimore Quaker. The story is atypical in the sense that the Quakers are a minority who participate in the mainstream of American life yet maintain their separate identity. The story of Moses Sheppard, from his uncertain beginnings to successful businessman to his latter years as a philanthropist, has a Horatio Alger quality about it. His activities, caught up as they were in Quaker concerns, seem to be a microcosm of the history of the early years of the republic.

The story has an unsensational beginning. A youth of humble origins came to Baltimore in 1793 to seek his fortune, and entered into general merchandising with John Mitchell. He prospered so spectacularly that by the 1820's he was able to retire, then to devote his attention to various directorships, to properties, leisure and study and, above all, to humanitarian concerns.

Moses Sheppard was an active member of the Society of Friends throughout his life. This fact profoundly affected his attitude toward business and personal asso-

9

ciations, and explained his dedication to the improvement of his community and particularly of the lot of the poor, the unfortunate and the underprivileged.

Vividly protrayed is the Quakers' concern of the early nineteenth century for the plight of the Negro and their continuing efforts to mitigate the evils of slavery. Moses Sheppard was very active in the affairs of the African Colonization Society, created for the purpose of removing the free colored population to Africa with their own consent. He was equally occupied with the plight of the Indian. The continuing and often ingenious efforts on the part of the Quakers to assist these unfortunate indigenous Americans met with steady frustration and failure—an illuminating though depressing tale.

These are but two of the many areas of humanitarian activity to which Moses Sheppard devoted himself. In his latter years he gave much thought to the way his fortune might best be utilized for the betterment of society. Increasingly he became interested in the problem of the mentally ill. He was particularly distressed by evidences of mental deterioration among the aged— perhaps a foreshadowing of modern geriatrics. Thus his last years were largely devoted to the conception and formation of an institution that would properly care for the mentally ill. The Sheppard and Enoch Pratt Hospital was the result. The funds provided at his death established the institution on a firm and unusual financial foundation. This prestigious and distinctive mental hospital stands as a permanent monument to the memory of Moses Sheppard, Baltimore Quaker philanthropist.

Dr. Forbush is uniquely qualified to write Sheppard's biography. He is himself an eminent Quaker whose

previous study of Elias Hicks testifies to his extensive
knowledge of Quaker history. In recent years he has
been Chairman of the Board of Trustees of the Sheppard
and Enoch Pratt Hospital, which post he took upon his
retirement as Headmaster of the Baltimore Friends
School. Living on the hospital grounds and in constant
communication with patients and staff, Dr. Forbush has
been able to absorb the tradition and appreciate the
present benefits of the bequest of Moses Sheppard.

The author had available to him an extensive collection of source materials, which until the present have
been relatively unexplored. He has mastered these
sources critically, imaginatively and sympathetically.

The resultant biography clearly depicts the life of an
admirable Quaker. It shows how greatly we as a people
are indebted to our Quaker minority. Their material
contribution to our society has been significant; their
moral and spiritual contribution has been even greater.
This biography makes understandable the fact that as
Americans we respect the Quakers so much. Perhaps it
also explains why most of us emulate them so little.

KENNETH O. WALKER
Professor and Chairman, Department of History
Goucher College

March 29, 1968

11

Preface

BALTIMORE was an unincorporated town of less than 20,000 inhabitants when Moses Sheppard made it his home. He was active in its commercial life as merchant, investor, and corporation director. He lived to see Baltimore become, for a brief period, the second largest city in the United States and, in his last years, grow to nearly 200,000. This bustling seaport possessed the fastest seagoing vessel of its day, the Baltimore Clipper, and projected the first commercial railroad in the country. The mixed population of Baltimore was strident, energetic, and boisterous; in Sheppard's lifetime it was dubbed "Mob Town." Like his philanthropically minded contemporaries, George Peabody and Johns Hopkins, Moses Sheppard began his business career in the provision business, and, like these two younger men, later moved into more important commercial ventures.

Moses Sheppard was a member of the Society of Friends and, as a Quaker, maintained the Society's testimonies of reverence for God and respect for the divine spark dwelling in all men. As outlined in the *Book of Discipline,* Quaker business men were urged to be industrious, frugal, simple in their living, and honest in their dealings. They were cautioned to avoid hazardous

12

enterprises, to honor their contracts, and to avoid entering into commercial affairs "beyond their ability to manage." [1] Men of ability, following these precepts, usually accumulated wealth and occupied positions of trust in the community.

Quakers were also reminded by their Discipline that "mercy, compassion and charity are eminently required by the gospel." [2] This advice Moses Sheppard never forgot. Late in life he wrote: "I am and long have been a drudge for the old and infirm, and the young and helpless, but if this had not occured something worse might have happened. . . . In every situation in which I find myself placed I conceive it to be my duty to do the best I can and leave or meet the consequences with all the magnanimity I can." [3] Having little formal education, he financed boys and girls, mostly orphans, in boarding schools, believing the best gift to any youth was education. On one occasion he wrote, "I have always believed it to be my duty to feel for human suffering and to mitigate it if I could, without reference to cause." [3] He was a Warden for the Poor in Baltimore, a member of the Inspection Commission of the City Jail—where he made a unique suggestion still followed—a member of the Indian Affairs Committee, and one of the Founders of Maryland in Liberia. Sheppard's most rewarding benevolence during his lifetime was his effort to provide for the free men of color a place where they could fully use their abilities without the handicaps of the white man's laws and customs. He was one of the few men whose wisdom and compassion were such that he left a final gift that, after his death, caused his benevolent ideas to continue for more than a century, and still causes his name to be remembered with gratitude. He wrote, "I am satisfied to be unnoticed and unknown." [4] A small circle of leading men of Baltimore cherished his friendship; his memory was a treasure held by many families in West Africa. Then for thirty years his name was forgotten. Now, after the commemoration of the seventy-fifth year of the opening of the institution provided for in his will, and the admission to it of patient 17,236, it is time to record a description of the manner of man Moses Sheppard was. The many quotations herein from Sheppard's letters delineate his Quaker philosophy and the warmth of his personality.

BLISS FORBUSH
The Sheppard and Enoch Pratt Hospital

April 5, 1968

Acknowledgments

In 1941, Lavens M. Thomas, 2nd, a member of the faculty of Emory University, deposited a manuscript biography of Moses Sheppard with the officials of the Sheppard and Enoch Pratt Hospital. This careful biography, *Moses Sheppard, 1775-1857: Humanitarian,* was well done and useful, his references accurate, and his grasp of the material available at that time excellent. My debt to Dr. Thomas is gratefully acknowledged. My familiarity with Quaker history, and the use of additional records of the Society of Friends, have enabled me to place Moses Sheppard primarily in the background of Quaker thinking and activity during the end of the eighteenth century and the first half of the nineteenth.

Most of the manuscript material concerning Moses Sheppard is in Friends Historical Library, Swarthmore College; the never-failing kindness of Frederick B. Tolles, Director, and Dorothy G. Harris, Associate Director, in making this material available was most valuable. LaVerne Hill Forbush, Custodian of the records of Baltimore Yearly Meeting, at the time deposited in the Record Room of Stony Run Meeting of Baltimore

15

and now in Swarthmore College, assisted me in using these extensive records.

The librarians in charge of the Maryland Room of the Enoch Pratt Free Library in Baltimore graciously located books, maps, and folders, as those of the Maryland Historical Society did also.

I wish to thank Dr. Tolles for reading parts of the manuscript and for his encouragement. Professor Kenneth Carroll of Southern Methodist University read the completed manuscript and made serviceable suggestions. Professor Kenneth O. Walker of Goucher College made an extensive study of the manuscript, and suggested a reorganization of the contents, which resulted in the story of Moses Sheppard moving more smoothly to its final conclusion; to Dr. Walker I am especially grateful for his labor and for his Foreword. For the meticulous typing of the pages, I owe my thanks to Mrs. Albrecht E. Stude.

In the background of every book there are always those who do the tedious reading and rereading, correcting and suggesting. How readable the book will be depends in large measure on their patience and care. To two members of my family I acknowledge grateful appreciation for this service—Ann Farquhar Forbush, and my wife, LaVerne Hill Forbush.

B.F.

Contents

List of Illustrations

MOSES SHEPPARD

Quaker Philanthropist of Baltimore

I

The Formative Years

W HEN MOSES SHEPPARD came to Baltimore in 1793, the Queen of the Chesapeake was a thriving, bustling, rather bumptious town on its way to becoming the most northern of southern cities and the most southern of northern cities. The early English settlers were joined by immigrants from Ireland, Germany, Sweden, and Bohemia. Acadians, driven from Nova Scotia by the British in 1756, took up a section of the area called French Town. A thousand Frenchmen, expelled from Haiti, enriched the life of the town. Early in the nineteenth century 6,870 servants and 1,981 convicts added a distinct lower-class flavor to Baltimore.[1] A steady influx of planters from the tobacco area below the Patapsco River took up residence in the town, bringing their Negro slaves from the fields as house or body servants. Baltimore town was destined to expand, since "Providence, working through geography, made it a funnel through which the products of the middle-eastern seaboard . . . and even of the lands on the other side of the mountains inevitably flow to the sea." [2]

Baltimore was not as old as many another port on the Chesapeake, such as Oxford or Annapolis, for nearly a century elasped between the landing of the first colo-

nists in 1634 and the founding of the town in 1729. But
in addition to its geographic advantage, iron deposits
were nearby of such superior grade that Englishmen
hoped to substitute them for Swedish ores; and the town
also lay directly on the belt of fine clay which runs from
New Jersey into western Virginia. The streams emptying into the harbor provided some of the best milling
sites in the country, and the lands to the north and west
produced ample wheat for grinding. By the time Moses
Sheppard settled in Baltimore, that enterprising port
had become "the general depot of imports and exports
for the middle part of the American States." [3]

On arriving in Baltimore, Moses was fascinated by the
wharves at the foot of Calvert Street, where ships
dropped anchor or hoisted sail. He felt at home with the
farmers unloading their produce at Marsh Market. Near
the Court House on upper Calvert Street, the stocks,
pillory and whipping post provided interest and served
as a deterrent to mischief makers. The exciting days of
the Revolutionary War were over, but Baltimore still was
"so conceited, so bustling and debonair" that it "seemed
growing up like a saucy boy, fat and mischievous, burst-
ing incontinently out of his clothes." [4] Rows of houses
were under construction, and in the older part of the
city, where Moses lived, the houses stood in disorderly
array, some blue, some yellow, some white, mostly one
or two stories tall. The owners of the ancient houses
practiced the colonial requirement of keeping a ladder,
a heavy broom, and a leather bucket of water by the
outside chimney in case of fire. Moses often passed the
large theater at York and Exeter Streets, but being a
well-brought-up Quaker boy, never dreamed of entering

its doors. The Quaker Meeting House (called Old Town Meeting) in which the Sheppard family worshipped was located at Fayette and Aisquith Streets.[5]

Except for official records of the Society of Friends, little is known about the ancestry of Moses Sheppard. Of his ancestors he wrote, "Those with whom I was connected by affinity of blood were distant, and generally unknown to me; placed among strangers, strangers became my relatives, my relatives were strangers. . . ." [6] In a somewhat melancholy vein, he added:

> I am indebted to my primogenitors for little more than life, no attentive hand recorded my birth hence I am as ignorant of the time I came into the world, as the period at which I shall leave it. . . . I have no local attachments from early recollections; hurried from place to place, always in penury and sometimes in want, those places of my transient sojourn are better forgotten or remembered with pain, hence I have no fond predilection for any favorite spot that gave me birth; thrown in the world I soon perceived I was the heir to nothing but its toil and labor. . . .

Moses, the grandfather for whom the young Quaker was named, had a two hundred and forty acre farm near Cohansey, New Jersey, and was a member of the Assembly.[7] He was a Baptist, married to Mary Dennis, who was a member of the Society of Friends. Of their six children, the three sons joined the Quakers. Nathan, the oldest, was the father of Moses of Baltimore.[8] Nathan was born November 13, 1726. He married Sarah Shoemaker, who "came of substantial Quaker stock," [9] her people for generations having been devout Friends. Moses was the youngest of their children who grew up: Mary, John, Nathan, Anne, and Moses. On April 11,

1761, Nathan Sheppard, father of Moses, purchased a farm of 126½ acres, and a mill, on the Wissahickon River in Pennsylvania.[10]

Before the outbreak of the Revolutionary War, the Sheppard family lived near Philadelphia "surrounded with the chief comforts of the life of the period." [11] But as excitement grew, feelings became more intense, and Sarah Sheppard became increasingly uneasy. She dreaded the possibility of war which might involve her family and so violate the peaceful testimony of the Quakers. Nathan shared her conviction. As emotions heightened, Friends were reminded that it was their belief that the Gospel message was one of peace and that they were expected to avoid taking part in war, defensive or offensive.[12] To escape the ravages of war and any possible violation of the Quaker testimony, the Sheppard family moved to Nova Scotia where they remained until some time in the 1780's. On their leaving Pennsylvania, the Sheppard property was lost or confiscated.

The return of the Sheppards to the United States was brought about by a first cousin, Elisha Tyson of Jericho Mills, Maryland. He offered Nathan and his family a plot of ground in Baltimore County on which stood a log cabin.[13] Little is known of Moses Sheppard's father after his coming to Maryland. His name appears in County records, and he was living in 1785, a few years before his youngest son went to Baltimore.[14] Sarah Sheppard, the mother of Moses,[15] attended Gunpowder Meeting of Friends at Sparks, Maryland. After the decease of her husband, she lived with her oldest son, John, a house carpenter in Baltimore, until her death on December 24, 1799. In the meantime she transferred

24

her membership, with that of her children Thomas, Anne, and Moses to the Baltimore Monthly Meeting of Friends at Old Town.[16]

The childhood and youth of Moses Sheppard are obscure. His earliest recollections are of "playing on an earthen floor in a log cabin" [17] at Jericho Mills, some seventeen miles north of Baltimore. He never spoke of going to school. It is likely, however, that he attended with other Quaker children the school held in the Gunpowder Meeting House. "His school education was of a most limited character," wrote his close friend, John Saurin Norris, "but possessed of extraordinary vigor of intellect, and with powers of mind capable of grasping the most subtle and profound questions which human minds can reach, he developed a mental capacity which few men possessed." [18] Another contemporary wrote: "The capacity and strength of mind of Moses Sheppard were of no ordinary character. Self taught, and self reliant, he evinced a boldness and originality of thought equaled by few." [19] In later years, other Baltimoreans noted the elegance of his style, the vigor of his writing, and his select but copious vocabulary.[20] Some of his essays and letters in manuscript are admirable specimens of the best writing of the day. "He became a well-read and well-informed man, always thinking on the great questions of religion, science, and politics that agitated society. . . ." [21]

John Mitchell, brother-in-law of Elisha Tyson, was a thriving provision merchant in Baltimore, with his store at 20 Cheapside. To him Moses Sheppard came as an errand boy in 1793. The city, with less than twenty thousand inhabitants, retained much of its rural atmo-

sphere, with tree-lined streets and many open spaces.
Moses enjoyed the view from the high point, now called
Federal Hill, where "with a telescope one could see
thirty-three miles down the bay." [22] Ships were constantly coming and going. Much of the produce sold by
John Mitchell came by water to the wharf below Cheapside, for the roads of Maryland, as elsewhere, were very
poor.

In Mitchell's store, "Moses Sheppard's work was characterized from the start by industry, intelligence and
faithfulness." [23] His business career was marked by
"order, punctuality, and fair dealing; these attributes
produced him business which he kept. . . . He had what
the world demands in its businessmen, steadiness of
purpose, [and] the power of adhering to a plan under
all vicissitudes." [24] *The Baltimore Patriot* later stated:
"His earlier years were marked by great business energy,
a prudent thrift, and undeviating rectitude. The son
of parents in humble circumstances, he was the architect
of his own fortune." [25]

Having been acquainted with poverty as a child,
Moses Sheppard determined early in life to lay aside
enough money to avoid economic adversity in old age.
He declared, "A youth of labor is essential to an old age
of ease." [26] Philosophizing at another time, he said,
"Youth is the dry season, or season of labor, and old
age is the rainy season, or season of rest in human life."
Moses added: "to me, it appears that a feeble old man
toiling or attempting to toil for a subsistence, that
should have been procured in his earlier years, is a
spectacle at which the very angels weep." [27]

Now in his eighteenth year, Moses Sheppard was

given every opportunity to assume responsibility. A quick learner, he rewarded the trust placed in him by his employer. In the second or third year of Moses' employment, John Mitchell offered to make the youth a "copartner and joint trader," [28] Mitchell to have a two-thirds interest in the partnership and Sheppard a one-third interest. As the younger man did not have this much capital, Mitchell loaned him the necessary amount at five per cent interest. In making the young man, with great business acumen yet with little capital, a copartner, Mitchell was both wise and kind. The partnership prospered, and in two years Sheppard's interest in the firm so increased that the name of the business was changed to Mitchell and Sheppard.[29] Mutual confidence and esteem always existed between the two associates, and at a far later time Moses Sheppard was named as one of the executors of John Mitchell's will.[30]

The year 1793 was most propitious for a young man to start business in Baltimore. The port served as a connecting link between America and Europe, and Baltimore shared in the extensive trade that developed. Commercial life in the port was greatly stimulated by the outbreak of a new war between England and France. This conflict eventually spread over most of the continent, and for the next twenty years the energies of Europe were wasted in war. During most of this period the United States remained neutral, and, possessing the only considerable merchant fleet not engaged as a combatant, became the principal carrier between the warring nations and the West. "While the great commercial nations were fighting one another for the carrying trade of the world, America ran away with the bone of contention." [31] The increase in volume of American business guaranteed enlarged business opportunities for Baltimore merchants, including Mitchell and Sheppard.

There was another and more subtle reason why the partnership of the two Quakers prospered.[32] As an offshoot of English Puritanism, the Quakers, perhaps unconsciously, adopted the ethics of John Calvin. All the outward marks of Christian ethics, as demonstrated by the best Protestantism, were practiced by the Quakers—honesty, integrity, frugality, simplicity, moderation, and industry. Calvin declared that God appointed a man's calling. This the Friend accepted, believing that "God's will . . . could be carried out as faithfully on the wharves and in the warehouses and counting rooms . . . as anywhere else." [33]

The Quakers were never permitted to forget the position of the Society of Friends in regard to right living. In their meetings for worship the ministers spoke of the virtues of both the inward and the outward expressions of a guided life. In each monthly business meeting some portion of the "Advices," part of the *Book of Discipline*, were read and commented on. The "Advices" urged members "such as trade by land and sea, or buy or contract" not to go "beyond their ability to manage"; they were urged to "keep their words or engagements in their dealings," so as not to "bring reproach to truth"; illicit trade, betting, gaming and horse racing were forbidden. They were advised "to keep to truth, and plainness . . . to be just in all dealings, and punctual in fulfilling their contracts. . . ." [34] As a result of practicing these virtues, most Friends prospered. Trade came to them because their neighbors believed in their honesty

and integrity. An honest, industrious, frugal businessman who exercised due caution in his transactions had
set out on a path toward the accumulation of wealth.
This was true of Moses Sheppard.

Membership in the Society of Friends was also useful
to Quaker businessmen. They were members of a
tightly knit religious body, widely spread over the East
and rapidly moving westward. Because of the general
reputation of Quaker businessmen, public knowledge of
a person's membership in the Society was valuable. "In
addition, Quakers themselves preferred to do business
with their coreligionists. Perhaps they were susceptible
to their own reputation." [35] Many of these advantages
were available to Moses Sheppard, and he eventually
equaled, in financial rewards, the results achieved by
many of the wealthiest Friends in Philadelphia, New
York, and Rhode Island.

The Friends Meeting played a predominant part in
the life of its members. Their outlook on the march of
events was molded by its ministers, their benevolent
impulses were stirred by its testimonies, and openings
were provided to harness these feelings to useful activities. The social life of most Quakers revolved around
the circle of Friends known through their Meeting.
Moses Sheppard, a quiet, thoughtful young man, was
accepted at once into the large Quaker group worship-
ing at Fayette and Aisquith Streets, on the eastern bor-
der of the city. Soon he had at least a speaking acquaintance with many of the leading citizens of Baltimore.
Saurin Norris later remarked of his friend:

His religious sentiments were in accord with the Society of Friends, of which he had been a consistent

29

member all his life; having been, in accordance with their rules, a member by birth. His attendance on their religious meetings was constant, and continued to about nine months before his death, when age and infirmity prevented his leaving his house. . . .[36]

Although Sheppard shared in the Meeting's business and committee work at a later date, his name does not appear in the records of the business sessions until he was of middle age. His shyness and lack of early education restrained him from vocal participation. Meetings for worship were held, according to the "plain language," on First days at 10:00 AM, with the Monthly Meeting for business on "the Sixth day before the 1st day in the month." [37] Many Quaker businessmen closed their shops in order to attend the Fifth day meeting for worship; John Mitchell and Moses Sheppard followed this custom.

The meetings for worship were an enriching experience. As Howard Brinton has said, "Quakerism is peculiar in being a group mysticism grounded in Christian concepts." [38] The Quakers believed that when they came together to wait on the Lord, "they might experience another Pentecost," and, as with the Church at Corinth, receive "the manifestation of the Spirit for the common good." [39] To some might be "given through the Spirit the utterance of wisdom, and to another the utterance of knowledge . . . to another prophecy . . . all these inspired by the Spirit."

There was a sense of expectancy when Moses, with the other young men, sat in the balcony of Old Town Meeting. The silence might be broken by a man kneeling, removing his hat (worn before), and offering vocal prayer. When this took place all others rose. Later a Recorded Minister, one noted for a life of rectitude and kindness, often rose from the facing benches saying how necessary it was for each individual to examine his own conduct. Another Friend might lay before his hearers, always in religious terms, some ethical problem or some pressing social deficiency, and exhort his fellows to be open to new understanding of the needs of others. After a solemn silence the Meeting was ended by two elders who shook hands. In good weather, Friends were accustomed to linger for a considerable time outside the Meeting House and within the yard, engaging in conversation. Perhaps, now and then, a little private business was transacted, informally.

Meetings for both worship and business were made more interesting by the presence of Recorded Ministers, who came with a minute of introduction, and were accompanied by another Friend. These visitors were entertained in the homes of local Quakers, a pleasant duty that Moses Sheppard shared as the years passed. In the fifteen years in which the young Quaker was in attendance at Aisquith Street Meeting, there were at least forty-two traveling ministers, both men and women, who came to Old Town. In the same period eight ministering Friends came from Great Britain to sojourn in Baltimore for a time.

In the business meetings, standards of conduct of individual members came under review. Moderation and simplicity were to be observed. Overseers cautioned those who failed to attend meetings for worship or were at strife with one another. And, "besides all the notorious crimes and gross wickedness . . . the following practices ought zealously to be taken care of and suppressed, viz: excessive drinking, swearing, cursing, lying, unlawful or unseemingly keeping company with women, or any other scandalous practice." [40] It was no wonder that Friends came to be known as "a peculiar people"—peculiar in the intensity with which they were required to practice their religion and in such nonessentials as dress and speech.

Like the Roman Catholic Church and Orthodox Jewry, the Friends in those days felt a happy and secure marriage was best served when the parties had the same religious background. Since a marriage outside the circle of the Society also involved the service of an ordained clergyman, this was considered a violation of the Quaker testimony for an unpaid ministry. During the lifetime of Moses Sheppard, members of the Society who thus "married out" lost their membership with Friends. This caused a great deal of suffering among Quaker families and aroused much resentment. Both Moses' sister Anne and his brother Thomas were disowned for "marrying out." Two years after her marriage by a clergyman, Anne Sheppard Allison asked to be restored to her place among Friends, and favorable action was taken. Twenty years elapsed before Thomas took similar action, perhaps at the instigation of his brother.[41]

As the population of Baltimore increased, Friends moved into the western part of the city. These Quakers desired a Meeting House on their side of Baltimore, one large enough to house the Yearly Meeting, which was outgrowing Old Town Meeting. A lot was purchased on Lombard Street, and a building constructed after the usual Quaker style, eighty by sixty feet overall. The brick building had a long porch, supported by five pillars, and a brick wall enclosed the property. A new Monthly Meeting was established, the Western District, with Philip E. Thomas as Clerk and Isaac Tyson as Recorder of vital statistics.[42] Moses Sheppard, his brother Thomas and wife Nancy, and their two children, Nathan and Mary Ann, chose to have their membership in the Western District.

As time passed, Moses Sheppard, whose residence was not far from the New Meeting House, took on definite responsibilities in the group. He served on committees at both the Monthly and Quarterly Meeting level, and was often a representative to a superior body. He collected subscriptions for projects undertaken by the membership and even investigated "clearness for marriage." The annual Yearly Meeting sessions, which lasted a week or more, were soon held at Lombard Street, and Friends came from Meetings in Maryland, Virginia, and central Pennsylvania. A representative group of Quakers also attended as informal delegates from the nearby Yearly Meetings of Philadelphia, New York, New England, and North Carolina. After Moses Sheppard purchased his home nearby, he took great pleasure in entertaining these visitors from a distance; and with some of them he corresponded for years.

In the Yearly Meeting sessions, there was much discussion concerning temperance, the Indians, peace, and the plight of the Negroes. Epistles expressing fraternal regard were prepared and sent annually to each Yearly Meeting in the United States and to Great Britain. These sessions drew Friends together and climaxed their religious year.

II

The Man of Business

From 1794 through 1816, the partnership of Mitchell and Sheppard prospered. As the war in Europe continued, the shipping industry in the United States entered upon a tremendous period of expansion, growing from 355,070 tons in 1790 to 1,089,876 in 1807. Large numbers of ships were built in the busy shipyards of Baltimore—many at Fells Point—until the merchant marine of the United States surpassed all but that of Great Britain. "The increase of American tonnage, during this period . . . has no parallel in the commercial annals of the world." [1] American ships moved into fields hitherto unknown to them. Trade was carried on with Venezuela, Brazil and Argentine; the flag of the Republic was taken through the Straits of Magellan, and on to the Pacific Islands and China. The *Chesapeake,* built near Baltimore, was the first vessel to fly the United States flag on the Ganges River.[2] A thriving trade developed with Scandinavia, and, by way of the Baltic, the German states. Ships from Baltimore passed into the Mediterranean. Mitchell and Sheppard handled merchandise that came from many of these ports and supplied the cargoes for a large number of vessels leaving for distant lands.

Baltimore schooners carried flour, barrel staves, dried fish, and manufactured articles from Maryland to the West Indies, and returned loaded with sugar, molasses, and also citrus fruits and coffee from South America. As sugar refiners in Baltimore produced far more sweetening than the area could consume, much was sent overseas to Germany and Holland.[3] In 1805-1806, Maryland exported $3,660,000 of her own products and reexported $10,919,000 of foreign products. Mitchell and Sheppard sold thousands of dollars worth of barrel staves each year to Isaac Tyson, son of Elisha, who was for forty years a merchant miller.

One of Sheppard's Journals indicates that the "grocery and provision store" was a true emporium; and an effort to classify the items as to probable place of origin indicates the extent to which the proprietors were engaged in world trade.

From Maryland, Pennsylvania, and nearby States came:

wheat, flour, rye, corn, barley, oats, buckwheat; ham, bacon, pot lard, butter, eggs, cheese, honey; beef, pork, chickens, corn meal, beans; pottery of many varieties; ships crackers, navy bread; vinegar; kegs of nails, fish hooks, axes, farm tools; plug and pound tobacco; whiskey, peach brandy; coil rope, seines; clay pipes, paints, paint brushes; powder, kegs of shot; wagons; horseshoes, horseblankets.

From Central and South America and the West Indies came coffee, cocoa; sugar, molasses; rum, gin; lemons, oranges. From Norfolk and the southern states came cotton, rice, indigo; yarn, thread, bags. From New England came potatoes; sweet oil, linseed oil; dried fish-cod, herring, mackerel; whale oil, sperm candles. From Mediterranean ports came figs, dates, almonds, salt. From European ports came salt; matches, wrapping paper, stationery; tinware; Madeira wine, French brandies, Scotch whiskey and ale. From Nova Scotia came dried fish and grindstones. From the Pacific came tea, ground pepper, allspice, nutmeg, mustard, cloves, cinnamon and ginger.

Some of the odd items carried by Mitchell and Sheppard included gun flints, hour glasses, painted buckets, "salt petra," candle wicks, and corn brooms. The only reference to clothing found in the few existing records is in a letter from Colonel George Sticker, written in 1794, in which he speaks of Sheppard, "who had just brought his materials for a Great Coat and Leggins." [4]

The profits made by John Mitchell and Moses Sheppard were steady rather than spectacular, as shown by their annual statements:

YEAR	PROFITS OF JOHN MITCHELL	PROFITS OF MOSES SHEPPARD
1795	£ 994 4s 9d	£ 497 2s 4½d
1797	£ 883 18s 0d	£ 883 18s 0d
1799	£ 1568 16s 7d	£ 1568 16s 7d
1800	$2,549.21	$2,549.21
1801	$2,326.84	$2,326.84
1802	$2,441.00	$4,653.69
1803	$2,602.11	$5,204.22
1805	$1,056.18	$2,112.38
1806	$2,148.60	$4,297.34
1809	$2,666.67	$5,333.33
1811	$1,512.45	$1,512.45
1812	$2,434.47	$2,434.47
1813	$5,864.13	$5,864.13 [5]

The amount of capital invested by the two partners

varied from year to year, remaining fairly constant at $20,000 to $31,000.

In a very few years, Moses Sheppard paid back the one-third loan that John Mitchell made to him on opening the partnership; by 1810 Mitchell's investment in the business was $6,910.50 and Sheppard's $22,287.47. The lower profit of Mitchell was in part due to the larger sums that he drew out for his personal expenses, as provided in the original indenture. As for Sheppard, "He never married; and if he lost the happiness of having a family, he saved the expense. He had one to provide for; and habits of rigid economy, early formed, adhered to him, as they usually do, after he became affluent." [6]

When either Great Britain or France blockaded each other's ports, the firm of Mitchell and Sheppard suffered, like other firms, but were able to maintain a sufficient amount of business. Evidently local and coastal trade formed the bulk of their commerce. There were frequent orders from ship captains, but these do not suggest a long ocean voyage. For example, the Captain of the schooner *Romp* bought from them a barrel of corn meal, a barrel of dried herring, a dozen fowls, twenty pounds of sugar, black-eyed beans, cheese, coffee, prunes, a barrel of prime pork, five bushels of potatoes, and three dozen eggs. The Master of the schooner *Pulaski* procured a barrel of navy bread, one-half barrel of pork, ships tea, five pounds of coffee, three gallons of molasses, hams, and twenty-five pounds of meal. The Captain of the *Alert* purchased a barrel of prime beef, a barrel of navy bread, pork, codfish, eggs, sugar, butter, pilot bread, raisins, coffee, and five bushels of potatoes.

The schooner *Elizabeth,* leaving with $1,325.08 worth of flour, might have set out on a longer voyage, however.[7]

As their business expanded, the partners purchased two warehouses. One was on Dugan's wharf, a few blocks from their store, for which they paid $1,300.00 a year on the mortgage; the other was at the foot of Cheapside, for which they paid $5,000 a year, over a considerable period of time. The records are not sufficient to tell the entire cost of either warehouse; one was carried at $14,010.95 in the inventory of 1806; one was rented out, off and on, for $400 a year.

Meanwhile Baltimore continued to grow: by 1830 the citizens of the incorporated city numbered 42,550, of whom 4,672 were slaves and 5,671 free men of color.

A group of 1,700 individuals, including Mitchell and Sheppard, formed an association to encourage the produce of their native country. All agreed not to purchase goods made abroad. This stimulated the erection of two cotton mills, one of them, the Union Manufacturing Company, on the Patapsco River. A Quaker, John Mc-Kim, was president of the corporation, which had a capital of a million dollars. It is not possible to ascertain when Moses Sheppard began to invest in this company, but he evidently purchased shares at an early date. He was a director for more than twenty-five years.[8]

Baltimore, and the firm of Mitchell and Sheppard, went through a trying period during and immediately after the War of 1812. The Federalists, strong in the City, were opposed to a conflict with Great Britain. Their point of view was set forth by Alexander C. Hanson, editor and publisher of the *Federal Republic,*

in vigorous articles lamenting the war fever. Baltimore
cast its votes for Republicans, and on June 27 a mob
attacked and wrecked the press of the *Federal Republic*.
The Mayor, who was present, took no action. Hanson
rented a house and prepared to continue the distribution of his paper, now printed in Georgetown. In July,
Hanson published a vigorous attack on the citizens, the
Mayor, and the Governor for not interfering with the
mob that destroyed his press or making any effort to
apprehend the members of the crowd. In the house of
Mr. Wagner on Charles Street, Hanson barricaded himself with a dozen Federalists. They were armed, a mob
gathered, and in the following melee two men were
killed. The authorities then intervened and the militia
arrived. The editor and his friends surrendered and
were conducted to the city jail, after which the militia
disappeared. In the night, the mob returned to the attack, broke into the jail, and manhandled the Federalists. General James M. Lingen was killed, and Light
Horse Harry Lee, famous for his activities in the Revolutionary War, was crippled for life.[9] This attack on the
freedom of the press was reminiscent of a similar event
during the Revolutionary War, when a mob attacked
William Goddard, editor of the *Maryland Journal and
Baltimore Advertiser,* and wrecked his press. Such epi-
sodes as these gave Baltimore the unsavory name of
"Mob Town." Moses Sheppard, who lived near Charles
Street, was cognizant of these events but took no part in
them.

Members of the Society of Friends were excused from
serving in the War of 1812; by an act of the Legislature
of 1808, their conscientious scruples against war were

recognized. As soon as the conflict began, the government commissioned privateers to attack British shipping, and of a total exceeding five hundred vessels, at least one hundred and twenty-six sailed from the Chesapeake. The privateers infested the shores of Great Britain and sailed up and down the channel and over the trade routes to the West Indies. Niles' *Register* listed 1,143 British ships captured by September, 1814.[10] The firm of Mitchell and Sheppard did not share in the wealth captured by Marylanders, nor did they handle goods sold in the harbor. The Friends Discipline stated, "members [must] carefully avoid engaging in any trade or business promotive of war, sharing or partaking of the spoils of war, by purchasing or selling prize goods. ..." [11]

At the conclusion of the War of 1812, major changes took place in American commerce. Until the war began, the States depended on Europe for most of their manufactured goods, now they turned to making their own. The centralized American factory system, soon to have power-driven machinery with interchangeable parts, slowly evolved. Cotton and woolen goods, iron, glass, headwear, and other articles, were made in new workshops in Baltimore. A period of depression came after the war, due to the dumping of goods, held in Great Britain during the conflict, on the ports of the East. Even American agriculture was hard hit; men released from the armies of Europe returned home to till the land, and the newly erected Corn Laws in England stopped the shipment of American wheat and flour to England and Ireland. These events caused Americans to turn their faces away from Europe, and to put forth strenuous efforts to develop internal trade. By the acquisition of the Louisiana Territory, the accession of Florida, and the potential expansion to the Northwest, the country suddenly discovered the limitless possibilities of agriculture and industrial development within its own borders.

Baltimore took full advantage of the new situation. Luxury goods continued to be shipped in from Europe, South America, and the Orient; but most of the outgoing cargoes went south and north along the coast. New manufacturing plants were built in Baltimore. The enterprising Quaker Ellicotts, whose mills were the first to produce flour, now established works for rolling and slitting bars of metal and making kegs of nails and iron utensils, purchased chiefly in the South. Isaac Tyson, Junior, with his partner established a laboratory for making chemicals and medicines on Pratt Street.[12] The many Quaker potters expanded their activities, developing new types of pottery and ceramics, including pressed hollowware. Samuel Kirk, a Quaker of Doylestown, Pennsylvania, with generations of goldsmiths in back of him, came to Baltimore to establish his firm of silversmiths.

Moses Sheppard branched out from the provision store at this time, purchasing and operating for many years a seine-twine factory at 64 West Pratt Street. When larger establishments featuring newly invented machinery made it unprofitable to continue this business, he did not close the doors of his plant, to the surprise of his friends, but continued manufacturing on a small scale, "so that he would not throw out of employment many elderly women who would become dependent on charity." [13]

In addition to the two warehouses originally purchased by the firm of Mitchell and Sheppard, on Cheapside street and Dugan's wharf, Sheppard erected one of the first private tobacco inspection warehouses in Baltimore, on the southeast corner of Light Street wharf and Camden Street.[14] This required an act of the Legislature. Sheppard agreed to keep the building in good repair, to provide scales and weights, brands and marking irons, for which he was entitled to one dollar for every hogshead of tobacco inspected by State officials. If a hogshead remained in the warehouse longer than one year, the owner of the warehouse received twelve and a half cents a month for storage. Moses Sheppard built this building at a cost of twenty thousand dollars, "both fire and water proof," plus a two-story house nearby for the keeper. Of this project he wrote: "It was obvious to me that an additional warehouse for the inspection of tobacco was wanted, where an article would remain in safety and where it would be insured at a small rate. . . . I built the best and most expensive house for the purpose in the State furnished with the best equipment." [15] There were other, poorly built tobacco warehouses in Baltimore, but they could not compete with Moses Sheppard's. In a six-month period the State collected $22,925.49 as duties on the hogsheads stored in the Quaker-owned warehouse; it is estimated that Moses Sheppard cleared at least $5,000 a year on the space rented. This considerable profit accrued to him until 1826, when the State purchased the property for the sum of $37,468.58, a gain to the owner of $17,468.58.[16]

An early letter preserved in the Sheppard file gives a rather unfavorable view of the Quaker businessman. A

Quaker farmer, John Worthington of Calverton Mills, Maryland, who sold a considerable quantity of flour to the Sheppard firm, declared that Moses had "picked his pockets." [17] Worthington claimed that Moses Sheppard purchased between 500 and 1,000 barrels of flour from him at a price fifty cents less than the flour was worth. He believed that Sheppard had early information, not available to the public, concerning a rise in the market value. The farmer went on to say that he knew such conduct was customary among merchants, but that it was not Christian. There is no copy of an answer from Sheppard to Worthington among Sheppard's correspondence, but Sheppard kept the letter, perhaps as a reminder of a non-Quaker slip that should not be repeated.

The Union Manufacturing Company decided, in 1821, to install more modern machinery, and as a newly appointed director, Moses Sheppard favored giving up handweaving for the newly invented British mechanism. He served on a committee to build a warehouse for the company, and on another that passed on the question of opening trade with the Orient. With the new machinery, the Union Manufacturing Company could manufacture sheeting, sail duck, and candlewick yarn.

With Philip E. Thomas, Sheppard was a director of the Baltimore Fire Company, founded in 1787. This was the oldest of the three main fire insurance companies, the others being the Equitable, of which Sheppard was a director, and the Phoenix. Unfortunately, there was always trouble between the volunteer firemen, which increased the difficulties of the insurance companies. Members of the companies often became locked in arguments with one another while the buildings they were called on to protect were consumed by flames. It was even said that some fires were set to see if street battles would take place.[18] On one night, there were five fires and five riots. Elisha Tyson was given credit for importing the first fire engine into Baltimore; he also gave a house in which to keep it.[19]

Baltimore was well supplied with banks, most of which had some Friends on the boards of directors. The Bank of Maryland was the earliest, founded in 1790 with a capital of three hundred thousand dollars; Moses Sheppard became a director in 1820, and served for many years. The Bank of Baltimore followed in 1795, with a capital of over a million, and then the Union Savings Bank. Thomas Ellicott, one of Moses Sheppard's closest friends and business associates, was for many years president of this bank, in which Sheppard invested heavily. Sheppard was also a director of the Savings Bank of Baltimore for repeated terms beginning in 1819. He was often reminded that "the duties of attending Director of the Savings Bank of Baltimore devolve upon you during the present month," or "you are requested to invest $7,500 for the Bank." [20] John Saurin Norris, a much younger man, for whom Moses had great respect, was later president of the Savings Bank.

A number of Sheppard's fellow Quakers, including his brother Thomas, William McKim, and Gerard T. Hopkins, invested in a trading company known as The East India Company of Baltimore; but it is uncertain whether Sheppard joined them. He did invest, and lost money, in the Temascaltepec Mining Company and the

Carralvo Mining Company, chartered in Maryland to mine in the southwest. As a reminder of a poor investment, Sheppard kept the worthless stock certificates.[21]

The merchant Quaker early became interested in purchasing land in and about Baltimore. In 1813, he secured 2½ acres of land in the western part of the city, on Fort Road, assessed at $450. Eventually he owned land and a mill on Solomon's Road; a farm near the falls of the Gunpowder River; land on Patapsco Neck valued at $5,000; and *Shipley,* a 38-acre tract purchased for $4,539. His favorite investment, however, was houses and lots within the city. He was partial to locations on Pratt Street, where he owned houses, stores, and warehouses valued at $20,500; and on Charles Street, where he secured houses and warehouses that cost him $24,000. His lots on Pratt Street and the neighborhood were valued at $89,000. He also accumulated ground rents, as well as stocks and bonds.[22] After John Mitchell retired from the firm of Mitchell and Sheppard in 1816, Moses continued the provision business alone for a number of years.

The *Baltimore City Directory* as early as 1817-18 lists Moses Sheppard as having a counting house. As he accumulated wealth, he loaned a considerable sum of money at interest. Many of these loans were made to his brother Thomas, of whom he was fond. This brother, however, appears to have been a poor businessman. He is listed in various city directories as a merchant, grocer, storekeeper, and flour middleman; at one time he became a health inspector. Often Thomas was unable to meet the interest on his loans. Moses later gave him a house on Sharp Street, on which Moses paid the taxes;

after his brother's death, Sheppard allowed Thomas' wife to collect rents from the house.

Moses Sheppard loaned considerable sums to Elisha Tyson, totaling over $10,000. It is doubtful whether the sums were repaid. Moses also loaned money to Isaac Tyson to assist him in expanding his business.[23]

Business contemporaries of Moses Sheppard recognized that he had an almost uncanny sense of making a profitable investment. At his death, the only papers in his portfolio that had no value were six shares of mining stock that had cost him $300; a few shares in the Bank of the United States, wrecked by Andrew Jackson; and notes signed by five individuals marked uncollectable, totaling $345. After giving up the provision business, Moses Sheppard gave active attention to the various directorships he held and to the care of his properties, and at a comparatively early age, when "in the prime of life," [24] he retired. Moses said his retirement was for two reasons: "to enable him to give his time to employment of his rapidly growing fortune, in judicious and remunerative investments," and "that he might have more time to read and study." [25]

III

Moses Sheppard and Quaker Concerns

THE SOCIETY OF FRIENDS, as its name suggests, was a community, an enlarged family unit. The Discipline of 1806, in use when Moses Sheppard was a young man, delineated the responsibility the Quakers should have towards one another: "As mercy, compassion and charity are eminently required by the gospel, it is desired that the cases of our members, who are in indigent circumstances, be duly inspected, in order that advice and relief may be seasonably extended, and assistance afforded them. . . ." [1] Sheppard was often asked to serve on committees to collect subscriptions for needy members and to distribute the funds secured.

The sums usually required ranged from ten to forty dollars.[2] Sometimes a barrel of flour was donated, frequently a cord of wood. The Meeting covered the expense of sawing, hauling, and splitting the wood. Now and then rent or taxes were paid. On one occasion, after loaning a woman funds to cover her living expenses for several years, a note was taken; still later this member conveyed her house to the Trustees, while Friends continued to pay her expenses as long as she lived. The last item on her account was "paid for grave and stone." [3]

From earliest times, Friends in Maryland were concerned with the education of their children, considering them "next to our own souls . . . the most immediate object of our care and concern." [4] A Friends' School was conducted in the Patapsco Meeting House on the Harford Road, and after Friends moved to Old Town, they constructed a brick, two-room school house and a house for the teacher. School was held in the Lombard Street Meeting House, and in time an addition was constructed for an enlarged school connected with the Meeting building.

Sheppard, who helped to raise money for the Friends' schools, was especially interested in the education of the children of the poor, there being no public system of education at this period. He heartily approved of the intent of John McKim, a member of Old Town Meeting, who left a fund yielding six hundred dollars a year to establish a free school. Isaac McKim, son of John, built a handsome structure—a copy of the famed Temple of Theseus in Athens—to house the school, located a block from Old Town Meeting.[5]

Traveling Quaker ministers, moving about the Yearly Meeting, noted that there were many Quaker youths who did not live close enough to a Friends' Meeting to attend a Quaker school. The Yearly Meeting was urged to establish a boarding school for such young people, similar to those flourishing in other Yearly Meetings.[6] In 1815, the Yearly Meeting agreed to establish such a boarding school, and appointed a committee, with membership in each local area, to collect funds for the purpose. Sheppard took up the task with enthusiasm. His account book shows that he secured $3,300 from Baltimore Quakers. He gave $500 himself, and obtained a like amount from Isaac Tyson, Philip Thomas, and Thomas and James Ellicott.

When enough money was pledged, Moses Sheppard was chosen as one of a large committee to purchase a location for the school and set it in operation. A farm not far from the Sandy Spring Meeting House in Montgomery County, Maryland, was purchased. Moses was interested in remodeling the existing buildings on the farm for the Fairhill Boarding School, as it was called.

The committee studied rules established by other Quaker boarding schools, which set forth the ideals and methods of Quaker education in the first half of the nineteenth century. The Superintendent and his wife served as heads of a family, supervising the pupils, the teachers, and the farm. "Corporal punishment could in no case be resorted to, but some place of seclusion [was] provided for refractory boys where they could not have much light, but plenty of air, and where they could be kept comfortably warm in pretty cold weather. . . ." [7] At a coeducational school, "the boys and girls [should] be at a proper distance from one another . . . to prevent undue familiarity; and yet not so far separated but that an innocent and cheerful intercourse would be allowed and encouraged at suitable seasons. Boys and girls were tenderly advised to . . . close the day with remembering their gracious Creator, that being the best preparation for quiet repose." Unnecessary noise was discouraged, orderly conduct expected; lessons were to be learned in silence, and moderation and decency were required at all times.

The Fairhill School opened as planned, and Sheppard, with other members of the committee, frequently drove from Baltimore to inspect its operations. From the beginning, however, there was a disappointing response from Friends. Some did not wish to send their children away from home, and a few preferred that their boys and girls attend long-established Friends' Schools in Pennsylvania and New York State.

In 1820, with an enrollment of thirty-three boys and eighteen girls, it seemed that the institution was about to enter upon a period of great usefulness; then the beloved Superintendent died, and the school never again felt the same sense of security. Gradually financial embarrassment dogged Fairhill, as the number of pupils did not remain high enough to cover expenses. Moses Sheppard was alarmed at the mounting deficits. In 1824, Isaac Tyson, then Chairman, reported: "the affairs of the school were conducted with economy and prudence, and the general deportment and improvement in the pupils was satisfactory," but added: "we doubt whether it would be more to the credit and reputation of the Society that it be suspended." [8] The school was closed and the property rented.

Now and then attempts were made to reopen it, but the establishment of the public school system of education brought about its final demise. Benjamin Hallowell, who maintained a well-known school in Alexandria, Virginia, wrote: "It is hard to support schools where the public school system exists, but Friends are encouraged to do so, so our children may be educated in accordance with the principles we profess. . . ." [9] The property of the Fairhill School was finally sold and the money set aside as a loan fund to assist young Quakers in securing an advanced education.

Sheppard's interest in the education of young people was not confined to the children of Friends. He realized the hardships that would have beset his own path if Elisha Tyson and John Mitchell had not befriended him, and the long hard study necessary for him to overcome his early lack of education. He was described as "a man of deeds not words. Quietly and unostentatiously he began by backing that boy or girl in school, lending a helping hand to some unfortunate person, and coming to the rescue of friends and relatives when economic adversity hit them." [10]

> How soon he began to devote a portion of his income to philanthropic purposes, we have not yet been able to learn; nor do we imagine, from the secrecy he imposed upon those he selected as his almoners, it would be ever possible to ascertain correctly. An utter enemy of show, parade, and ostentation, he pursued the noiseless tenor of his ways doing good by stealth, and rigidly enjoining that his acts of benevolence should remain unknown, not only to the world at large, but to the recipient of his bounty.[11]

More information is known, however, concerning his aid to young people than about other of his benevolent acts. Letters have been preserved indicating that Moses Sheppard for many decades supported talented young people in their educational efforts. Usually he was paying the tuition and board of one to three young people at school; once he mentions that the number was increased to five. Except in rare cases, he paid the expenses through a third party. At a much later date the editor of the *Baltimore Patriot* wrote:

> Many orphan children, and young girls, thrown early upon the world for means of livelihood, have reason to

bless their secret benefactor. Some he educated and supported, partly or wholly, until they were capable of maintaining themselves. The others he advanced sufficient funds to enable them to engage in business in a moderate way.[11]

One of the favorite schools in which girls were educated by the Quaker was Sharon Boarding School, in Darby, Pennsylvania. Rachel Tyson Jackson, a daughter of Isaac Tyson, married John Jackson, a Quaker minister of Darby, and together they conducted Sharon. In the 1830's, Moses Sheppard, also a distant cousin, began to send some young people in whom he was interested to Sharon. On one occasion, John Jackson wrote to Moses: "Thanks for the one hundred and fifty dollars received . . . to be applied at my discretion to the education of deserving young women who are likely to leave school for the want of the means to remain and pursue their education." [12] In order that his benefactor might have some choice in the matter, the principal sent him the names of three likely candidates—Moses decided to pay the tuition of all three. In another case, Jackson wrote: "I am satisfied that a small sum of money appropriated in this manner, is calculated to do much good, it gives the capital on which they [the young people] can commence business that will accord them all their lives; and it is not the individual alone who will be benefitted, by the charity, the blessings extend wherever their influence as a teacher is felt, as they impart knowledge they have received from others." [12] Again the principal wrote: "S.B.C. has been here a year, her tuition paid from a small legacy. She had first rate ability, and is anxious to pursue her studies, but is without means as her tuition is paid only through the month . . . her improvement is very great. She is one of the best pupils, and will get a good situation as a teacher." [12] Sheppard sent the required amount.

Sheppard agreed with John Jackson when he wrote, "we can do more good with our school . . . to a class of females, who without such aid would be left to struggle with the adversities of life, but have the mental powers, if properly developed, to be a great blessing to themselves and of extreme usefulness to others." [13] When sending money to help a student about whom he had received an especially favorable report, Moses wrote: "When Napolean asked Madame de Staël what he could do to benefit the French people, she replied, 'educate the mothers.' " He added "This brings to mind a sentiment of my own, written to the manager of a female charity school, 'I challenge the history of mankind for a single instance of a savage and barbaric race whose Mothers were enlightened and virtuous.' " [14]

Sheppard not only sent money to Sharon over a period of twenty-five or more years but interested others to do likewise. In one case, he forwarded $100 from a Mr. B. M. High.[15] The principal of Sharon visited in Moses' home, and later wrote how much he had enjoyed the occasion. The two men talked about religion, and both agreed it was difficult to reconcile the practices of men with their religious professions. "Virtue consists in the practice of goodness and truth," wrote Moses, "religion is more than a profession of faith, it is a *rule* of life." Jackson was surprised that his friend was well acquainted with the writings of the ancient Greek and Oriental philosophers.

Rather late in his association with the Sharon school, Sheppard expressed his pleasure that the principal had used good Quaker [and adolescent] psychology in supplying one of the girls with clothing out of the funds he sent, "to make her appear like the other girls, by which she is relieved from the mortification she at first had to endure." [16]

Rachel Jackson once sent Moses Sheppard a copy of the proceedings of the Teacher's Institute of Delaware County. His comments on reading the pamphlet indicated his open-mindedness. He wrote to Rachel: "It has been alleged, that learned ladies are not good domestic women; if they were taught general literature instead of science, one would make them broad, the other keep them at home. . . . It is more important that a mother understand her own stature, than to know a hundred thousand veterans fell in battle. . . . I propose that no woman should be marriageable until she possesses a comprehensive knowledge of anatomy and physiology." [17]

There was a growing interest in temperance among Friends in the early nineteenth century. Farmers at that time customarily provided their men working in the fields with rum or whiskey; on the frontier the brown whiskey jug became standard equipment. At social gatherings, elections, logrollings, funerals, and weddings, alcohol was freely used. This the Friends frowned on, believing the use of strong beverages "increased vice and dissolution in the land . . . to the impoverishment of many. . . ." [18] As early as 1794, the Baltimore *Book of Discipline* read: "Are friends clear of importing, vending, distilling, and the unnecessary use of spirituous liquors . . . frequenting taverns unnecessarily, and do they keep to moderation and temperance on all occasions?" [19] As this query began to be more rigorously enforced, it is possible that Moses Sheppard's early retirement from the provision business was hastened by the enforcement of this query. Other provision dealers belonging to the Meeting were disowned for "vending" whiskey.[20]

Of greater importance to Friends was their testimony against war. They expected their members "to walk wisely and circumspectly towards all men, in the peaceable spirit of Christ." [20] It was not expected, "as the world was circumstanced," that Friends should condemn non-Quakers for bearing arms.[21] During the War of 1812, Friends had an opportunity to test their principles of nonviolence, as they had in the Revolutionary War and the many conflicts with the Indians. Richard H. Townsend, who many years later became private secretary to Moses Sheppard, wrote in his diary at the time:

> Citizens were conscripted to help with the fortifications [of Baltimore] or to man the works. . . . I remember to have seen Uncle Jacob [Townsend], Thomas Matthews, and Joseph Davenport brought up into the ranks on Gay Street; where they stood, quiet and unresisting; refusing to take arms, when they were commanded, or to go through any infantry exercises; till at last, they subdued the spirit of persecution; and those in power ceased to molest them.[22]

After the attempt of the British to destroy Fort McHenry and capture Baltimore failed, Townsend added a description of the usual aftermath of every battle. "I

Friends Meeting House, Lombard Street, Baltimore
Interior, C. Y. Turner.
Courtesy, Stony Run Friends Meeting, Baltimore

remember to have seen some of the volunteer soldiers, brought to the town on litters . . . a day or two after the battle . . . thirty or forty never returned." [22]

The Quakers did not close their books on the War of 1812 when peace was declared. At Monthly Meeting in Lombard Street, Moses Sheppard and other fellow members sat in judgment on those Friends who had deviated from the Quaker peace testimony. One by one, eleven young members were disowned because they took some part in the defense of the city. One served on a ship of war, one volunteered for the Battle of North Point, one helped build the new fortifications, one hired a substitute to do military duty for him, and another paid a military fine for not doing active service. One of the eleven young Friends was retained as a member—perhaps more were—because he sent an "offering" [apology] to the Meeting for his conduct. He wrote that he felt himself convinced "that the principles of Friends were founded on the purest precepts of the Gospel . . . and [believed] it the duty of all men to live in harmony and peace. . . . He condemned his deviation in this respect." [23]

It was inevitable that the Quakers, who believed that there was a divine spark in every man, should extend their care beyond their own membership. Throughout the nineteenth century, the chief concerns of the Friends were the unjust treatment given the Indians, the disadvantaged position of the freed Negroes, and the degradation that was the lot of the slaves.

The efforts of Baltimore Friends on behalf of the Indians began shortly after Moses Sheppard came to Baltimore. Plans were made to promote education and share agricultural and mechanical knowledge among the tribes of western Pennsylvania and Ohio, areas at that time within the boundaries of Baltimore Yearly Meeting. Moses helped raise "subscriptions" to maintain these efforts. These early attempts to soften the lot of the Indians were frustrating. The Shawnee, Wyandotte, and Delaware Tribes then roamed a wide area northwest of the Ohio River. To reach them, Friends had to travel by horseback, carrying supplies and gifts for the chiefs by pack animals. On reaching the Indian country, the representatives of the Meetings were often unable to find the tribal chiefs, as information concerning the whereabouts of local councils was confusing and vague. But eventually agricultural tools were forwarded to the Indians, and for a number of years couples from western areas in the Yearly Meeting—Redstone and West Branch, Pennsylvania—lived among the tribes for one or two years at a time. On several occasions, Indian chiefs stayed with Moses Sheppard on their way to ask aid from the President for their people. They called him "Son of Onas." [24]

The efforts of the Quakers were not very fruitful. Chiefs Little Turtle and Five Medals reported: "We are sorry to say that the minds of our people are not much inclined towards the cultivation of the earth as we would wish." [25] During the War of 1812, the tribes whom the Friends were assisting were attacked by other Indians and their settlements destroyed. Having lost their homes and mills the Friends constructed for them, these tribes decided to accept an offer of the government to give them lands west of the Mississippi, where they would be unmolested, as they thought, by the white men.[26]

Reticent though he was said to be, the name of Moses Sheppard began to appear more and more frequently in the records of the Lombard Street Meeting. He was appointed a representative from the Preparative Meeting to the Monthly Meeting, then to the Quarterly Meeting, and finally to the Yearly Meeting. In time he became a member of the Yearly Meeting's Committee for Sufferings, the highest authoritative body in the Society. Created originally when Friends were persecuted for not going to war or for nonpayment of tithes to churches, this committee continued to defend Friends who violated any State or Federal law because of conscience. Between sessions of the Yearly Meeting it met in one of the country Meetings such as Pipe Creek in Maryland or Hopewell in Virginia.

Sheppard served in many capacities in his local Meeting. He assisted in selection of Elders, a new Recorder, or a new Clerk; he was asked to serve as an overseer at weddings—surprising, because he was a bachelor. It was natural, with his business experience, that he should be appointed to look into the titles of Friends' property in Baltimore and to secure land for a school house. Repeatedly he was requested to work with others on collection of funds to carry out some concern of the Meeting— Friends never taking collections during the periods of worship or business.

In the early days of the Society in America, the Friends, with the same economic interests as other Americans, held slaves, accepting slavery "as they found

it, without qualm or question." [27] By the end of the
Revolutionary War, the consciences of Maryland Quakers were so troubled by this denial of human rights that
they urged their members to free their slaves, and finally
made it a disownable offense for any member to keep a
slave. This provided a great hardship on Quaker plantation owners—the Yearly Meeting made no effort to
reimburse the slave owners—and some left the Society or
were disowned. Others sold their properties, moved to
the city to choose other avenues of earning, or mi-
grated to Ohio where neither cotton nor tobacco was
raised in any quantity. Apparently, "Quaker planters
without slaves could not survive in a region where
slavery prevailed." [28] Although the Society freed itself
from the evils of slavery by 1784, Maryland Quakers did
not find a permanent solution to the racial problem, for
most "American Quakers confined their fellowship with
red and black men to benevolence." [29] A few Quaker
idealists hoped that the Negro, after securing an education, might achieve equality with the majority group.
"But Friends only reluctantly opened their Society to
colored members, and wished no more than other
whites of their day and generation to associate with
different races on terms of social intimacy." [29]

For a period, Friends in Maryland were content with
having cleared themselves of slave owning, but found
they could not live in the midst of slaveholders without
continued uneasiness. Elias Hicks, the famous Quaker
preacher of New York state, who spoke strongly against
the institution of slavery, made seven trips to Maryland.[30] Moses Sheppard purchased a copy of his powerful antislavery pamphlet, *Observations on the Slavery of*

Africans and Their Descendants, issued in 1811. But the Quakers of Maryland were never so united in their attack on slavery outside the Society as they were in the struggle to free their own membership of this blight. Thomas Drake summed up the condition: "No immediate steps on their behalf seemed to be required of Friends in a collective capacity. American Yearly Meetings allowed the question to rest." [31]

The first serious effort to solve the problem of slavery in Maryland was made just before Moses Sheppard came to Baltimore, through the founding of the Maryland Society for the Abolition of Slavery, in which Elisha Tyson was a moving figure. Although in existence only seven years, the Society succeeded in having repealed the law of the state that prohibited manumission of slaves by last will and testament.

Elisha Tyson was the driving force in another effort to help the Negroes. He worked effectively to prevent the illegal detention of people of color, which so often resulted in their being sold as slaves.[32] Sometimes he became aware of manumissions long suppressed; sometimes of attempts to kidnap free Negroes in order to transport them by stealth out of the State and sell them to slavers. In tracking down kidnappers, Elisha Tyson faced dangers many times. On one occasion, seeking six freemen who had been spirited away and hidden in the cellar of a tavern, his life was threatened if he opened the door leading to their hiding place. His answer was: "Shoot if thee dares, but thee dare not, cowards as thou art, for well dost thou know that the gallows would be thy portion." [33] The six men were released. In spite of threats to burn his house or to take his life, Elisha continued his work to thwart the kidnappers. It was stated that "he saved over two thousand Negroes from enslavement. . . ." [34]

A second group of men, including Moses Sheppard, formed The Protective Society of Maryland, which paralleled and continued the work of Elisha Tyson. They were especially concerned with those Negroes who, freed in their master's will, were not set free by the heirs, and by those who were picked up as runaways, held in jail, and then handed over to slave dealers. The members of the Association agreed to visit the jails as soon as word reached them that a runaway was being held or a Negro claimed to be in this category. Sheppard had among his papers long lists of names of individuals to be manumitted in different parts of the state, and he spent much time in alerting county officials when the manumissions should legally take place. The Association members also worked to secure a law that made it necessary to discharge all colored people confined as runaways from such custody if, within a time limit, no one stepped forward to claim them as slaves. The second law secured "made it a penitentiary offense to sell out of the State of Maryland a slave entitled by manumission to secure his freedom on the expiration of a term of years." [35] As time passed, more and more of the activities carried on by Elisha Tyson for the good of the Negroes were taken up by Moses Sheppard. One biographer wrote, "In the Biblical record it was young Elisha who shouldered the mantle of the aged Elijah (2 Kings 2:13f); in this case, however, it was Moses Sheppard who shouldered Elisha's mantle." [36]

IV

The Brick House on Pratt Street

WHEN MOSES SHEPPARD was in his middle years, a close friend, John Saurin Norris, wrote of his appearance:

> He was remarkably of middle height, proportionally robust, with features cast in a massive mould, particularly the nose and ears, while his eyes were small, gray and twinkling, set under heavy brows; he was a man, who when seen, could never be mistaken for another. As he was used to pass about the streets, he was one the passerby would stop to look at, and would, perhaps instinctively, think there was something out of the common order about him, yet there was nothing in his appearance, dress or demeanor, that was outré or singular. . . .[1]

On May first, 1821, Sheppard purchased the brick house on the corner of Pratt and Sharp Street from the estate of John Mitchell. For many years this had been the home of John Mitchell and his kindly wife Tacy Tyson Mitchell, in which the younger man had often been entertained. Thinking back over his early days in the city, when he began his career without money of his own or financial help from his family, Moses Sheppard must have taken considerable pride in owning the home of the former head of the Mitchell and Sheppard provision store.

The Brick House on Pratt Street
Courtesy, *The Baltimore Sun*

The spacious 3½ story house faced south and east, allowing the sunlight to stream in through the many windows. Fireplaces warmed each floor. Leaning on the deep window sills, a visitor could study the street below or catch a glimpse of the harbor. Steep staircases, with slender carved spindles and rounded balustrades, led from floor to floor. Wide baseboards and strong mouldings lent dignity to many of the rooms. There was an extensive yard in the back of the house, surrounded by a brick wall, built in such fashion that the pump over the well could be used by people passing down the street. "There were two long handles and a spout on a pivot, so the water flowed in the yard, or in the street as desired. There was a contrivance there by which butter, eggs, and milk could be lowered into the well to keep cool; also by turning a crank a clean cedar bucket was raised to the surface." [2] As Sheppard was an honorary member of three fire companies, the members did not hesitate to make use of the well when water was desired.

Moses Sheppard's furniture was marked by "simple elegance and elegant simplicity." [3] Purchased over several decades, Moses secured distinguished examples of eighteenth and nineteenth century craftsmanship. His first important purchase was a grandfather clock, which he owned for nearly sixty years.[4] This unusually tall clock, seven feet five inches from the floor to the delicate fretwork that crowned the decorated face of the time piece, marked the day of the month as well as the time of day. A Chippendale love seat and Hepplewhite sofa with unbroken curved back graced the living room.[5] Sheppard kept his choicest books in a tall two-section Baltimore-made bookcase; the paneled doors had both clear and frosted glass set in cross-banded edges. The supper table, its six foot top made of pie-shaped pieces of burled mahogany, could be tilted up and placed against the wall, but was usually piled high with books and papers. Sheppard's own chair was an unusually deep Chippendale wingback; the wings protected him from the draft, holding the warmth from the fire. He owned two perfectly matched card tables, made in 1802 by William Cyeetuosi, decorated with inlaid medallions of contrasting wood, exemplifying the rich and elegant taste of Baltimore cabinetmakers between 1790 and 1820.

Sheppard's most remarkable piece of furniture was a Hepplewhite sideboard, forty inches tall and sixty-one inches long, of brilliantly curved, grained mahogany, skilfully inlaid. His extension dining room table, with

Moses Sheppard's Bookcase

heavy reed carved legs, had room for a goodly company. Two smaller tables, Sheraton and Pembroke, were used as serving tables. The cellarette, an oblong wine cooler with inlaid decorations, was divided into sections to hold the various etched bottles.

Sheppard slept in a cherrywood and mahogany bed with high headboard, a scrolled top broken by an urn, and smooth tapering sideposts holding the tester poles. The sweeping curtains and valances kept the draft away from the occupant. A Sheraton corner washstand, with one drawer, high splash board and flat top, was a necessary accessory of the period. Other bedroom furniture included a six-drawer mahogany chest with handles of Birmingham brass, a tremendous inlaid wardrobe, and a small bidet for convenience.

Other articles of furniture that have survived from the Pratt Street House are a small Sheraton ladder back chair; a long wicker back settee, a gift from Liberia; and a heavy Chippendale mirror surmounted by a golden eagle ornament. On the walls of his home hung several noteworthy pictures, carefully chosen prints from the extensive collection he accumulated.

One of the remarkable characteristics of Moses Sheppard—raised in a log cabin, a clerk in a provision store, later director of banks and industries—was his passion for reading. Denied much formal schooling, he eagerly made up this deficit by prolonged study. All his life he was a reader, and his library, much of which is still intact, attests to the breadth of his interest and to his choice of good literature. He treasured his books, and made careful provision that his library should be placed where it would do the most good.[6] However, he formed the habit of giving a great many books to his friends. When he purchased something that especially pleased him, he secured extra copies and distributed them where he thought they would be enjoyed. For example, in one of his notebooks is a list of 109 books and pamphlets, which he gave, at various times, to Benjamin F. Taylor of Hughesville, Loudoun County, Virginia, a friend of his later years.[7] Over a period of two decades, the philanthropist sent more than 200 books to a Negro physician in Africa.[8] Thus it is impossible to estimate the number of books that the Quaker purchased; nearly 800 are still intact, part of a much more extensive collection. Not content with purchasing books through dealers in Baltimore and Philadelphia, Sheppard imported choice books from England.

In addition to reading in his own extensive library, Sheppard spent many hours—"almost every day"—in the reading rooms of the Maryland Historical Society, of which he was a member; and in the rooms of the Baltimore Library, which he supported. His ideas on many subjects are set forth in the voluminous correspondence conducted after he retired from active business, and in essays he wrote and gave to his friends. His only published essay, however, was a paper, read before the Maryland Historical Society, entitled *African Trade in Jamaica and Comparative Treatment of Slaves.*[9] He refers occasionally to articles from his pen published anonymously in various papers of the day, but these cannot be identified. His friends commented on Sheppard's facility in the use of the English language, due to his extensive reading and to his care in writing.[10]

The prosperous Friend owned the writings of the

leading Quaker authors, five versions of the Bible, and many aids to the study of the Scriptures. Of contemporary leaders outside the Society, the humanitarian possessed the works of Edward Beecher, Theodore Parker, and William E. Channing. He gave away many copies of the writings of his friend George W. Burnap, who for thirty-two years was minister of the First (Unitarian) Church of Baltimore. Six of Burnap's books contain notes jotted down in the back, as well as a list of individuals to whom copies were sent. Sheppard possessed books on the Roman Catholic Church, on Universalism, Unitarianism, Mormonism, Swedenborgism, and Hinduism. His erudition, commented upon by many contemporaries, may have been the result of his prolific reading of sermons, religious essays, and religious disputations.

There were nearly fifty books in the Brick House devoted to the Negro. Sheppard owned books and sermons of Southerners defending slavery, the writings of Frederick Douglass, and the denunciations of William Lloyd Garrison.

He imported from London a very good telescope at a cost of £100, with a number of special lenses.[11] His library contained books in the field of geology, mineralogy, astronomy, anthropology and physiology; for a time he read a good deal on phrenology, but later wrote to Benjamin Taylor that evidence did not support the theories advanced in this subject. He secured the four volumes of Benjamin Rush, the famous Philadelphia physician and scientist, reports of the Pennsylvania Hospital, Friends Hospital for the Insane, and works on body and mind. Since Quakers were advised by the Discipline to shun works of fiction and playwriting, these were absent from Sheppard's collection, but a surprising amount of poetry was included.[12]

Sheppard subscribed to the current newspapers and magazines in Baltimore, the State of Maryland, and Philadelphia. For sixty years he kept an index of articles that interested him the most, having many of the publications bound, or neatly tied in bundles.[13] He made a special collection of newspapers and journals published between 1775 and 1810, representing editors in Baltimore, Norfolk, Philadelphia, and Boston. Among the bound volumes kept over a period of years were the *Pennsylvania Mercury and Universal Advertiser,* the *Colonization and General Advertiser,* the *African Repository and Colonial Journal (20 bound volumes), Niles' Register (13), The Reformer,* the *American Register,* and the *Christian Examiner.*

Supported by his books and papers, Sheppard spent many a quiet evening before the open fire in the back parlor of the brick house on Pratt Street. Likely as not, he munched on a Jonathan apple sent him by one of his Pennsylvania friends. He had a well-stocked mind. The editor of the *Baltimore Patriot* commented:

> The capacity and strength of mind of Moses Sheppard, were of no ordinary character. Self taught, and self reliant, he evinced a boldness and originality of thought equalled by few. . . . Those with whom he was intimate remarked a peculiar faculty of analyzing an argument, that stripped it of all extrinsic, and reduced the proposition to its mere self. . . .[14]

A later writer summed up Moses Sheppard's love of literature:

70

Books he read with discriminating taste, and his comments upon them, especially upon those containing
theological questions, evince a refreshing independence of thought and belief. No subject appears to have
been unworthy of his notice, and his frequent applications for information to numerous correspondents and
his inquiries as to books containing such information
exhibit an eager search for knowledge, a search which
did not slacken even when he had long passed the age
of three score years and ten.[15]

Nothing pleased Sheppard more than having his close
friends drop in for an evening chat; many an interesting
discussion took place on economic problems, social
needs, religion, and natural science. The Quaker "sat as
an interested listener, but when solicited for an opinion, he would [in later years] deliver it with a fiat of an
oracle." [16] It was said of Sheppard that he could trace
with the precision of a professor the migrations of nations from Asia to Europe, or recite Pope's "Universal
Prayer" or lines from his "Essay on Man." His words
were few but "he had the habit of enunciating apho-
risms, or propositions, that would at times startle his
hearers." [17]

After one of these spirited discussions, a visiting
Friend wrote: "he had never heard the subject presented in a light so striking and conclusive, and yet in a
manner so simple and natural." [18] A Philadelphia
Quaker on a visit found Moses' anecdotes so amusing
and instructive that he urged Sheppard to pay him a
visit because of the "cheering tonic-like affect" of his
presence." [19]

Not always did the conversation center around things
historical and theological, for Sheppard mentioned that

there was often what might be called business gossip, especially about business failures, which were not infrequent. Moses wrote a business friend:

> We don't descend to notice small fry that are Gazetted; we will not waste time on them. A person uninformed might suppose that the current events might occupy our attention . . . no, the war is distant, the Planet lately discovered more so, the one belongs to the warrior, the other to the astronomer; trading men want a subject connected with trade, and failures are as necessary a topic for the men as scandal is for the ladies.[20]

Sheppard the humanitarian could unbend with children and delighted to have them come to his house; he planned afternoon teas for youngsters in the neighborhood, who played with the large collection of African curios that eventually filled his room. After the railroad was built in front of his house, now and then he took neighbors' children to ride with him as far as Ellicott City and back. At twilight, some had the opportunity to gaze at the heavens through his big telescope, which always stood ready for use on its tall tripod.

Many of his contemporaries were entertained by Sheppard's collection of several hundred English and American prints. Among them were political cartoons, as well as cartoons having to do with reform measures in the United States—the Missouri Compromise, the Nebraska Bill, the Fugitive Slave Law—and a vicious collection expressive of the Southern opinion concerning the amalgamation of the races.

Sheppard was not lonely in the large brick house on Pratt Street. When he moved in, he took with him his brother Thomas and Nancy his wife, and their two chil-

dren, Nathan and Mary. As a housekeeper, there was
Eveline Scott, a free colored woman, who served in the
household for more than forty years. There was a colored cook to assist Eveline, and a Negro servant named
George Barton. A second colored man helped with the
outside work and inside cleaning. Quarterly and Yearly
Meeting times were opportunities for Sheppard to entertain his out-of-town Quaker friends and to make new
acquaintances.

> Sheppard was temperate in all things. He seldom in-
> dulged in luxuries (save for his furniture), yet when
> he had guests . . . during the annual gathering of
> Friends . . . a noted caterer was employed to furnish
> the table with the substantials and delicacies of the
> season.[21]

Sometimes Moses' hospitality was somewhat taxed, as
when he wrote a friend in Philadelphia, "I must consider myself favored at our last Yearly Meeting. . . .
Benjamin Warden, his wife, his two sisters, and a niece
of his wife, stopped with me. It was more than I looked
for, for I did not expect them to tabernacle with me.
They stayed for two weeks." [22] On another occasion he
mentioned: "I did not propose to have but two or three
[guests], but eight or ten pushed in." On the other
hand, some of his closest friends, with whom he corresponded for years, were first met at Yearly Meeting
times. Among these were John Sheppard, Benjamin
Hallowell, Dr. Nathan Shoemaker, and Thomas Ellicott.

John Sheppard (1767-1855), of Greenwich, New
Jersey, was a first cousin. The two men corresponded
from 1801 to 1855 and exchanged visits. John Sheppard
was a farmer, and for a season a member of the State

Assembly. On acknowledging Moses' invitation to stay
with him during Yearly Meeting, John wrote: "I have
received thy kind invitation to visit. . . . my daughter
and self may attend the sessions next month . . . write if
it will be convenient to lodge us, and if so how many of
the Sheppard tribe you can conveniently accommodate." [23] They made the trip, stayed a week, and on
return wrote, "We arrived home in the morning. . . .
your unremitting kindness and attention to us while
there demands our sincere acknowledgement, and I feel
much indebted for it. Mary in a particular manner
thanks her cousin Moses for her beautiful box, over and
above the general kindness that was lavished upon
us." [24] He added, "I have sent a barrel of apples which I
hope will prove good to your taste. . . . I am also
sending a small cheese to Cousin Ann."

After another visit to Baltimore, John Sheppard became ill and both men blamed it on the water. Moses
sent a rather humorous letter to his cousin, saying, "If
thee will pay us a visit in the spring, I will have something better than water—champagne, the Temperance
Society notwithstanding!" [25]

The many kinship ties among the Quakers was shown
by another guest to the Brick House. Benjamin Hallowell of Alexandria, Virginia, was a distant relative, an
able educator, and a recognized minister of the Society
of Friends. His school—The Alexandria Boarding
School—offered exceptional training in mathematics,
and many boys who desired to attend the United States
Military Academy, at West Point, including Robert
E. Lee, were trained by Benjamin Hallowell. This
teacher, like Moses Sheppard, had a great interest in the

rapidly developing study of the natural sciences. On one occasion, he told Moses: "The more we study the Book of Nature and become acquainted with the important lessons it teaches, and the interesting truths to be learned from this source alone, the more we Admire, love and adore the great Author of Nature." [26]

Sheppard frequently attended lectures on geology and anthropology and sent summaries to Hallowell. After hearing a talk by Professor Sillian of Harvard University, Moses exclaimed, "The Deity performs his wonders, and the fountains of the great deeps are broken up." He added, "the duration of time is beyond the comprehension of man, a thousand years are but as one day . . . and the future creations may produce a human race as superior to us as we are to the meanest reptile." [27] Listening to different speakers who told of the wonders of Egypt, and the new discoveries in geology, Sheppard said he enjoyed the talks on Egypt the most, because it was almost necessary to learn a new language to understand geology. He was surprised to note in a series of illustrated lectures on Egypt, "a koffle of black slaves tied by the neck to a pole, precisely as they now bring them out of the interior of Africa . . . and other evidence of their servility and degradation." [27] He added, "man's inhumanity to man has made countless millions mourn."

Sheppard read an original essay on the subject of reason and religion to a group that included Benjamin Hallowell. Hallowell felt that his views were expressed "with great force and clarity," [28] and urged Moses to publish the essay, saying: "Thy views appear to me to be eminently calculated not only to reconcile conflicting opinions, but to advance the true notions of the relation of man to Deity and his fellow creatures." [28] The Baltimorean replied that "he had never thought of giving public expression to abstract religious ideas. I cannot believe my pen can produce anything beyond the use of my immediate friends," he answered; "born in a class 'doomed to know little of life but labor,' I had not dared to question accepted doctrines or opinions consecrated by time until lately. I have slightly applied myself and I am surprised to find how far my opinions are taken as authority." [29] He expressed his belief that the human mind "was on its way upward," and the general conclusion "that truth and usefulness are more essential than faith and belief."

When Samuel F. B. Morse perfected his "electric-magnetic telegraph," whose wires came a short distance from Sheppard's home, the latter hastened to notify Benjamin Hallowell of the first failure caused by using lead pipe underground to carry the wires, and the success when wires were strung on poles through which "the fluid would pass." [30]

Benjamin Hallowell lectured at the Smithsonian Institution and was a pleasing speaker at Quaker lyceums.[31] Dr. Shoemaker wrote from Frankfort: "Benjamin Hallowell will take his leave of us on Fourth-day. He will leave a pleasant savour; all classes, both abolitionists and non-abolitionists, Jacksonian and anti-Jacksonians, appear to have been well satisfied with him." [32] Sheppard, who was shy of receiving praise for any of his own acts of kindness, wrote, perhaps humorously, "If I am correctly informed, Benjamin Hallowell is on the road to ruin. I am told he is becoming popular,

and popularity will ruin a Quaker." [33] Both Hallowell
and Sheppard continued to enjoy each other's com-
panionship for many years.

At Yearly Meeting, Sheppard first met Dr. Nathan
Shoemaker, another distant cousin, who was a practicing
physician in the City of Brotherly Love and a recognized minister of the Society of Friends. Dr. Shoemaker
was associated with the Pennsylvania Hospital, and was
one of the founders of the Friends Hospital for the Insane at Frankford. Sheppard wrote Thomas Ellicott: "I
believe he is a worthy man, and if thee should become
acquainted with him, I have no doubt thee will form
the same opinion." [34] On another occasion, Moses wrote
of his cousin, "He is an estimable man and his acquaintance is desirable. He is one of the few relatives that I am
always gratified to meet and associate with." [35]

The two Quakers began an extensive correspondence
lasting for many years. They often discussed religious
topics. Moses was the more liberal, but found he could
talk over any differences of opinion candidly with the
doctor. They both held to the generally expressed ideas
of the less evangelical Friends and united in their understanding of the needs for progressive social action.
Once the doctor wrote Moses, however:

> There is a convention sitting here for the reorganizing
> of society, to discuss the evils of the present social sys-
> tem, and the best means of reorganizing it so that
> conflicting interests now existing may be avoided. I
> think it will evaporate in smoke. There are many rest-
> less spirits amongst us who are dissatisfied with their
> present condition, and anxious to be doing something
> to overthrow the existing organized society.[36]

77

Among the Baltimoreans closest to Moses Sheppard were Elisha Tyson and his son Isaac, Thomas Ellicott, Philip E. Thomas, Benjamin Latrobe, and John Saurin Norris. Elisha Tyson (1750-1824) was a frequent visitor to the home of Sheppard, and Moses was always grateful to the older man for the assistance rendered to him as a youth and for his wise advice concerning humanitarian services. Elisha lived around the corner from the Brick House. Elisha's son Isaac (1777-1864) was an active figure in the Lombard Street Meeting. He was a merchant miller, and a director of the Union Savings Bank, interested in the Savings Bank of Baltimore, President of the Merchant's Fire Insurance Company, and later a director of the Baltimore and Ohio Railroad. For some years he made his home in the Brick House with his friend.

Of the Ellicott brothers, Thomas (1779-1859) was the intimate friend of Moses. He, like all the members of his family, was a miller, one-time President of the Union Savings Bank, and later a founder of the Baltimore and Ohio Railroad. In 1834, he moved to his wife's estate in Bucks County, Pennsylvania. Many letters passed between the two Quakers, and they frequently visited one another. Ellicott could entice Moses to make him a visit by writing, "There is an abundance of strawberries, and the prospect of a bountiful crop of raspberries." [37] To which Moses answered, "These constitute an almost irresistible invitation to a lover of good things to transport himself to the scene of plenty." [38] On his part, Moses would comment in a different season of the year, "The mercury is seven this morning, and was ten above in the backyard. We keep a fire in our rooms, coal in the front . . . we are enough heated, and every evening some of our friends come in. . . . we have many comforts, as I believe are useful and necessary." [39] On that occasion he wrote that he did not have any of Thomas Ellicott's favorite "crab apple cider, but in lieu of it we have lemonade." In later years, Moses would visit as long as two weeks at a time at Avondale, Ellicott's home.

Philip E. Thomas (1776-1861) was closely associated with Moses Sheppard in several undertakings, and often came to the Brick House to talk over their business and Quaker affairs. Thomas was Clerk, first of Old Town Meeting and then of Lombard Street Meeting when it was established; later he became Clerk of the Yearly Meeting, and at various times of its Meeting for Sufferings. Thomas was a "man whom people listened to with conviction," and one "in whom the prosperous merchants of Baltimore had unbounded confidence." [40] It was said of him that "he was a man of pious and benevolent heart, ever forward in efforts to advance the moral and religious conditions of men." [41] He was at one time Overseer of the Poor and active on a committee to assist free Negroes to emigrate to the Republic of Haiti. He became the first President of the Maryland Bible Society. Philip Thomas was one of the most active, far-sighted, and able businessmen in Baltimore; he quickened and consolidated interest in the development of the Baltimore and Ohio Railroad, of which he was the first President. He was President of the Merchants Bank, contributed $25,000 towards the construction of the Washington Monument, and presented Franklin Park to his native city. [42]

One of the most dynamic Baltimoreans well know to

Moses Sheppard was John H. B. Latrobe. He had many
talents, for he was a painter, musician, poet, author,
inventor, engineer, organizer, and soldier.[43] Latrobe
was tremendously interested in the plight of the Negroes. Next to his law practice—he was for decades the
General Counsel of the Baltimore and Ohio Railroad—
he gave most time to bettering the lot of the free men of
color. He was President of the Maryland Colonization
Society, a Vice President of the American Colonization
Society, and followed Henry Clay in its Presidency. He
shared both of these activities with Moses Sheppard. Of
Sheppard he wrote: "A friend of mine . . . attracted by
the part I took in Colonization, was Moses Sheppard, a
Quaker, who was my friend for life, and he and I were
delegates to the annual meeting of the American Colonization Society. He was a man whose wisdom was
sententious and profound. I think he loved me as much
as he loved anyone. . . ." [44] Once on leaving for Europe,
Latrobe wrote to Moses:

> I cannot leave the country without saying goodbye to
> one, so old and true a friend as you have been . . . even
> though the toil and trouble of the last ten days have
> forced me to put on paper what, otherwise, I would
> have expressed in person. Charlotte is by me, as I
> write, and she begs me to say to you, that she looks
> upon you as one of the visitors to Fanny Knowe during
> my absence. Bound myself for the Old World, I shall
> not forget my friends in the New. . . . Goodbye, my
> dear sir, goodbye." [45]

Moses often stopped at Latrobe's town house on the
corner of Charles and Reed streets, and often visited the
lovely house, with its spacious lawns, that the lawyer

built at Relay, Maryland, overlooking the valley through which the B & O Railroad passed.

Another welcomed visitor in the back parlor of the Brick House was John Saurin Norris (1813-1882), a much younger contemporary. Norris entered the employment of Isaac Tyson in the milling business, and married his daughter Henrietta. He became Treasurer of the Savings Bank of Baltimore, later President of the First National Bank, and Recording Secretary of the Maryland Historical Society. At the request of Moses Sheppard he became, at a much later date, the second President of the institution that Sheppard founded.

The caliber of these men of affairs suggests the worth of Moses Sheppard himself and the contribution he made in returning their friendship. It is interesting that, although Moses received (and saved) invitations to tea or other hospitality from some women in Baltimore and Philadelphia, he corresponded with few. None were his close friends, as their husbands or brothers were.

V

Religious Ferment

AT THE END of the eighteenth and through the first half of the nineteenth century, Maryland played an important part in the ebb and flow of religious life in America. Important conferences had assisted in reorganizing the Episcopal Church, the Methodist Episcopal Church was launched in the Lovely Lane Church in Baltimore, the United Brethren Church came into being in the city, the first Catholic Bishop in the United States chose Baltimore as his ecclesiastical see, and Unitarianism began by the Patapsco River.¹ Through most of this early period of religious ferment, the Society of Friends went its placid way, holding itself aloof from the disturbing movements about it. Sheltered behind a hedge erected through a strict enforcement of the Discipline, Quakers maintained their own way of life, dress, manner of speech, and habits.²

Members of the Society, however, were steadily widening their commercial outreach. John Sykes, a recent Quaker historian, has pointed out that the Quakers, through their skill in business, banking, and manufacturing, "were becoming over-involved in making money, and more than that in maintaining the attitudes

and status their prosperity conferred upon them." [3]
"Not all Friends were in business," Sykes admits, "but
the growing majority were, and it consumed them; it
veiled, except in certain individuals, the pressing in-
sights that were waiting to be realized within their
meetings for worship—that most delicate of instruments,
that became clumsy in their hands." Sykes says, "From
being the shock troops of the Spirit, they were becoming
the shock troops of commerce." Baltimore Yearly Meeting, with its large majority of rural Quakers, was less
caught up in this overpowering commercial activity
than London and Philadelphia Yearly Meetings; but
the condition existed even in Baltimore.

With the great revival campaigns and the counter liberal movements, waves of theological thinking pressed
about the Friends. For his own ideas, Moses Sheppard
drew heavily on the rationalists, Unitarians, and the
Quaker concept of the Inner Light. He rejected, with
many liberals of his day, the infallibility of the Scriptures and protested Calvin's theory of the depravity of
man. He made much of the laws of nature as an expression of the Creator. He declared: "When those laws are
understood, they will be found to be in perfect harmony
with the doctrines [Christ] promulgated. . . . the laws of
the universe and the doctrines of Christ will prove to be
one and the same." [4] He added: "The ethics of Christ
had been dimly perceived before the advent; his mission
was to confirm them, and accelerate their propagation.
. . . Christianity has never flourished among a people who
were destitute of science, with them it became a debasing
superstition or vindictive bigotry." In the same essay,
Sheppard wrote, "My views do not detract from the

authority of Christ, but they make the laws of nature and his doctrine coincide, and confirm one another."

Concerning the miracles, the Baltimorean did not go as far as many liberals. After reading Theodore Parker's book on the Scriptures, Moses wrote to Dr. Nathan Shoemaker, who sent him the Unitarian's book: "It contains some excellent views and substantial truths. I am rather of the opinion he entertains some doubts with regard to the miracles of the blessed Jesus, as we find them recorded in the four gospels." [5] He continued, "I admit that there are some things recorded in the Old Testament that tax my credulity pretty heavy, but I have never been disposed to call in question anything that I find in the New." To his friend, Thomas Ellicott, he wrote: "If we do what we believe is right, and abstain from injuring others, we have, I believe, the rudiments of religion, Bible or no Bible, and the effect would certainly be harmony and good will." [6]

The Society of Friends could not escape the new currents in religious thought, rationalistic or evangelical. In the Baltimore *Book of Discipline* there was no direct statement of theological belief, though it spoke of the "good works of Christ," and urged Friends "to stand open to the leadings of the love of God, through Jesus Christ our Lord." [7] The new edition of the *Discipline,* issued in 1821 when Moses was forty-six, stated: "The Apostles and Disciples of our Lord and Savior Jesus Christ, found it necessary to meet together for the consolation and strength of one another . . . pursuant to the design of the Gospel, the nature of which is to produce peace on earth and goodwill to men." [8] The nearest approach to theological doctrine was found in the section on Blasphemy, which stated:

> If any in our membership shall Blaspheme, or speak profanely of Almighty God, Jesus Christ, or the Holy Spirit; they ought to be timely and earnestly treated with . . . and if [any] deny the divinity of our Lord and Savior Jesus Christ, the immediate revelation of the Holy Spirit, or the authenticity of the Scriptures . . . they are not one in faith with us.[9]

In comparison with the Articles of the Church of England or Calvin's Catechism, the Quaker *Discipline* was exceedingly simple. Its very simplicity, however, made for contention between conflicting points of view. Ministers and others who had been influenced by quite different religious movements, speaking in the Quaker meetings for worship, produced disharmony and contention.

Living in the early period of textual criticism of biblical documents, Moses Sheppard was influenced as well by the discoveries of archeologists and scholars of his day. He wrote to Benjamin Hallowell that "the original manuscripts of the Bible passed through the hands of ignorant scribes who made many mistakes in copying the documents, and that in some cases designing men, who wished to impress their points of view, tampered with the originals." [10] Benjamin agreed that the Bible contained the most exalted concepts of God; "yet he found many statements which were irreconcilable with the character of God." [11] He added, "the most noble pictures of what man ought to be, and . . . his high destiny . . . with the means by which this high destiny can be achieved" are found in the New Testament.

Sheppard expressed himself very strongly on the Old Testament:

> It is valuable history, but taken as a whole unprofitable, if not an injurious book to place in the hands of persons, either young or old, whose minds are not mature, and well grounded in the New Testament. It contains many eternal truths, no doubt, in relation to the duties and spiritual condition of men [however] there is such a mixture of crime and violence in the Old Testament that it is difficult for the young and immature mind to harmonize the acts of the best Jews and Gentiles with the ideas we have formed of "pure religion and undefiled, which is to visit the widows and the fatherless in their affliction and to keep unspotted from the world." [12]

As the years passed, traveling ministers eloquently presented opposite ideas. Many visiting English Quakers, representing a warm evangelical position, stressed the Virgin Birth, the deity of Christ, the depravity of man, the substitutionary atonement, and the bodily resurrection. These doctrines, only occasionally stressed in the past, were now considered essential by the evangelicals. On the other hand, the most eloquent liberal ministers to visit Baltimore—such as Elias Hicks and John Comly of Philadelphia—grafted the liberal thinking of the day onto the stream of thought uttered by the early Quakers. They taught that the only essential was to believe that the Light of Christ, indwelling in the soul of man, was a sufficient guide to point the way to the good, to warn men of evil, and to give men the strength to achieve the good life. Their motto was: "Christ in you the hope of glory." This indwelling light, they declared, came from God and was the same divine power that illuminated the prophets and came to its fullest expression in Jesus of Nazareth.[13] The Baltimore businessman found the messages of Elias Hicks, John Comly and other liberals congenial to his way of thinking. It was said "that Sheppard rather gloried on being charged as a heretic." [14] Once he wrote, "there is hardly a man who is not a heretic to one other man." [15]

Matters came to a head in Philadelphia Yearly Meeting in 1827, where the Quakers divided, not only because of the conflict over religious views, but because the city and rural Friends had drifted apart. Some two-thirds of the membership conducted "an orderly retreat" to form a new organization, which came to be called the Hicksites or Liberals. Later in the same year, a separation followed in New York Yearly Meeting.

The separation in Baltimore Yearly Meeting, which took place in 1828, was without the bitterness and animosity engendered in the northern bodies. So few left to form an Orthodox Yearly Meeting that William Foster, an evangelical, wrote acquaintances in England: "Baltimore is the only Yearly Meeting on this continent, who can be said as a body to espouse the cause of the Hicksites." [16] Only two of the fifty-three representatives withdrew and, when joined by a small body of Quakers, organized a new Orthodox Yearly Meeting in the nearby McKendrean School House. Richard Townsend, a member of Old Town Meeting, wrote in his diary:

No uproar or commotion attended this division. . . . It is a good feature of our past history, and pleasant to remember that in our borders, all was quietness, and steadiness, in this movement; it seemed as if each party was fully aware of the magnitude and importance of the step it was taking; and that it had sufficient self-esteem to maintain its dignity and demeanor.[17]

Later Townsend added: "The waves of the ecclesiastical sea never ran as high in Baltimore as in the cities of New York and Philadelphia. The Separation itself was marked by dignity and courtesy in our bodies."[18]

According to Townsend, the large majority of the members in Baltimore, including Moses Sheppard, remained with the Hicksites. Anna B. Thomas, an Orthodox Friend, wrote that "at least four-fifths of the membership remained with the Liberals [Hicksites]."[19] The meeting houses and their records remained in the hands of the liberals.

Irrevocable harm was done to the Society of Friends by this division.[20] For many months following the separation in Baltimore—in fact as late as 1853—it was reported in Lombard Street Meeting that additional Friends had "withdrawn" to join the Orthodox Friends. Among these members were such strong and able Quakers as Gerard T. Hopkins, James Gillingham, and Hugh Balderston, all of whom were greatly missed. Moses Sheppard continued his regular attendance at Lombard Street, but felt the division keenly. Later he wrote to Thomas Ellicott, "the reduced and broken community of Quakers no longer affords a social circle, in neither segment of the Society is there enough similarity of character or persons to give a zest to the evening fireside."[21] He especially regretted that the absence of members caused the younger Friends to extend their acquaintanceship with those outside the Society of

Friends, "which led off from the habits and principles of the Society." As another consequence, Sheppard's own list of associates was broadened, and he was surprised to find that he "seemed to be welcome in a different class, but in such company [he] discovered he had more of Quakerism than [he] was aware of. . . ." [21]

As the Hicksite Friends did not insist on a rigid interpretation of doctrinal statements, there were no further separations in their societies, but within twenty years the Orthodox Friends were troubled by a second division. This grew out of the lively evangelical movement among English Friends, forwarded in this country by Joseph John Gurney, an eloquent scholar trained in a system of evangelical theology. Many Friends accepted his interpretation and became "Gurneyite Friends." They became the largest body of Quakers in the United States, and took his name. In New England, however, John Wilbur of Hopkinton, Rhode Island, vigorously opposed Gurney, championing the older ways. He trusted in the Inner Light as strongly as the Hicksites, but coupled with this "the usual doctrines of Orthodox Christianity." A division eventually took place in the East, but only one small group in Baltimore Yearly Meeting was involved. Dr. Shoemaker wrote Moses: "There are divisions amongst us [in Philadelphia], as was the case with the Apostles. . . . for my part, I am determined not to quarrel with my brethren about it. I have passed through one campaign, that of 1827/28, and I desire never to engage in another." [22] The doctor expressed a sentiment with which Sheppard agreed, "I trust there is something above all Scripture . . . and that is the mediation of God's law in the soul of man. . . . to live in obedience to this, that is required of us." Moses replied: "I entertain Gurneyites, Hixites, Wilburites, Congregational Quakers, Progressive Quakers, Quakers in practice and Quakers out of practice. I require none of them to pronounce Shibboleths." [23]

Outside Quaker circles, the religious world was in a turmoil during the 1840's, with the growth of new denominations and the division of old. Spiritualism, much in vogue during this decade, affected only one frontier Meeting. Baltimore Yearly Meeting felt it necessary to issue a statement on the matter. "The practice of attempting to hold communion with the Spirits of the deceased persons was a cause of much exercise. . . . Friends are cautioned against this manifest delusion. . . . let the subject entirely alone." [24] The Church of the Latter Day Saints (Mormons) "which sprouted in the revival-singed soil of . . . western New York among an uncouth and unstable people, pitifully eager for signs and wonders," [25] grew as fast as, if not faster than, the Society of Friends, but there is no record of Quaker converts to Mormonism. Most evangelical ministers preached the second coming of Christ, but none fixed the exact date. William Miller, a Baptist farmer-preacher of Low Hampton, New York, found in the Book of Daniel that the event would take place in 1843.

Sheppard sent word to his Avondale friend, "The final conflagration of the world is a bugbear renewed, in some quarters in every age. Miller has brought it to public attention." [26] The Unitarian minister in Baltimore preached a sermon refuting the technique of using the Book of Daniel for divination, and Sheppard had a thousand copies printed and distributed. He sent one to Benjamin Taylor with the comment, "Any absurdity, however apparent, any system of theology, however absurd, will find favor with the credulous multitude." [27] He continued, "At the present time, the Christian religion is in a state of effervescence, at least the Protestant part. Storms purify the atmosphere . . . all great religious movements are produced by and accompanied with convulsive throes." He commented further, "[Organized] Christianity is far in the rear of the Christian character, perhaps the present turmoil may produce a forward movement, I am decidedly of the belief that Protestantism cannot remain stationary where it is, it must either advance or recede." [27]

In his personal religious practice, Sheppard never neglected attendance at meetings for worship or business. His service on committees became almost continuous. He audited the accounts of the Treasurer, served as a representative to overhead bodies, nominated members to act as clerks, elders, and overseers, and gave advice on discipline committees. Young men in the meeting lost their membership for accepting service in the militia; others were disowned for using profanity, selling liquor, or for the excessive use of alcohol. In 1843, a member was disowned for hiring a slave and acting as an agent when the master was absent. The Monthly Meeting records were filled with judgments on members who were married by a "hireling teacher"; efforts were made to soften the rule, and it is obvious from the records of the Monthly Meeting that an acknowledgment of error and a desire to retain membership were sufficient to gain reinstatement. When a young Friend was under discipline for having attended a wedding accomplished by a clergyman, Moses Sheppard wrote, "Deal gently with the young man . . . important consequences resulting from an apparent trifling circumstance in youth . . . may give a direction to determine the character of the man through life." [28]

The spiritual well-being of Lombard Street Meeting was strengthened by the messages from the recorded ministers who were "moved by the Spirit." Of a Friend appearing in the ministry, Moses wrote: "We have a new member in our gallery; whose exhortations are frequent and earnest; she generally speaks twice in a session, and speaks as one having authority, and not as a scribe. . . . She visited Francis Cockran, and he has been much more depressed since!" [29]

At home and by correspondence, Sheppard carried on lengthy religious discussions with his older friends, adding to the list Benjamin F. Taylor, a teacher in Loudoun County, Virginia. Sheppard was an optimist. He believed that man was on an upward journey, with some backsliding, but, he declared, "the progress of mankind is ad infinitum, when we consider who is the teacher, and the unending period of time through which the human race may be taught." [30] The humanitarian's sturdy belief in progress was traceable to the ancient Quaker insistence on the perfectibility of mankind. With Elias Hicks, he believed that the work of redemption, carried out in Palestine in the first century, could be repeated in each heart. "Those who desire it . . . crucify the sins of the flesh, and do the will of God." [31]

The passing of the years allowed Sheppard to spend more time with his books. "He read much, and of the best authors; and not merely for amusement, nor for variety or show, but for the honest purpose of finding truth, and cultivating his own mind." [32] In the community of his friends, "there were few more original or fearless thinkers than he, few more sincere lovers of the truth, few who abhored utterly all sophistry and sham."

Sheppard insisted that the human mind should not be trammeled by dogma or ecclesiastical statements of the past. When Dr. Shoemaker wrote Moses that a visiting Quaker minister had declared that "reason was a stumbling block in religion," [33] Moses replied, "The present tendency of the human mind is onward, we set no bounds to its attainment, the impossibilities of today are overcome tomorrow." Benjamin Taylor wrote, "Orthodoxy cannot expect to sustain itself by saying to the honest inquirer after truth 'here is something you must not look into. . . .'" [34] To which Moses replied, "You and Rev. George W. Burnap, according to the Orthodox, are both rank heretics. Will not my character, already suspect, suffer from the association!" [35]

Philadelphia Yearly Meeting considered the publication of some advices on the use of the Scriptures. Sheppard doubted the wisdom of such publications, because, he felt, such pronouncements led to disagreements and schisms. "We have not heretofore understood," he wrote, "the fact that our Society has been as much under clerical influence as any other Protestant church." [36] Looking back on the division of 1828, he added, "Our clergy have made one schism and they may make another. . . . If they would propound the duties of Christianity instead of their notions of is doctrines they would do more good, by thus giving precedence to acts rather than belief." On another occasion he wrote, "Thee will perceive by the answers to the questions on the miracles that all kinds of opinions and forms of belief are entertained in our Society, hence it is best to publish nothing." [37]

Sheppard considered publishing a well-printed copy of the Sermon on the Mount, somewhat like Thomas Jefferson's *Extracts from the Moral Principles of Jesus.* This he considered because he felt the ordinary person did not have the time nor the inclination to "labor through the thousand pages of the Bible." [38] In the end, however, he gave up the plan.

He and his friends became quite philosophic in their correspondence, Moses sometimes taking a pessimistic position. "It is true, I have large rooms and warm fires. . . . I have the elements of contentment, and I fear it is equally true that I am not duly grateful when I see men in everyway superior not so well furnished . . . but, when love gives us life, he gave us woe. . . . The journey of life is but one of trial and perplexity." Moses then added, "This partial view of mankind is surely not the last. . . . our laboring and suffering shall be compensated in a way we cannot comprehend . . . those who must suffer here, will meet to enjoy hereafter." [39]

Sheppard kept an open mind on the subject of immortality. "Mounds of granite or marble seem, for their strength and structure, to imprison the body and soul . . . the body only is enclosed, and the mind is disengaged and left at large, unrestrained and unconfined. Immortality may be obtained, and we hope has been obtained by those we love." [40] Dr. Shoemaker wrote Moses, "Time is but the beginning of Eternity"; and Moses replied, "Of that bourne we know nothing except by deduction and analogy, not by evidence, no voyager has returned to narrate celestial scenes, and if one were to return I believe it would be impossible for us to comprehend existence apart from substance, time and space." [41]

VI

The Exciting Thirties

In 1830 BALTIMORE, with a population of 80,625, was the second city in size in the United States. There were 14,788 free men of color and 4,123 slaves. As Moses Sheppard took his daily walk, he could see to the north the new brick shot tower, conspicuous because of its height of 234 feet. Passing up Charles Street, he could take pleasure from the colonial rectory of St. Paul's Episcopal Church, with its palladian window and white trim. Further along, the Roman Catholic Cathedral, with its solid walls of Patapsco granite, impressive portico and gilded dome, made a dignified contrast to the surrounding brick houses. The tall spire of the First Presbyterian Church and the delicate pediment of the First Independent Church caught Sheppard's eye. On Howard's Hill (now Mt. Vernon Place), the stately monument to the Father of his Country dominated the landscape. The white marble statue of George Washington, incongruous in Roman toga, topped the impressive shaft. From Howard's Hill, he could see the harbor as far as Fort McHenry. The Quaker physician and artist, Robert Sutcliff, from York, wrote, "I do not know any city in England superior in beauty." [1]

After a visit to Baltimore, William Wirt, Attorney General of the United States, wrote his daughter; "No city in the world has a more beautiful country around it . . . in the directions west, north, and east . . . the ground rising and falling in forms of endless variety, sometimes soft and gentle, at others bold and commanding . . . the fields richly covered with grass . . . clumps of trees, groves and forests [all] flourishing. . . ." [2]

It was only three blocks from the Brick House to the Lombard Street Meeting House, surrounded with Linden trees; a bit south stood the Otterbein United Brethren Church, with wide windows and stately colonial tower. If he was after kitchen supplies, Moses Sheppard traveled four blocks south to the Hanover Street market. William Wirt said of this place that he saw "quantities of superb beef, mutton, lamb, veal, and all sorts of hogsheads of wild duck, geese, pheasants, and partridge." [2] He noted that across the lane there were "wagons and carts, groaning under the loads of country production," while nearby were "loads of sweet-cakes of all sorts. . . ."

The foundation of the city's prosperity was still in its port. Although there were short wharves between Light and Calvert Streets, the larger wharves, including those opposite the warehouses owned by Sheppard, extended out from the land lying between Cheapside and the Fallsway. Ships from many countries could be seen loading and unloading from the broad windows of the Brick House on Pratt Street.

Exports of American products from Baltimore, in 1830, amounted to just over $4,000,000 and of foreign products re-exported to nearly a million more; imports were over four million, a rather neat balance.[3] Flour was still the chief export, amounting to 308,116 barrels that year; 14,200 hogsheads of tobacco were shipped out, as well as 4,000 barrels of beef and pork, nearly as many of fish, 148,210 kegs of butter, 480,210 kegs of lard, and 34,120 gallons of whisky.[3] Sugar from the Caribbean Islands was still the most important import. Valuable cargoes of silver, copper, and gold came in from South America, and shiploads of guano, much needed to refertilize the tobacco fields of Maryland and Virginia, came from the Chincha Islands off Peru. Baltimore imported so much coffee from Brazil that it was said the chief smell about the harbor for decades was that of roasting coffee.[4] China silks, satins, and tea, now came in at Canton, an area east of Fells Point. More than 300 pairs of millstones in or within ten miles of the city enabled Baltimore to be called "the granary of the West Indies." [3] Mitchell and Sheppard assisted in importing and transporting many of these products.

Baltimore's chief contribution to ocean transportation was "the Baltimore Clipper," an almost perfect vessel and the fastest of her day. From the time the Quaker, William Fell, started his boat yard on the point that bears his name, large numbers of ships were launched there. These included the log canoe, the bugeye, the ketch, and the schooner; also such large ships as the twenty-eight gun frigate *Virginia*, ordered by the Continental Congress, and the *Constellation*, sistership of the *Constitution* (*Old Ironsides*).[5] The pride of Baltimore was the clipper, "a small schooner, usually seventy-five to one hundred feet long, with two very tall, slender masts, sharply raked, and very light stayed." [6] The speed of this vessel depended on her streamlining, "she had a hull which surpassed any other of her time in slipping through the water." [7] She could sail closer to the wind than the broad tublike boats of her day. Chartered as a privateer, the clipper ship made herself at home off the coast of Great Britain.

According to Hamilton Owens, the most beautiful, and perhaps the fastest, ship ever built in the Baltimore area was the *Ann McKim,* ordered by Isaac McKim in 1831. She was a luxury ship, the largest of the clippers, with frame of live oak, and her bottom sheathed in copper. In June, 1833, the *Ann McKim,* loaded with three thousand barrels of flour, rounded the Cape of Magellan and unloaded in Callao, Peru, returning in a year with a cargo of copper. The outgoing trip took 95 days, and the voyage home 72.[8]

Unfortunately, to the distress of men like Moses Sheppard, the clipper ships could be used for evil purposes; to the slave trader they "were a divine answer to prayer." [9] The slave trade was outlawed by the United States government, but the clipper could outsail any man-of-war seeking to stop the traffic in slaves. Human cargoes were landed in the West Indies and then smuggled into the southern states. "Capable as the Baltimore clipper was in the eyes of the owner," wrote Hamilton Owens, "she must have been a hell afloat to the black wretches who were taken aboard her on the Gold Coast for shipment." [9] Her hold was relatively shallow, and much space was occupied by the stores necessary for the crew and for goods to trade in Africa with the native chiefs who sold the slaves. A temporary platform was erected on a scaffolding some three or four feet below the main deck, and on this improvised platform the Negroes slept in spoon fashion.[10]

Fortunately, many Baltimore clippers were engaged in bringing European immigrants to the city. From the earliest days when the Irish Carrolls came to Maryland, there was a steady influx of Irishmen; after 1830, this influx became a flood. In the thirties the numbers of immigrants from Germany increased sharply; first the skilled clock makers, cobblers, smiths, weavers and bakers, then the more affluent groups who brought the noble Protestant and Catholic cultures. The Germans did business with the Quakers, but they never understood why the Quakers did not praise the Lord with cymbal and harp, as the psalmists and the German Liederkranz did.

Sheppard was in the provision business when the first steamship was commissioned for the Baltimore trade. In 1813, six years after Robert Fulton sailed the *Clermont* up the Hudson River, the ship *Chesapeake* transported passengers and freight from Baltimore to Frenchtown at the head of the bay. It was not long before many boats, powered by steam, were taking the goods of Mitchell and Sheppard to rivers on the Eastern Shore, up the bay to Elkton, down to Norfolk, up the Rappahannock to Fredericksburg, Virginia, and up the Potomac to Washington. By 1830, the Union Line had ships steaming between Baltimore and Philadelphia, leaving one city at six AM and reaching the other at noon the next day. Sheppard often took this line as a comfortable way to reach Philadelphia Yearly Meeting.

Merchants like Moses Sheppard, eager as they were to extend the shipping of the city, did not neglect the profitable trade with the expanding West. Baltimore had an early advantage when the Federal government constructed the National Pike, which by the 1830's was built over the Allegheny Mountains and as far west as Columbus, Ohio. This excellent road cut the cost of freight from the West to Baltimore in half. Baltimore was thus brought nearer to Ohio than its rival Philadelphia, and a large quantity of goods that once went down the Ohio and Mississippi rivers came directly east to the Chesapeake Bay. Still earlier, when main roads were fingering their way out of Baltimore in increasing numbers, Sheppard had helped to establish a chartered turnpike to Frederick, Maryland. He owned stock in the Baltimore and Frederick Turnpike Company, and was a "manager." [11]

The early advantage of Baltimore over its rivals to the north was lost before the middle of the century. "New York possessed a land-locked harbor, which offered more perfect natural shelter than that of any other major American port as close to the sea." [12] In 1818, the Black Ball line began a weekly schedule of sailings between New York and Liverpool. "At that critical period of port rivalry, these sailing packets [leaving on schedule] did much to cause the channels of trade with Europe to flow towards New York rather than Boston or Philadelphia" [13]—or Baltimore. In addition, the clever New York merchants diverted the handling of the southern cotton crop from the nearby ports to New York; returning vessels brought back English manufactured goods, which were then transshipped to the South, to the benefit of New York traders. The final blow came with the opening of the Erie Canal in 1825. The success of this undertaking can hardly be exaggerated; the entire Great Lake district now found a new outlet to the East. The results are shown in the commerce that flowed into and out of New York, Philadelphia, and Baltimore. In 1815 exports from New York were $10 million, from Philadelphia $4 million, and from Baltimore $5 million; in 1840, the exports from New York were $132 million, from Philadelphia $10 million, and from Baltimore still $5 million. Imports to New York amounted to $23 million in 1821, to Philadelphia $8 million, and Baltimore $4 million; in 1840 imports at New York were $60 million, to Philadelphia $16 million, and to Baltimore $8 million.[14]

Baltimore merchants, stimulated by a Chamber of Commerce, of which Sheppard was a member, tried to meet this new competition. The first attempt was to dig the Chesapeake and Delaware Canal cutting across the land separating the two bays. When completed the new passageway opened an inland waterway from Philadelphia to Baltimore, and on to Norfolk, Virginia. The second attempt, less successful, was to construct a canal from Havre de Grace, on the lower reaches of the Susquehanna River, north to the Pennsylvania line. This tapped a large wheat-growing area. The third project was a revival of the older plan to dig a waterway from Georgetown, on the Potomac River, to Cumberland, Maryland.[15] The Maryland legislature appropriated a considerable sum to further this project, but since the terminal of the canal was some distance from Baltimore, merchants in the city were not so enthusiastic.

Still more trade was lost by Baltimore when a remarkable canal system was built connecting Philadelphia with Pittsburgh; this included an incline railroad that took canal boats over the ridges of the Alleghenies. Moses Sheppard and his fellow merchants, alarmed at this situation, sought a new answer to the problem of east-west transportation.

In 1821, a group of Quakers in Darlington, England, built a railroad, primarily for the transportation of coal, from Bishop Auckland to Darlington. George Stevenson constructed a successful steam engine, and by 1825 the Quaker Line was in operation. Evan Thomas, brother of Philip E. Thomas, then President of the Merchants Bank, went to England and returned enthusiastic about the possibilities of developing a railroad in Maryland. Colonel John Eager Howard, the largest landowner in Baltimore, called together a group of businessmen, including the financier George Brown, to hear a report from the returned Quaker. It was decided "to take under consideration the best means to restore to the City of Baltimore, that portion of the Western trade which had recently been diverted from it by the introduction of steam navigation and by other means. . . ." [16] A committee, including Philip Thomas and Thomas Ellicott, was appointed to develop plans; and when they reported that it was feasible to build a railroad from Baltimore to the Ohio River, it was decided to seek incorporation for the purpose. As Baltimore was one hundred miles nearer the West than Philadelphia and two hundred miles nearer than New York City, the merchants were assured that a successful railroad would return Baltimore to her preeminence as a center of trade.

On February 28, 1827, a charter was secured for the Baltimore and Ohio Railroad, with the right to issue three million dollars worth of stock. Philip E. Thomas was named President of the corporation, and J. H. B. Latrobe, who was now Moses Sheppard's lawyer, counsel. In addition to the stock purchased by individuals, the City and State invested several million dollars in the enterprise. Many mechanical problems concerning railroading were worked out, and on January 1, 1830, a party of ladies and gentlemen, including the Postmaster General of the United States, was drawn by a single horse from the city terminus to the Carroll viaduct, a distance of six miles.[17] Five months later, the line was extended to Ellicott's mills, with passenger trains running on schedule. A new era in transportation in the United States thus began in Maryland. Moses Sheppard was much interested in the enterprise, and was an early investor and later a director.[18]

Locomotives soon succeeded horses as the motive power on the railroad, the first practical commercial engine being constructed by Phineas Davis, a Quaker living in York, Pennsylvania. This engine, named *The York*, safely ran at a speed of thirty miles an hour; by 1831, it was hauling passengers and freight to Frederick, Maryland. Tracks were laid past Moses Sheppard's house on Pratt Street, but when steam engines took the place of horses, the City Council would not allow them to operate within the city limits. Horses continued to pull the cars along Pratt Street and down to the docks.[19]

It was said of the originators of the American railroad, that Philip Thomas and his associates "were in fact, competent, resourceful, and determined American business men. . . . at the risk of their reputations, they gathered together a great aggregate of private capital for the general good. . . ." [20]

A period of great speculation began in the thirties, speculation in farms, town lots, banks, canals, and railroads. This was followed by an extensive depression in 1837, which lasted for five years. Sheppard wrote Thomas Ellicott: "When I observe the prevailing anxiety and distress, the general discontent and trouble, there seems grounds for an opinion that this world is the penitentiary of the solar system." [21]

Moses Sheppard's gloom was heightened by his experience with the Bank of Maryland, of which he was a director.[22] The President of the Bank was Evan Poultney, a respected member of the Society of Friends, and on the board, in addition to Sheppard, were other Quakers. "The officers and directors were among the elect, at least in popular estimation." [23] But in 1833, President Andrew Jackson refused to recharter the Bank of the United States, a panic developed, and in March of 1834, the officials of the bank announced that, because of the withdrawal of Federal funds from the institution, business could no longer be continued. William Ellicott headed a committee to make an accounting of the bank's assets, but before a full report could be made a riot broke out in the city. A mob gathered in front of the imposing residence of Reverdy Johnson, counsel for the bank. At first the mob was content with throwing stones through the windows of the house, but as the mob grew they broke into the dwelling, "threw its contents, including a valuable library, into the street, and set fire to the books." [24] They began to tear the house itself to pieces "even toppling over the marble columns of the Greek portico which adorned it." Other mobs, undisturbed by the authorities, attacked the homes of officials and directors of the bank; even the house of the Mayor was broken into, the furniture piled in the street and burned. Finally, well-armed men met at the Washington Monument, and led by eighty-three-year-old General Sam Smith, defender of Baltimore in 1813, paraded through the town and intimidated the mob. But it was not until regular soldiers were brought from Annapolis and Washington that order was restored. Eventually the State Legislature paid one hundred thousand dollars to the property owners, because of the failure of the city authorities to protect its citizens.[25] Again Baltimore lived up to its reputation of "Mob Town."

From its inception, Moses Sheppard watched the continued growth of the Baltimore and Ohio Railroad. Through Philip Thomas and J. H. B. Latrobe, he kept in close touch with the plans and progress of this new means of transportation. As long as Philip Thomas retained the presidency, Sheppard was confident of the railroad's future. When the line reached Frederick, it was the longest railroad in the United States; Washington was tied in by a branch in 1835. For a time, during the depression, the public lost interest in the B & O. Meanwhile Baltimore's transportation was extended to Harrisburg by the Baltimore and Susquehanna Railroad, and to Philadelphia by the Philadelphia, Baltimore and Wilmington Railroad. Owners of canal stock fought the railroads—for example, as when the owners of Erie Canal stock secured a law in the New York Legislature forbidding the railroad, whose tracks now extended to the western part of the State, to carry freight except in the winter when ice closed the Canal.[26]

In 1836, Philip Thomas told Latrobe that he was "tired and discouraged" [27] and would like to resign as president. It is possible that his resignation was hastened by a letter from Elias Hicks, in which the famous preacher questioned whether an Elder of the Meeting should spend so much time on business. Elias was certain that "preoccupation with roadbeds, bridges, tunnels, ties, and railroad carriages, would stifle religious life." [28] The Long Island minister wrote at the same time to another Quaker, James P. Stabler, the Assistant Superintendent of the B & O, that railroading "belonged principally to men of this world, but not to the children of the light, whose kingdom was not of this world." [28]

Latrobe declared that Philip Thomas was "more instrumental in starting the enterprise than anyone else," [27] and that "no other person in the community would have done what [Thomas] did more honestly, more prudently, or in any respect better, during the period of his presidency." In accepting Thomas' resignation, the Board passed a resolution, stating "that he was the father and projector of the Baltimore and Ohio Railroad, and thus could be regarded as the father of the railroad system in the United States." [29]

After his friend gave up the presidency of the railroad, Sheppard became increasingly uneasy about the conduct of its business. Frequently the management spent more money than it took in from revenues; for several decades the corporation could pay its interest only in railroad stock or script. After a brief tenure by Joseph Patterson, Louis W. McLane was named to the presidency at an annual salary of four thousand dollars. He was a man of wide experience, a former Secretary of the Treasury of the United States and Ambassador to Great Britain. Latrobe said that "he possessed great and statesman-like qualities." [30] Yet Latrobe did not have confidence in him. "I never was quite sure that he took much interest in his office . . . he was not a pleasant person to get along with. He was peremptory and at times uncertain, and would not abide opposition or difference of opinion."

The general public, however, had confidence in McLane, and as the depression eased, the railroad pushed up the mountains to Cumberland. Latrobe, the engineer, laid out the last sixty-five difficult miles to the top of the Alleghenies. Moses Sheppard was one of the first to make the trip to Cumberland. This was still a primitive town, with the railroad tracks running through its center. On each side were mountains from which coal was taken to be shipped eastward. Moses noticed the coal cars were loaded so high that coal was spilled along the tracks, making the right of way unsightly; and he asked that the condition be remedied.

Sheppard did not like President McLane; he felt he was "too aristocratic, too great a man, too unapproachable." [31] The Quaker resented doing business with an official who required his callers to send in their names by a porter; often the reply came that the president was engaged and was unable to see his callers. The directors of the railroad knew of Moses' interest in the line, and were well acquainted with his business ability. In 1842, while Moses was out of town, they elected him a director. Moses replied, on his return, "I have no wish for a directorship of any kind, a private state suits both my genius and my taste best." [32] To Thomas Ellicott, he wrote, "I long ago discovered I was designed to occupy the shady part of the picture, and I am contented there." He also told Thomas, "I knew I was too stubborn to be made a tool or catspaw, to which situation the president had reduced the directors," and added, "The directors were afraid of McLane, who had acquired a singular and commanding influence over the Board; he issued orders from his chambers, and his subordinates seldom approached him, and when they did it was with trepidation, like his majesty King George the First." Sheppard thought that McLane "was more unapproachable than the President of the United States."

By 1848, Sheppard changed his mind about a directorship in the railroad. He declared that the stock holders were dissatisfied and the corporation "was badly managed at enormous expense." [33] He recognized that revenues were large, but said the funds received were divided among the people employed. Some of the directors, who felt it was time for new leadership, asked Moses Sheppard to give them his advice, and to become a director. In October of that year, the Quaker wrote to his Avondale friend that he was "in the market as a candidate for a directorship in the Baltimore and Ohio Railroad," though he admitted his election was in doubt. "I will not electioneer," he said, "if they see proper to elect me very well, but it shall not be at my solicitation. If I do no good," he continued, "I may keep a man out that would do harm." [34] He and Johns Hopkins were elected.

Moses Sheppard was named to the Committee on Construction and Reconstruction. This group immediately decided to push the right of way west of Cumberland. Meanwhile, Louis McLane, sensing opposition to his management, resigned, and was succeeded by Thomas Swann, later a mayor of Baltimore City. The tracks of the B & O were laid down to Wheeling, on the Ohio River.

Men of keen insight, like Sheppard, saw that the railroad would now outdistance the canals as the means of transportation in America. In spite of this, the State of Maryland continued to vote large sums to complete the Chesapeake and Ohio canal as far as Cumberland. The cost of transporting produce growing west of the Alleghenies was much reduced, and the West, previously tied with the economy of the South by way of the Mississippi River, was now joined economically with the East, thus isolating the South. "Had it not been for the railroads," Ernest Bogart has written, "[like the Baltimore and Ohio] the full development of the Far West, and of other parts of our country, untouchable and inaccessible by river and canal, would have been impossible." [35] Sheppard may not have contemplated the vast extension and usefulness of the developing railroads in the United States, but never lost faith in them as a financial venture. He was, by 1849, the seventh largest stockholder in the Baltimore and Ohio Railroad.[36]

Merchants like Sheppard were "still the most important men [in the city], and, as always they continued to look longingly toward the lush countryside and think of themselves as landed proprietors." [37] Although Sheppard owned land in the country, on the Gunpowder River and to the west of Baltimore, he remembered the hard days at Jericho Mills and the log cabin with its dirt floor. He was content to sit by his open fire, surrounded by his books and visited by his friends, in the Brick House on Pratt Street.

VII

Care for the Indians

THE EARLY ATTEMPTS of Baltimore Friends to aid the Indians came to an end when the tribes north of the Ohio River were driven beyond the Mississippi. Commenting on these efforts on behalf of the red men, Benjamin Taylor wrote: "The success of the Society's efforts in this cause . . . have never been commensurate to the zeal and disinterestedness which have promoted the exertions. . . ." [1] As new opportunities to aid the Indians became evident, the Indian Affairs Committee was reactivated: Philip E. Thomas was continued as Chairman, with Moses Sheppard and Isaac Tyson added to the membership. In 1839, a deputation of the northern Yearly Meetings solicited the aid of Southern Quakers in the assistance they were rendering the Six Nations in western New York. This began a new work in which Sheppard played an important part.

Baltimore Friends at first concentrated on establishing schools for Indian children and raising the standard of living of the adults. Sheppard wrote a friend, "I am decidedly in favor of conferring comfort on the body, and intelligence on the mind simultaneously." [2] He added, "I consider comfort essential to mental culture,

112

and mental culture essential to civilization." He was not sure that it was practical to attempt to civilize the Indians, for he undertsood that "the Indians look down on the labors of civilized life." He agreed with Benjamin Taylor, who was astonished at the tenacity with which the tribes clung to their original habits, as well as "the stern and unyielding resistance they make to all efforts to bring them within the pale of civilization." [3] It seemed to Taylor that instead of partaking of civilization, the Indians seemed to wither and die when exposed to the white man's culture.

Although the educational program had some success, the most important contribution the Friends made was their effort to protect the treaty rights of the red men. White men, going west along the Mohawk Valley, continued to press in on the Six Nations.[4] The Ogden Land Company, a group of unscrupulous and influential men, secured a preemptive claim to purchase the Indian lands in western New York, should the tribes be persuaded to give them up. The company sought in every way possible to bring this about and sent agents to the reservations for that purpose. Some of the Indian chiefs believed that the tribes would be better off if they had no contact with the white population; the Government's stated policy was to move all the Eastern tribes west of the Mississippi River. Some chiefs were bribed by agents of the Ogden Company to give up their ancestral acres.[5]

In 1838, the Ogden Company claimed it had the signatures of a majority of the chiefs to release the four reservations they held, although these signatures were

113

not secured in open Council as required by the laws of the tribes. This treaty was presented to President Van Buren for his approval, and placed before the Senate.

Fearful that this treaty would be ratified, delegates from the four Yearly Meetings (Baltimore, New York, Philadelphia, and the new Yearly Meeting of Genesee) waited on President Van Buren to plead that the Iroquoian Indians be allowed to retain their lands. They declared the proposed treaty fraudulent, secured by bribery and misrepresentation. Convinced of the rightness of their case, the President notified the Senate that "he could not . . . consistently cause the treaty to be carried into effect." [6] A document summarizing the material laid before the President was also prepared and given to each Senator. The Quakers were dismayed a few weeks later to learn that the Senate, by one vote, ratified the treaty giving the Indian lands to the Ogden company. Legally the Six Nations were now dispossessed of their territory and, within five years, required to move beyond the Great River.

The Quakers were appalled at the action of the Senate, and determined to arouse public opinion. They issued a *Narrative of the Proceedings . . . in Relation to the Indians,* recounting the illegal steps taken by the Ogden Company to secure the signatures of the chiefs to this Treaty of 1838. A great council was held at Farmington, New York, at which the chief Sachem solicited the aid and advice of the Friends. He reported that surveyors of the Ogden Company were already surveying their lands for the purpose of selling them to new settlers. The Quaker representatives advised the tribes not to resist even an unjust decree by force. "That path is a bloody one," they said, "it is strewed with the dead and dying. The Great Spirit leads no one of his children in that path." [7] They added, "We have seen your tears, and we weep with you." Meanwhile, efforts to right the wrong were set in motion.

Committees were formed in the three main cities, and Moses Sheppard became familiar with Philadelphia, New York, and Washington. Copies of the *Narrative* were sent to the Governor of Massachusetts, whose interest was aroused because his State had retained certain rights affecting the Indians of western New York when that territory was ceded to Albany. He issued a statement, saying, "If [the] Governor and Council of Massachusetts . . . had known all that had occurred in this unhappy business . . . they would not have approved it." [8] The Governor of New York also issued a statement, declaring, "I am fully satisfied that the consent of the Senecas was obtained by fraud, corruption, and violence, and that therefore [the treaty] ought to be held void." [9]

Eastern newspapers took up the cause of the Six Nations, and wrote of "the dark and mischievous spirit that actuated the land company" [9]; public opinion became aroused. President Van Buren listened with attention to Philip Thomas and Moses Sheppard when, on several occasions, they presented the case for the Indians. The two Baltimore Friends pleaded with the Secretary of War "that this small remnant of a once numerous nation, be rescued from the melancholy fate that has befallen all the other tribes of Indians east of the Mississippi." [10]

Those associated with the Ogden Land Company were alarmed at the rising public outcry, and as a result of the publicity given their conduct by the Quakers, worked out a compromise through the mediation of the Secretary of War. Moses Sheppard said earlier: "The black man and the Indian cannot get justice here, and they had better go where they can find it, if there is such a place;" but he was happy to work on the suggested solution, which would save a portion of the land for the tribes. The suggested formula, which Sheppard helped to draw up and the Ogden Land Company agreed to accept, included the following items: 1. Those members of the Six Nations who desired to go beyond the Missouri River would be paid a fair price for their lands. 2. Two of the four reservations, at Cattaraugus and Allegheny, would be restored to the Indians. 3. For the other two reservations of Tonawanda and Buffalo, the Ogden Land Company would pay at the rate agreed upon in the Treaty of 1838. 4. A proper portion of the $102,000, claimed to have been spent by the tribes on improvements to lands and buildings at Tonawanda and Buffalo, would be paid to the tribes.[11] Philip Thomas and Moses Sheppard, on behalf of Baltimore Yearly Meeting, signed this Supplementary Treaty.[12]

The Supplementary Treaty provided that the Six Nations would have 52,000 acres of fertile land. As there were only 2,500 individuals in the member tribes, this amounted to a goodly acreage per family. If the tribes rejected the Treaty, they would be required to leave New York State for western territory. An advantage in the new treaty was the concentration of the tribes and government support for their schools. The Secretary of War promised an annual support of $10,000 for this purpose.[13]

Moses Sheppard pointed out to the Indian Affairs Committee that the Secretary of War had been induced to exert his influence on the Ogden Land Company "under a sincere desire to afford the Friends a full opportunity to carry out their views in relation to the improvement of the Indians." [14] This being the case, "it was expected by the Government that the influence and cooperation of the Society would be exerted towards obtaining an early ratification of the proposed treaty." Sheppard thought if the Indians accepted the treaty it would place a heavy responsibility upon Quakers to expand their work of civilizing the tribes, and that their efforts "would be observed with great interest by the public at large . . ." He felt that if the attempt failed, "it probably would be the last effort that would be made in behalf of this injured and suffering race." Philip Thomas and Sheppard were appointed to represent Baltimore on the group that would present the Supplementary Treaty to the Iroquois and the associated tribes.

The two men put their business in order and set out on the long journey to the Buffalo Creek Reservation. The Baltimore and Ohio Railroad had not yet reached Cumberland, and the Stockton and Falls Line of stage coaches went north over very indifferent roads, so Thomas and Sheppard decided to go most of the way by water. They went by steam to New York, and then up the Hudson River by boat to the terminal of what, up to that time, was the greatest engineering wonder of the country, the Erie Canal. The canal packet used by the two Quakers was the most elaborate and best equipped boat on the Big Ditch.[15] It was strictly for passengers and took precedence over all other crafts in passing at midstream or on entering one of the eighty-three locks between the Hudson River and Lake Erie. The men spent the day on deck watching the cultivated fields and dense woods slip by, now and then making short visits to the towns that lined the canal—Schenectady, Utica, Rome, Syracuse, Rochester, and Lockport. The two railroad men were astonished by the eighteen ac-queducts that carried the canal over small and large rivers; one took the boat over the Mohawk River and another over the Genesee River.[16] They wondered if their projected railroad, now approaching the top of the Allegheny Mountains, would ever carry as much traffic as the Erie Canal.

When the Grand Council Assembled on the Buffalo Creek Reservation, many chiefs were present as well as representatives of the four Yearly Meetings. The Friends explained the background history of the present situation, the validity of the Treaty of 1838-39 signed by forty-five Seneca chiefs, the efforts of Friends to nul-lify this treaty, and the willingness of the Ogden Land Company to accept the Supplementary Treaty. To the members of the emigrant party, the Quakers said: "The white men are now very numerous and powerful—the red men are few in number and very feeble. Some of their nations are entirely extinct—their council-fires are gone out forever. Others have been greatly reduced—and the little remnants yet living, are poor, and weak, and scattered abroad. . . ."[17] The Friends also re-minded the Indians that if they remained on the Res-ervations, they must turn chiefly to farming and away from hunting, give up the use of intoxicating liquor, and educate their children. The Supplementary Treaty was explained article by article. It was made plain that the tribes had but two choices, to go West or to concentrate their numbers on two of the four Reservations.

The Grand Council then adjourned for two days to provide opportunity for the chiefs to discuss all that was placed before them. During the hours when the chiefs deliberated, Moses Sheppard and Philip Thomas visited the Reservations. They noted that many of the Indians wore the old costumes, with blankets girded about them, tomahawks and scalping knives hanging from their belts, their faces painted in glaring colors, and many with ear rings and silver bracelets. A large number lived in wigwams or poor log huts, many made of bark, with dirt floors, on which they slept in buffalo robes. Sheppard went inside several houses and found large fireplaces but few chairs or stools. At meal times, Indians dipped into iron pots over the fire. These were filled with beans, hominy, and an occasional piece of meat. Clothing, harness, and agricultural implements hung on the walls of the huts. They noted many aged and infirm Indians on the two Reservations.

When the Grand Council, with ten Quaker representatives, met the second time, a chief of the Tonawandas declared: "the white people will resort to any means to deceive the Indians. Because we are few and weak, they think they can do as they please with us— they take advantage of our weakness to cheat and deceive us." [18] John Blacksmith, another Tonawanda chief, said his tribe would never consent to part with their lands.

After the Friends left, the Grand Council remained in session for four days. Griffith M. Cooper, the agent for the four Yearly Meetings, later returned with the acceptance of the Supplementary Treaty, signed by seventy-nine of the eighty-one chiefs who were present at the Council. This was taken to the Secretary of War. The chiefs did ask, however, that a second formal Grand Council be held a month later, at the same place, for a final ratification of the document. "[The Indians] as an injured and oppressed people, threw themselves on the mercy of the government, asking that the alterations in the original treaty be accepted." [19]

The two Baltimore representatives reported to the Indian Affairs Committee all that had taken place at the Grand Council, adding "that a meeting for divine worship was held on the Reservation, attended by a large number of Senecas," in which "occasion was afforded to open some views relating to the nature of true religion . . . and the necessity of following the promptings of the Holy Spirit."[20] An aged chief augmented this teaching, speaking in his native language, and drawing illustrations from his own experience. The Baltimore Committee decided to publish one thousand copies of an account of what took place. Sheppard called attention to the number of aged and infirm Indians on the Tonawanda Reservation, and one thousand dollars was granted to assist them when they were forced to move. The Committee also appointed Philip Thomas and Moses Sheppard to attend the second Grand Council, with a directive to see that "no interpolation or alterations will be introduced into this treaty injurious to the Indians."[20]

The second Grand Council, held from May 16 to 22, 1842, was attended by the original parties, plus representatives of the Government: Samuel Hoare, a noted lawyer, represented Massachusetts, and two delegates from the New York State Legislature were present. Again the Supplementary Treaty was explained, questions answered, and in the end fifty-five chiefs signed the document, sixteen refusing. It was obvious that some of the Tonawanda Indians planned to join a portion of their tribe living in Canada. In a concluding address, the Commissioner of the United States stated that he believed "the real friends of the Indians, the Quakers, had done everything they could to obtain, and had obtained, the very best terms for them that they could." [21] The agent for the Ogden Land Company declared, "The Quakers, who do not hold to fighting, have fought your battle valiantly." [22] Benjamin Ferris, for the Friends, made the final statement:

> Brothers! It was our concern for the happiness and welfare of your people, that brought us here. If we had not thought your best interests would be promoted by the treaty . . . we would not have been here. For it appeared to us that if this compromise should not be accepted, you must, inevitably, be driven from your present homes into the wilderness beyond the Mississippi.[23]

Ferris reminded the chiefs that their lands were now secure, that they were rich and fertile, amply sufficient for the comfortable maintenance of their families. He ended, "We greatly desire your prosperity, and that you may live on [the] land in peace and harmony."

At the fall meeting of Baltimore Yearly Meeting, Thomas and Sheppard reported on the successful conclusion of the Buffalo Creek Council. They recounted that 345 Indian children were in various schools, maintained by Friends and different missionary bodies, and that soon public schools would be established. They knew that Griffith Cooper would help with the removal of the aged, infirm Indians and the widowed members of the tribes who needed assistance. They could also report that the Council had agreed to give their income from the Government, over a period of five years, to assist those families that would now move to the Buffalo Creek and Allegheny Reservations.

Soon the Indians from the two lost reservations began to move to Cattaraugus and Allegheny. "The hand of industry was seen on all sides. New Settlements were made, commodious dwellings erected, barns built, and the [Indian] fields enclosed." [24] Moses Sheppard and Philip Thomas reported that the Indian women lagged far behind the men in adopting civilized ways, and cared with indifference for their children. Several Quaker women were added to the Indian Affairs Committee. They immediately proceeded to establish a Manual Labor School on the Cattaraugus Reservation, where the Indian women were taught the elements of housekeeping and child care. Clothing was provided for destitute children in the School, and sufficient money granted to provide one hot meal a day.[25] Several Indian girls were placed in the homes of Friends, and the committee paid the tuition of a bright young Indian woman to attend John Jackson's school at Darby, Pennsylvania.

Shortly after the close of the Grand Council of 1842, sixty-two Senecas, belonging to the old emigration party, left New York for the West. Within six months, word came that almost half of them were dead, and "some of the rest, in a miserable emaciated condition, struggled back to their [former] homes." [26]

When the removal of the tribes began, many of the Indians were uneasy. They had lost half of their territory to the Ogden Land Company, and they had no assurance that the white men would not find ways to steal the rest of their ancestral property from them. The Friends sought to reassure the chiefs that "they held an absolute and indefeasible title to their remaining lands," [27] but the red men were not satisfied. They recalled that as far back as 1784, George Washington had declared, "In the future you cannot be defrauded of your lands"; and only recently Governor Dewitt Clinton had given similar assurance. The chiefs knew that their once princely domain, which had included millions of acres of fertile land stretching from the Finger Lake country to Lake Erie, had been steadily reduced. To them, "the avarice of the white man was as insatiable as death." In addition, the warriors of the tribes were afraid that their chiefs might, wittingly or no, betray them, since any treaty signed by a majority of the chiefs was binding on the nation as a whole.

Moses Sheppard and Philip Thomas were appointed to attend a meeting of delegates of the four Yearly Meetings in Philadelphia to consider ways in which the Friends could be of further service to the Six Nations. Out of these sessions came many suggestions, the most important of which were. 1. that the white men who were settled on Indian lands, and "by their influence and example do more harm than good," be removed from the Reservations, their dwellings to be used for the

Indians from the lost Reservations, and that the white men be paid for removing, and 2. that the Indians, for better security, convey their title to the two Reservations in trust to the State of New York, "that the Seneca nation cannot hereafter alienate it but with the consent of the State, and that the State cannot eliminate it without the consent of the Seneca nation." [28]

When the suggestion reached the assembled tribes, discussion was long and heated, especially on the part of members of the Tonawanda Reservation, who so far had not cooperated in any of the recent moves, and who insisted that they would not, in spite of the Supplementary Treaty, leave their old homes. They were supported in their stand by white men hostile to the Quakers. Finally the proposition of placing the title of their lands in trust in the State of New York was approved, with the provision that "the State cannot hereafter alienate the land without the consent of *two thirds* of the male population of the Senecas." [29] This removed the matter from the dictates of the chiefs. The Council asked the Friends to have the proper papers drawn and laid before the Legislature. This was done and the chiefs sent with it the statement, "That the Seneca nation, once the powerful and courted ally of sovereign nations, has dwindled away to a weak band. . . . Their lands too have been torn from them, and they stand now upon only four insignificant parcels of . . . territory." [30] They appealed to the legislators as "the guardians of the nation," and asked the government to "protect and shelter [them]." Their petition declared, "The Great Spirit made the red man as well as the white man, we are brothers. . . ." [The Great Spirit] will ask, "where is your weak red brother whom I put in your hands that you might guide and guard him? . . . We are poor and ignorant. We know not what will be good for us. We ask you to think for us and act for us. . . . Let not all the land be taken from us." [30]

In 1844, Moses Sheppard reported to the Baltimore committee that a Cayuga Indian, whom the Friends had assisted, was finishing his medical education at Geneva College, "during which time his deportment had been uniformly correct and exemplary." [31] The young man wished to return to his tribe, but needed books and equipment for dental surgery. Sheppard received fifty dollars from the funds of the Indian Affairs Committee to purchase the instruments needed, and collected medical books for the doctor's use. The young Indian woman who attended Sharon school finished her education after "acquiring a good deal of valuable information," and returned to her reservation to begin work.

Fearful that the Friends might become tired of assisting the tribes, Chief Harry Two-guns, who had visited Sheppard some years before, urged the Society not to grow impatient with the conduct of the Seneca nation. "If you go back," he sent word, "who are we to look to for advice?" He continued, "Brothers! be not discouraged by the dark clouds that hang over us; we think it will settle away, and a bright and clear sky appear, so that the sun and moon will gladden our hearts." [32] The chief mentioned steady progress in farming at Cattaraugus, one warrior having a wheat harvest of 300 bushels. Every three months, ten new girls were enrolled to live in the reservation school, while learning to spin, knit, sew, and cook. At the next general committee session,

Sheppard approved of an additional appropriation of $1,000 to extend the educational work on the reservations.

The following year, a delegation of Indians, supported by members of the four Yearly Meetings, requested the New York Legislature to give them a new constitution and so erect a more democratic government covering the tribes.[33] This was approved, and a member of the Supreme Court of the State was appointed to assist the Indians as counsel. This document provided for annual elections, by plurality vote, of a Clerk for the nation, a marshall, and three peacekeepers on each reservation. The peacekeepers were to settle disputes not only between members of the tribes but also between the red and white men, and also to allot land for individual improvement and to locate new highways. Sheppard went with a delegation to President James K. Polk to present a copy of the new constitution to be placed in the archives of the nation.[34]

Although the principal work of the Indian Affairs Committee was now accomplished, its members were not ready to terminate the educational work for the Indian women and children. They urged the chiefs to release the squaws from the heavy farm work, so that they might devote more time to the care of their children and their homes. In a long council meeting, Young Chief, a distinguished sachem, promised that they would "call our women from the fields," but added, "their habits and duties have been so long fixed, that it may be some time before they consent." [35] At the conclusion of this council the chiefs announced, "In order to express the high regard we entertain for the friendship so long existing between the Friends and the Seneca Indians, we have solemnly concluded to adopt into the nation one of their number." Philip E. Thomas was chosen, and with proper rites was taken into the tribes with the name Sagouan, meaning the Benevolent One.

During the next few years, the Indian Affairs Committee continued to keep in close contact with the Six Nations. A conflict broke out between the Indians Christianized by the missionaries, and the so-called Pagan Party, which was in the majority. For a time, this conflict threatened to close the educational work of the Friends. A Christian chief declared in council that he had been told by a missionary that it would be a crime to send his children to the Quaker school. Henry Two-guns spoke for the Friends, when he declared that they did not come to teach religion, but to give the children useful information for better living. Philip Thomas assured the tribes that the Friends were not desirous of teaching the Indians to be Quakers, but only to teach them how to cultivate their lands, to build houses, and to raise their food. He said, "With your religious concerns we have studiously avoided to interfere, not because we have deemed Religion an unimportant subject, but because we have not been called upon . . . or sent among you to teach it. If you faithfully conform to the will of God, so far as he is pleased to make it known to you . . . it will teach you to be *practical* Christians." [36]

Meanwhile, a group of more than two hundred Senecas went beyond the Missouri River. "Many were decoyed away by various unfair contrivances and gross misrepresentations." [37] As with most of the red men who went to the West, the group suffered heavily and, in the end, asked the Friends for money to help them return to New York State.

Philip Thomas, who had been created Ambassador to the United States by the Six Nations—with a new name Hai-wa-nob, meaning ambassador—continued to watch over the interests of the tribes. On one occasion, as he related to the group meeting in the Brick House on Pratt Street, he discovered that an agent of the Federal Government had cheated the tribes out of nearly twenty-nine thousand dollars of annuity money. He went to President Millard Fillmore, who declared he would see that the money was refunded. The President appreciated all the Quakers had done for the remnant of the red men who "occupied a small portion of his native State." [38]

Shortly thereafter, the Friends decided that their educational work for the Seneca Nation could come to an end. Much progress had been made. The men of the tribes now mostly wore the dress of the white man and engaged in farm work. The Indian women spent most of their time caring for their children and their homes. The fields of the Six Nations produced more food than the tribes could consume, and the annuities provided by the United States were sufficient to cover the expenses of their government and any public works undertaken. It was time for the Quakers to withdraw and "leave them to walk alone." [39]

In January of 1849, the chiefs sent a long letter of appreciation to the Friends, summing up all that had been done for the tribes over the years. They hoped the members of the Society would still be ready to assist them if occasion arose. They urged the Friends "to extend their fostering care over our people . . . not to abandon them to become the prey to the heartless enemies, and land speculators." [40] The school was now turned into an orphanage and named after Philip Thomas. Sheppard agreed that the funds of the Society should no longer be spent to carry on educational work in the Reservations, which now would be covered by appropriations from the public treasury. Thus the Friends' active work among the Seneca Indians on the Cattaraugus and Allegheny reservations came to an end.

VIII

A New Mandate

THE AMERICAN COLONIZATION SOCIETY, of which Moses Sheppard was a Vice President, was founded in Washington in 1816 for the purpose of removing the free colored population of the United States, with their own consent, to Africa. As early as 1827, the Legislature of Maryland agreed to an annual appropriation of $1,000 to assist in "the great and laudable objects of the [American Colonization] association." [1] In Virginia, $90,000 were spent by the State in a span of five years for the same purpose. Considerable sums were raised in Maryland and forwarded to the national headquarters, and it was claimed that "no where in the United States had colonization been regarded with more interest than in Maryland." [1]

The settlement of free Negroes in Africa proved to be a slow process; five years elapsed before the national association succeeded in purchasing land from the natives of Africa to begin a settlement. This land, on the west coast south of the British colony of Sierra Leone, was secured "for the compliment of a half dozen gallons of rum, and an equal amount of African trade-cloth and tobacco." [2] General Robert Goodloe Harper of Baltimore suggested Liberia as the name for the colony, and

John H. B. Latrobe thought it would be suitable to name the future capital city after President James Monroe; hence Monrovia. Claims of ownership on the coast were very vague, and a dozen warlike tribes united to attack the American settlement, and only with great difficulty were beaten off. The annual rainy season came before the colonists had time to put roofs on their thatched huts, tropical fever took its toll, and some immigrants, frightened by the savage attacks of the natives, fled to Sierra Leone. Just when provisions and ammunition were running low, a Government ship, the brig *Strong,* arrived from Baltimore with assistance. The colony survived these birth pains.

By 1821, the American Colonization Society had transported 2,000 free men to Liberia. The settlement owned a strip one hundred miles along the coast, with a depth of some fifty miles. Many acres were placed under cultivation, schools established, churches founded, and trade with the native population encouraged. Congress gave permission to land any slaves captured from slave traders off the coast of Africa—such trade with the United States being prohibited—and appropriated $100,000 for the use of such captives taken to the new colony.[3] Sheppard was vitally interested in these developments: "Nothing seemed to have challenged Moses Sheppard more than the question of Colonization." [4]

Friends as a whole were generous in providing money and assistance to remove freed Negroes from southern States to areas where they could make a new start and not be resold into slavery. The Yearly Meeting of North Carolina transported 300 slaves, whose freedom was purchased or manumission secured, out of that State in a single year at a cost of $3,500. Rhode Island appropriated $1,000 for the same purpose; New York sent Friends of North Carolina $250 to help with their program; Philadelphia Yearly Meeting forwarded nearly $3,000 in the same period.[5] Agents for the Colonization Society collected funds from churches and civic organizations both North and South. The First Presbyterian Church of Baltimore in one collection gave $57.37; an Eastern Shore church collected $100; Masonic lodges in Baltimore contributed a like amount. The pages of the *African Repository*, magazine of the American Colonization Society, were filled with the lists of contributors.

In order to expedite sending freed Negroes from the State, the Maryland State Colonization Society was organized, with Moses Sheppard as one of the incorporators, in 1831. The next year the State Legislature appointed a "Board of Managers, whose duty it should be to remove from the State the people of colour then free, and such as should thereafter become so, to the Colony of Liberia in Africa, or such other place out of the limits of Maryland as they should consent to go." [6] The Board was further authorized to provide and support the emigrants until they should be able to provide for themselves; and to place before the colored population of the State correct information concerning the conditions and life in the Colony of Liberia, "or such other place or places to which they might recommend emigration." To implement the action of the Legislature, the sum of $200,000 was appropriated. The Legislature acted because:

> the whole subject of slavery, at this time, was beginning to assume an angry aspect. What has since been known as modern abolition was putting on a definite,

and to slave-holding States, offensive shape; and even among Colonizationists, a discrepancy of opinion, in regard to the subject of slavery, threatened to paralize effective action.[7]

It was felt that since slavery was a matter of State judgment alone, each State might well have its own plan for the removal of freed Negroes. A Board of Managers, was named to dispense the funds appropriated over a period of twenty years. Sheppard, known as a careful businessman and a cautious Quaker, was named Chairman of the Commission.

Certainly in the beginning, Sheppard shared the enthusiasm of William H. Fitzhugh of Virginia, who wrote in *The Repository:*

> Our design was . . . to induce the voluntary emigration of that portion of the people of color already free, and to throw open to individuals and states a wider door for voluntary and legal emancipation. The operation . . . ought to be gradual. But we entertained the hope, founded on our knowledge of the South, that this operation . . . would *in the end* remove from our country every vestige of domestic slavery, without a single violation of individual wishes or rights.[8]

The Virginia gentleman believed that the resources of the country were equal to the task, either by using the annual surplus then accumulating in the national treasury, or by the sale of public lands. He estimated that the annual increase of colored population in the nation was under forty thousand and was convinced that provision could be made to remove fifty thousand Negroes each year.

Southerners varied in their reasons for supporting colonization. John H. B. Latrobe thought that through colonization Maryland could in a reasonable length of time be "numbered with the free States of the Nation . . . without the ill-timed and injudicious interference of others in [Maryland's] internal course." [9] Charles C. Harper, who served with Sheppard in disbursing the State's funds for emigrants, expressed the view generally held by Marylanders at the time:

> No scheme of abolition will meet my support, that leaves the emancipated blacks among us. Experience has proved that they become a corrupt and degraded class burdensome to themselves as they are hurtful to the rest of society. Shut out from the privileges of citizenship, separate from us by the unsurmountable barrier of color, they can never amalgamate with us, but must remain a distinct and inferior race . . . dangerous to our republican institutions. To transfer them from slavery into such a condition, would be a mockery of freedom.[10]

Harper thought slavery a "foul reproach" to the nation, and urged gradual emancipation, with immediate removal to Africa, where he believed the Negro could be a "flourishing and enlightened people, enjoying [American] protection [and] the free institutions we enjoy." [10] Harper's point of view seemed to be held by many Maryland free Negroes at this time. At a convention in which they expressed their interest in colonization, they passed a memorial:

> We reside among you as strangers; natives yet not citizens; surrounded by the freest people and most republican institutions in the world. . . . Our differences in color, the servitude of many . . . will not let us hope to mingle with you one day, in the benefits of citizenship. As long as we remain with you, we must, and shall, be

content to be a distinct caste, exposed to the indigni-
ties and dangers, physical and moral, to which our
situation makes us liable. All that we can expect, is to
merit by our peaceable and orderly behavior, your consideration and the protection of law.[11]

These memorialists admitted that Marylanders were
opposed to slavery as such, shown in the State's stringent
laws against the slave trade, but felt they would always
be excluded from citizenship, and that "they could
never participate in the enviable privileges which they
continually witnessed." Thus they favored immigration
to Liberia, already accomplished by many free Negroes
of the State.

Moses believed that if the freed Negroes were sent to
Africa, unhampered by white people and their discrim-
inatory laws, they would soon learn the arts of government and commerce. When someone asked him if he
thought the Negroes had the ability to build a country
of their own, he replied: "I will make no comparisons
and conjectures concerning the mentality of the Blacks
and the Whites. Let them first be educated alike. The
Irish, if educated, will have some peculiarities, but
some, as we have seen, exhibit brilliant minds." [12] Many
non-Friends fervently hoped that through the efforts of
Christian men of color, a beginning would be made towards evangelizing all the African continent.

In the early days of the Republic, many thinking men
in the South considered slavery a wasteful system of
labor and one incompatible with the genius of American liberty. Even as late as 1820, the planter interests
were pliant enough to accept the Missouri Compromise,
which "dedicated the lion's share of the Louisiana terri-

tory to freedom." [13] But as the cotton empire continued to expand, absorbing more of the fertile areas in the South and most of the manpower, the institution of slavery became sacrosanct in the eyes of all Southern statesmen. Previous existing antislavery societies disappeared, and a demand to reopen the slave trade with Africa began to be heard.

Until the organization of the American Anti-Slavery Society in 1833, the activities of the various colonization societies were supported in nearly all parts of the country. Members of the Anti-Slavery societies, however, vehemently attacked the colonization movement. These radical abolitionists declared colonization was only a means of draining from the country the troublesome Negroes who might cause a rebellion; and that it took from the land the best minds among the Negro body who could furnish the leadership in the battle to secure emancipation and the elevation of the race at home. Not agreeing with the position taken by the radical abolitionists, Sheppard resented their attack on the colonization movement.

With State funds available, an agent of the Maryland Colonization Society was sent through the counties of Maryland, and 146 free people of color were secured to sail for Monrovia in December, 1832. Moses Sheppard was on the dock to see immigrants off on the ship *Lafayette*. The first letter that reached him from Africa was from Joseph Bringhurst, telling him of their safe arrival, and adding, "Shall I ever forget, I think not, the morning when you came on board the brig . . . and shook my hand, and my wife's hand, and my son's hand." [14]

136

Sheppard had sent with these colonists seeds, tools, clothing, and books. Personal letters, inquiring concerning their welfare, went on the next boat, accompanied by gifts for their children.

A constant stream of letters passed back and forth between the Brick House and the colonists. Later Sheppard wrote, "Until I got hold of Colonization, or rather until it got hold of me, I very seldom wrote a letter except on business" [15]; from then on his correspondence became voluminous. Sheppard continued to send needed supplies; and in return came presents from the immigrants—rare plants and unusual wood, a leopard skin, newly canned goods of native production, a snake's skin, and a red monkey. The home on Pratt Street gradually filled with curios, which were of general interest to Sheppard's neighbors and the friends of Colonization. Young and old came to see these strange articles and carved figures. "Moses Sheppard served [refreshments] to the delight of younger friends." [16]

Unfortunately, the emigrants from the *Lafayette* felt that they were not well treated in Monrovia; their supplies were put into the common stock, and the provisions they received were old and of poor quality. Dr. James Hall, a medical official of the American Colonization Society, who explored land to the south of Monrovia, reported that he found that Cape Palmas would make an excellent site for a new colony. The Board of the Maryland State Colonization Society, made up, as John H. B. Latrobe declared, not "of clergymen . . . but of men of business intelligence and character," [17] determined with the cooperation of the managers of the State fund to found a new colony, to be called Maryland in Liberia, the seat of whose government should be at Cape Palmas.[18]

On November 23, 1833, seventeen emigrants sailed on the brig *Ann* to begin this new colony. This group took with them a Constitution for Maryland in Liberia, drafted by Latrobe. The preamble stated that the founding Society [desired] "to hasten, as far as they can, the period when slavery shall cease to exist in Maryland. . . , believing the cause of Colonization, as the safest, truest, and most efficient auxiliary of Freedom, under existing circumstances." [19] The Constitution promised laws founded on justice and humanity, election by ballot, freedom of worship, of speech, of assembly, and trial by jury. Two unusual sections placed the final power in the hands of the Maryland Society, and forbade anyone holding office who used "ardent spirits." Moses Sheppard was one of the seventeen officers and managers who signed and witnessed this document. In doing so he said, "we will plant slow oaks, posterity will have the shade." [20]

Sheppard believed that Maryland would some day be numbered with the free States. He wrote to the Society's agent, Robert Finley, "slavery will be done away with in Maryland when the voice of the people is heard." [19] He was also certain that in those counties with a large number of Negroes, freedom would be granted to the colored people only if the freed Negroes would agree to emigrate. He added, "The feudal Barons of the lower counties, wrapped in their coat of mail, will defend their castles to the last extremities, but . . . the convincing voice of the age . . . will insure their fall." He declared, "Maryland is numerically a free State, politically a slave State. The majority of the voters are for freedom, the majority of the legislators, I fear, are against it."

In an essay wrîtten for a northern paper to encourage contributions for the cause, the humanitarian wrote, "A new era is beginning in Colonization [the Maryland plan of separate State colonies] in which those interested in freeing the slaves, in establishing temperance societies, in promoting missions and education, could unite in one endeavor." [19] He pointed out that a series of colonies on the west coast of Africa would advance Christianity, and serve to arrest the illegal slave traffic. To those who felt the task too great, he said that in an era which saw the development of canals, the invention of railroads and steamships, colonization was not impossible. He concluded his essay with the sentence, "It is not in mortals to command success, but they may deserve it." Sheppard thought the new venture at Cape Palmas was "a great undertaking, with many difficulties to overcome, and many disappointments"; to him the deciding factor would be the character of the emigrants. If they would work, as many did not in Monrovia, the effort would succeed, if not it would fail.

In later years, Latrobe wrote, "Moses Sheppard did not give so much money to this cause as some others, but he got others to give; also his major gifts were directed to the colonists themselves, either as personal gifts or in support of their work." [21] As a representative of the State dispensing money, Sheppard solicited accurate information about the settlement. He wrote a colonist: "It is desirable that we have correct information to enable us to adapt our conduct to the actual situation of things, and to institute such means as will correct abuse and place the colony in an improved state . . . write me your opinion, and advise me frankly and fully." [22] He added: "I have thought of you frequently, I feared you didn't find the society that you have been accustomed to here . . . but among the people who went out were a number of respectable and correct individuals." The Baltimorean accompanied this letter with rope, clothing, wheels, and other articles for his correspondent to distribute. He marked each item with the name of the recipient, and sent a special message, that these articles "were not as a compensation, but as a mark of respect." [22]

To Stephen Tippet, the businessman wrote: "I feel much interest in your success and happiness. You will find some books and writing paper in the box; try to learn to read and write, do your best and you will do well." [23] With this letter went a pair of shoes, two bleached cotton shirts, one brown shirt, four ruled copy books, two quire of paper, five yards of cotton cloth, and four school books. To a young shoemaker, the Quaker sent an outfit of tools and some leather, at a cost of $100, so that the young man could begin business. To seven different women he sent "a spinning wheel, with two flyers and three spools, a pair of cotton cards, and a pat of cotton." [24] Thomas Jackson received a spade, a shovel, three hoes, and a supply of iron, which was scarce in Liberia. To Willoughby White's daughter went a tin bucket, a tin case, and a bag of dried apples.

Repeatedly, Moses Sheppard expressed strong solicitude for the welfare of the emigrants, but did not hesitate to remind them that they must maintain themselves by hard work. He wrote to James Reese, whom he evidently knew very well, "I heard from your Uncle Stephen Sheppard lately, and his family were all in good health." [25] Moses then dispatched a humorous letter to his own Uncle Samuel Sheppard, who had assisted in sending supplies to James Reese:

> James Reese to whom those things were sent, is the nephew of Stephen Sheppard of Somerset, Maryland. I expect this branch of the family is unknown in Pennsylvania. The color of Stephen is dark mulatto, he is nevertheless a respectable man, and his traditions of the family does not differ greatly from my own; in another generation, or two, the family may shine in ebony! [26]

In many letters, Sheppard stressed the necessity of developing agriculture and the use of native products. He complained to an emigrant who wrote asking for a shipment of lumber, "I cannot understand the need to send lumber across the ocean to be carried into the *woods* of Liberia." [27] Now and then he sent a stern letter, as the one he sent Susan Hyman:

> I sent in a chest, twelve yards of cotton cloth to make a working dress for you. I want you to cultivate a large garden . . . such a garden will nearly support your family, with a flock of goats . . . Don't think you went to Africa to live without working . . . You complain of the high price of flour and other American provisions. You have nothing to do with flour or other articles from America. If you cannot live off the products of the country, you had better leave it. I am dissatisfied with the whole tone of your letter . . . nothing indicates industry or usefulness. I believe you have set up as a lady, and I assure you I will not work in America for a lazy Negro lady in Africa. [28]

To Susan's husband, Sheppard added, "You say you are

working hard and living low; pursue that course and you will hereafter live better and work less. You write for a box of candles, why cannot you use palm oil." [29]

Sheppard wrote a long letter to Thomas Jackson, detailing the careful manner in which the ship *Lafayette* had been fitted out for her voyage. "No ship," he declared, "had ever sailed for Liberia more abundantly supplied; everything was done here to make the voyage pleasant and to insure the health and comfort of all." [30] He added:

> I shall be extremely mortified if the emigrants on the *Lafayette* do not do well. They were not the miserable slaves [from the deep South] taken from the tobacco and cotton fields, ignorant and dirty, thoughtless and improvident, and thrown on the shores of Liberia without any means or preparation to begin with; they were men of intelligence who had been accustomed to provide for themselves and not one of them was totally destitute. If Liberia is not a country where such men cannot soon be in a comfortable situation, I am greatly deceived. We have no better men to send.[30]

The land about Cape Palmas was fertile, the climate suitable, and it was thought trade would soon flow around the peninsula. Land was purchased from native kings, and through the wise and firm conduct of Dr. James Hall, there never was any physical conflict with the tribes in this area. After the *Ann* sailed, Moses Sheppard wrote to the father of a Negro boy who lived in New Market, Maryland, informing the father that the boy had stayed with him for several weeks before sailing, and that he had outfitted him for the trip. He secured from interested individuals a trunk, three shirts, a pair of shoes, a mattress, and a blanket. But Moses wrote the county agent of the Society that local friends should secure proper outfits for such young people sent on to Baltimore for emigration. "The cost will be trifling," he wrote, "compared to the sacrifice [by emancipation] made by the benevolent Master, and such equipment [is essential] to the health and comfort of the passage, and after arrival in Africa." [31]

When it was reported to Sheppard that a blacksmith whom he had assisted was drinking, Moses warned, "He is a freeman and has a right to drink, and I am free and have a right to withhold from him my aid." [32] To Henry Hyman, who was complaining, the Baltimorean wrote, "If you are not content, very few in Liberia could be expected to be so, for very few of them were as well provided . . . you cost as much as you would have sold for in Norfolk. I have, in fact, been working here to establish you there." [32] Sheppard sent Hyman a small chest containing various useful articles, including a Bible, with the suggestion that he read a chapter a day, adding, "it will not be time lost." He continued, "I hear you have two [native] servants. I am compelled to ask myself if I am the third. If you keep two there, I must discharge myself here." [32] To Ann Polk, another complainer, he sent word, "No doubt there will be privations to suffer, and hardships to encounter, but these privations and hardships ought not to discourage you, for these are the price that all, white and black, in America and Africa, at some time and in some way, pay for freedom and independence." [33]

In considering his own part in advancing the cause of colonization, Moses Sheppard wrote to Robert Finley, the main agent of the American Society, "John H. B.

Latrobe is in Washington, where by a kind of agreement, he is Minister of Foreign Affairs, and I, for the
time being, am the Home Department." [34] Sheppard
did all he could to publicize the Cape Palmas colony,
sending copies of reports and news items to judges,
heads of Maryland corporations, prominent merchants,
the clergy, and members of the bar throughout the
State. He sent material to English Friends, hoping they,
who strongly advocated immediate emancipation, might
better understand the situation as it existed in the
South.

To the Reverend George McGill at Cape Palmas,
Sheppard wrote: "I have for the last three years devoted
nearly all my time and spent from four to five hundred
dollars of my own money a year in connection with
colonization. . . . I am now convinced the land of Liberia is good and the climate healthy for all but the
white man. If carefully selected emigrants fail, the
whole idea fails." [35] He was forced to admit, however,
"Founding a colony is no trifling business." [36]

IX

Sheppard and Maryland in Liberia

THE INDEPENDENT COLONY of Maryland in Liberia prospered from the beginning; the Board of Managers took a lively interest in the settlement—none more than Moses Sheppard. It was their aim to make the colony as attractive to the free people of color in America as the United States was to the increasing flood of emigrants from Europe. Between 1831 and 1839, eleven ships carried colonists and supplies from Baltimore to Cape Palmas. A colony at Grand Basa, established chiefly through the efforts of Pennsylvania Quakers, was wiped out by native tribes.[1]

In June of 1834, Sheppard received a letter from a young man in Liberia, Samuel Ford McGill, which he acknowledged: "I am glad to receive so well written a letter from the son of an old friend."[2] This was the beginning of one of the most rewarding experiences in the life of the Baltimorean. In a second letter, McGill wrote that he hoped to study medicine, but did not have the means to do so, and inquired whether the Colonization Society would assist a young man who desired to be useful to Cape Palmas. Moses Sheppard took the matter up with the Young Men's Colonization Society, meeting in his home, and they pledged two hundred and fifty dollars a year toward the education of the young Liberian, with the stipulation that when his education was completed he return to the colony. Details were left to Moses Sheppard to work out.

Being a realist, Sheppard made sure that the young African knew exactly what lay ahead if he came to the States. "I think it my duty to inform you," he wrote, "what your situation will be, and what will be expected of you." [3] He pointed out that in Baltimore his associations would be entirely with Negroes, and that no white man would call him "Mister." If admitted to college his attendance would be as a servant, though he would receive the same instruction as the other students. Sheppard declared, "In proportion as you waive the claim to equality, it will be conceded you, in proportion as you urge it, it will be denied." He mentioned that to secure a medical education would require unremitting application and toil. "The object you have in view is an elevated one," he added, "the golden apples of science grow high on the tree of human knowledge." The warnings advanced were to prevent future disappointments.

If McGill had the stamina, Moses Sheppard felt that his goal would be reached. Meanwhile, the Quaker encouraged influential people—judges, lawyers, and doctors—to urge the officials of the Washington Medical College in Baltimore to admit Samuel McGill when he arrived. Dr. Edrington said that the young man could use his personal medical library, and arrangements were made for him to do his clinical work in the almshouse. The faculty of the college agreed "to teach without regard to cast or color." [4]

When McGill arrived, all the carefully laid plans

were defeated by the conduct of the student body, who refused to associate with Samuel McGill. They passed a set of Resolutions:

> Resolved that . . . the city faculty has admitted a Negro boy as a student for the purpose of instructing him, and have admitted him to all the rights and privileges of the College.

> Resolved that, any persons who professed any degree of self esteem cannot conceive that the faculty would consent, that students of fair complexion should mingle with those of dark skin.

> Resolved that, the faculty be requested to dismiss this boy, and never again permit the introduction of such persons, as it tends not only to its injury, but to its everlasting prostration . . . from our known sentiments of our friends in the South, even in this State, we would represent a danger not only incurred by the Institution in his abiding with us, but would forcibly exert upon our future professional prospects." [5]

The Board of the Maryland Colonization Society urged the faculty to reconsider the student's action, but student representatives said "it would be illusory to entertain the hope of reconciliation, or rather the readmission of Samuel McGill to the school . . . their feeling of humanity had had to succumb to the superior influence of public opinion and their own self interest." [6]

Sheppard reached Dr. Edward Phelps of the University of Vermont, who became much interested, and volunteered to take the young man as his private student. He offered McGill room and board in his own home while the young man pursued his education. "Africa ought not always to be dependent on America for knowledge of medical science," he wrote; "we should

147

send them genuine stock . . . in our lifetime we might know that true knowledge has taken root . . . where superstition has for ages held undisputed sway." [7] Dr. Phelps, a deeply religious man, thought that a medical doctor could reach the savage mind "and medicine carry conviction to the heart of the heathen. . . ."

Sheppard contacted Matthew and Hopkins, a Baltimore firm, for McGill's passage north. Because of the strict Maryland laws concerning transportation of Negroes out of the State, it was necessary for Sheppard to secure from Judge Brice a document declaring McGill a free man, and also to post a bond protecting the captain of the ship. The Quaker paid for a cabin and requested the firm to see that their captain treated the lad "without reference to color." [8]

Ira Easter, agent for the Maryland Society, wrote the young student stating the interest of the group in his success, and urging him to secure all knowledge possible, to be prudent and circumspect in his conduct because of "the excited state of the public mind in regard to the African race." [9] "You must never forget," he added, "that you are an African in America. It is due to Mr. Sheppard to state, that from the time of your arrival in this city, until you took your departure for Vermont, he has given his time and influence to secure the object for which you were invited to this country."

The reports that came from Dr. Phelps during the next few months were very gratifying. Samuel McGill applied himself with diligence and demonstrated excellent ability. Moses Sheppard collected thirty medical books from Baltimore doctors who were interested in the young student; out of his own pocket he paid for a four-volume study of chemistry, a French dictionary, drawing apparatus, surgical instruments, a prism, microscope, and a black silk vest.[10]

Samuel McGill wrote of the enjoyment he was taking in his studies, and the kindness of his instructors. "I must succeed," he exclaimed, "if life lasts; to fail in my attempt with the eyes of so many placed upon me, would be too disgraceful to utter. Ten thousand thoughts and reasons urge me onward, and failure is not to be thought of." [11] He was surprised to find snow on the ground in Vermont in May, and to learn that at the same time the temperature in Liberia was one hundred degrees warmer. Sheppard was pleased at the kindness of Dr. Phelps and the other young students. "It was the students that obstructed your way here," he wrote, "I do not know of a physician in Baltimore who would not willingly have taught you. . . . men of science belong to a community of minds, where complexion is unregarded." [12] He reported that the Young Men's Colonization Society had disbanded, but agreed personally to assume financial responsibility for McGill's continued education.

Sheppard told the young student that in his absence, some old buildings on the lot between his house and Howard Street had been torn down, and the lot purchased by a slave dealer. There was a sign at Charles Street and Pratt, "Harris & Company, Slave Agency." A heavy business in Negroes was carried on, not over fifty feet from the African Meeting House, and "wenches" sold for $500 and "fellers" for $700. He added, "Five years ago the town would have been in a ferment at the erection of such an establishment, and it would not have been permitted, now it is scarcely noticed, a few people grumble. I am one." [13]

Samuel McGill wrote his patron that his professors had notified him that he must secure a cadaver for study and dissection in the anatomy laboratory. He appealed to Sheppard to come to his aid, as he could not meet the requirement; so Sheppard and a medical student approached a Negro who often provided Washington College with cadavers. "This man was more than half drunk every time we saw him but the bodies were at last secured." [14] Taken to a local doctor's private laboratory, the body was placed in a cask of spirits; a master cooper ascertained that the cask was perfectly tight; and it was placed in a larger cask, with the intervening space packed with bran. "I asked the agent if the captain who would ship the cask should know what was on board," wrote Moses, "but he replied that if the captain knew what was on board he would be sure the ship would sink. Even the owner of the ship in Boston must not know." After the ocean voyage, the cask was hauled a hundred miles overland by horse and wagon.

The young medical student wrote appreciative letters to Sheppard, thanking him for his interest, for the candor with which he wrote, as well as for his sound advice. McGill reported that he witnessed a considerable number of medical operations by Dr. Phelps, and was intensely engaged in the study of anatomy and physiology, spending as much as five hours a day in the dissecting room. He reported that several social invitations came to him from townspeople, but he did not accept them because he felt they were "momentary acts of condescension on the part of the giver . . . as well as a desire to see and confer with a half savage character." [15] He now realized that Sheppard was right when he warned that people in Vermont would come to see him as they might go to look at the animals in a zoo.

Although Samuel McGill could secure a diploma from Dr. Phelps, since he was a private student (this being the custom at that time), the African wanted a degree. For this it was necessary to attend a college, so arrangements were made to have him continue his studies in Dartmouth College, an institution founded originally to educate American Indians. Here there was no hesitation on the part of either faculty or student body to receive Samuel McGill.

The young man moved into a college dormitory where he paid $8 for his room, and $2 a week for his board and washing in a private family. He felt competent to handle his courses, and wrote to Baltimore, "From the slight acquaintance I have with the students, I judge confidently that I am not the most ignorant one of the whole, and in a year I hope to be attached to the Senior Class." [16] He reported that he was very careful about his expenditures, always consulting Dr. Phelps before spending any money. When smallpox broke out in the neighborhood, the future doctor went with his professor to inoculate townspeople. "It was simple," he declared, "but with me a matter of some importance, for when I drew my lancet to scarify the arms of human beings, my feelings were indescribable." [17] He added, "I fear without a little practice in this country, I shall make an awkward beginning in Africa. There is a degree of timidity in the actions of a young practitioner which constant practice can alone remove. . . . without this I fear I shall become confused and frustrated."

As letters continued to pass between the younger and the older man, the Quaker had his secretary copy the correspondence, made a small volume of the letters bound in leather, and sent them to the young man's father in Liberia. Sheppard mentioned that he still acted as Elisha Tyson's successor in prosecuting the claims of free Negroes whose freedom was questioned by men who would sell them into slavery.[18]

Moses Sheppard's interest in Samuel McGill did not lessen his concern for the colonists in Maryland in Liberia. He was especially fond of Henry Hyman, who, as a lad, lived in the Brick House for five years. When Henry became twenty-one, the humanitarian outfitted him to go to Africa. Hyman, who had been taught the blacksmith's trade, was provided with $500 worth of iron with which to set up shop in the colony. To another colonist, Sheppard wrote, "If Henry succeeds I shall think the money well spent. I have consistently told him he must repay me a part; but if he establishes himself as a useful and respectable man, I will freely forgive the whole, and if he does not succeed he will be unable to pay me." [19] To Hyman he wrote, "I am desirous that you may be economical, industrious, and sober . . . here the way is shut to you, the most correct deportment would leave you a rank below the most worthless white man. Where you are the way is open to you to the first rank in society, and hence you have every inducement to aspire to good character." [20] The Quaker urged the young man to attend Sunday School, church, and day school. He sent him paper, books, and seeds. Later, when Henry's wife sent their benefactor two pieces of needle work, Moses had them framed and placed on the walls of the Brick House. In a letter to Hyman, the Baltimorean added, "I saw your mother yesterday, and she thanked me for my kindnesses to you, but grumbled because I sent her child to Africa." [21]

At one time, Hyman asked for "hog bells," to which Sheppard replied, "There are no bells made for hogs that I can find or hear of. I have sent three kinds. How would it be to bore their ears, and put a bell in each, or make ear rings? Ladies wear ornaments in their ears, and hogs should be proud to wear theirs. . . ." [22] After a letter in which Moses scolded Henry Hyman for not working more diligently, Henry felt hurt, but the Quaker answered:

> You complain of my severe language. It shows my solicitude for you. I feel a deep interest in you. I feel the fine little boy who came to live with me can not be other than a prudent, correct, and respectable man. . . . The advice of others may be useful to you, but it is only your judgment and understanding on which you can rely. Advice is like a seed, when it is placed in bad soil, it is unproductive and useless. [23]

During the next few months, Sheppard sent Hyman $50 worth of medicine, fishing tackle, and a grindstone. He explained, "Your brother is still with his mother, without a chance of education. I would give him some learning, and an outfit for Liberia, if she would let him go, but she will not." [24]

As the attack of the abolitionists on the colonizationists began to take effect, the colored population of Baltimore showed less inclination to emigrate. James Stewart, an early colonist, sent word to Baltimore: "I don't see what the colored people are about that they do not emigrate to this country faster than they do. . . . There are eminent characters in Baltimore that would be useful here, their ignorance keeps them back." [25]

To Sarah Russwurm, wife of the Governor of the colony of Maryland in Liberia, Sheppard sent a "whimsical box of odds and ends," including some toys for the children, with a letter in which he said, "You stand well here . . . Latrobe is your friend. There is a feeling of pride here, I confess to share, in having the first colored governor in Liberia. . . ." [26] To many other colonists went seeds, agricultural tools, paper, books, quills, shoes, cotton shirts, and other useful articles. [27]

From professors in Dartmouth College, Moses Sheppard often received excellent reports of Samuel McGill's work. More books and a set of surgical instruments were forwarded. Additional specimens for dissecting arrived in Hanover. In one case, Sheppard said the cadaver was "pickled in eighteen gallons of whiskey, and packed in four bushels of bran around the inner cask." [28] In October of 1838, Dr. Phelps wrote that McGill had successfully passed all examinations and received his medical degree. Samuel suggested that he work in Baltimore for a period, but Moses did not approve of this. [29] Dr. Phelps wrote to the Maryland Colonization Society praising the gentlemanly conduct, the industry, and the perseverance of the Liberian; he reported that the young doctor was an honor to his patron and would provide an excellent service to society.

154

Dr. McGill stopped for a few days in Baltimore, awaiting a ship for Cape Palmas, often visiting his chief patron, who arranged and paid for the doctor's passage on the brig *Oberon,* which sailed in November, 1838. As a further gift, Sheppard added more medical books, a stethoscope, and a framed picture of Dartmouth College. To the new doctor's father, he sent word: "It is unnecessary for me to write, Samuel will tell you everything. He has acquitted himself to the satisfaction of his teachers, and the gratification of his patrons." [30] In a final note to the young man, the Quaker philosopher commented, "I have very little to say. You have been taught that the Lord made man, remember and forget it not; it is equally true, in another sense, that man makes himself, keep that also in remembrance." [31]

On reaching Cape Palmas, Dr. McGill found many improvements had taken place in his absence. He now was the official physician for Maryland in Liberia, at an honorarium of $500 a year. He plunged with enthusiasm into the task of healing the sick and practicing as much preventive medicine as possible. He told Moses Sheppard that he was certain he could do more for the people than a temporary resident sent out by the Society. Dr. McGill secured a small vessel that enabled him to cover quickly the ocean front of the colony and to sail up the rivers. He made a study of the fever so dangerous to the health of new colonists, and soon discovered that the directives in the medical books did not apply—in fact, the purgings and bleedings prescribed left the patient in a dangerously debilitated state. McGill wrote that he spent two thirds of every day visiting the sick, and returned home exhausted by the demands of his practice. In the evenings he studied the excellent books his patron sent out to him. At first the old women laughed at him and even taunted him, but by using great patience and sagacity he felt that "the Rubicon was passed." [32]

From the beginning he was in conflict with the native witch doctors, whose time was devoted entirely to driving out witches and devils and distributing fetishes supposed to ward off evil. The practice of testing an individual charged with being a witch was a barbarous one. He saw a woman so accused forced to drink two gallons of water in which a pound of crushed sausay [33] wood was steeped, then forced to walk over hot sands and sharp rocks, while men of the tribe prodded her with their spears, howling at the top of their lungs. In the end the individual was left half dead on the shores of Lake Sheppard.[34] Dr. McGill pleaded to be allowed to tend the so-called culprit, but was threatened with death if he interfered. The ordeal was frequent, for ten men and women were forced to undergo it in a three weeks period. Sheppard asked the doctor to send him samples of sausay wood in order to have it chemically analyzed.

While Samuel McGill was in Baltimore, he became engaged to a young lady, Lydia Nicholson. Evidently she could not make up her mind concerning matrimony, for the young doctor sailed back to Liberia without her. McGill corresponded with several Maryland friends concerning Lydia, and finally appealed to Sheppard for advice. The bachelor answered, "I am now writing to you on a subject I am not qualified. I cannot transfer myself into a youth in love. . . . It is plain to me, and I think it must be obvious to you, that she never had any affection for you, all her conduct demonstrated . . . a cool, calculating policy. . . ."[35] Sheppard thought that "scarcely any other colored girl in town would have repelled your advances." Then the businessman added an item unknown to his younger friend, "When you were in Dartmouth, I formed a plan to complete her education, which would have been greatly to her advantage, but I prudently abandoned it [for] I had no confidence in her." He went on to give the advice requested. "My suggestion is that you had better abandon the case at once and forever, to me Miss Lydia's conduct appears prudish, self conceited, vacillating, and insincere. . . ." But, he hastened to add, he could not define the philosophy of love; "hence I never interfere in matches beyond the giving an opinion, and I do not do that unasked. Matches are made in heaven, but some garrulous husbands and carping old bachelors aver they are sadly mixed on the way down." As a final word of comment he wrote, "I do not want to discourage you about getting married, and highly approve of it."

Dr. McGill had several sharp disagreements with the clergymen who had been sent out by the various missionary bodies. They established schools for the native population, but would not permit the children of emigrants to attend their classes. The doctor felt that all children in the Maryland colony should have the same educational advantages. He was especially alarmed at the thought that at some future period the emigrants might be less well educated than the natives. Moses

Sheppard felt the main effort in the schools ought to be placed on teaching good citizenship, stressing the necessity of industry. "My maxim," he said, "was that a contented colony must be formed by contented individuals . . . a portion of the friends of the blacks are so interested in saving the soul, that they give no attention to their bodies." [36] Sheppard thought that the duties of Christianity should be inculcated, and "make good works a part of the system as well as faith and belief, so conducted as to teach Christianity by the exhibition of a Christian life." The Quaker trusted that he was not bigoted in his views, stating, "I am satisfied that a great difference, an actual contrariety of opinion may exist among persons equally sincere; my conviction that I am right is no evidence that another is wrong. . . . I should regret to find myself opposed to the efforts of the pious and benevolent." [37]

Finding himself in opposition to the missionary faction of the Maryland Board, Sheppard thought it wise to resign from that organization. This withdrawal was not a complete break with the colonization movement. Sheppard remained a Vice President of the National Society into the 1850's. He was asked to return to the local body as its Secretary, and he served as a delegate to the colonization convention held in Baltimore in 1841. He never gave up his interest in Maryland in Liberia, and his correspondence and contributions to the welfare of individuals at Cape Palmas continued until his death. As he wrote to Dr. McGill, "I am constantly quitting this cause, but I never quit." [38]

After several years of practice, Dr. McGill sailed to Baltimore in the spring of 1842. He brought his patron up to date on current events in the colony, wrote articles for publication, and lectured to some groups on the Maryland colony. His chief purpose, however, was to pursue his matrimonial venture. Moses Sheppard wrote a mutual friend, "She agreed to marry him. The time was fixed, the parson engaged, when behold! she declined. Another appointment was made subsequently, and another disappointment followed; a third arrangement was made more successfully; they got married, and I am glad of it." [39] Sheppard admitted that he did not understand the activities of Cupid, "but I suppose love laughs at reason as well as at the locksmith."

Dr. McGill and his wife returned to Liberia on the bark *Globe* with one hundred and ten emigrants, one of the largest groups sent out at one time by the Maryland Society. Unfortunately, Mrs. McGill and her newborn baby died the following year. Sheppard sent a letter of condolence to his friend, and forwarded a gravestone on which was carved the words, "Here I am Lord with the child thou hast given me. Time sweeps away the weeper and the wept." [40] With the death soon afterwards of his father, Rev. George McGill, the doctor's responsibilities were increased by the care of his mother and several younger brothers and sisters. He opened a warehouse and store at the Cape to supplement his income, receiving excellent advice from his merchant friend. He wrote later, "The stern realities of life meet me at every turn, they neither appall nor discourage, if by exertion they can be overcome, my spirits rise with the emergencies." [41] He added, "The death of my wife left me a crushed and sorrowing man, without definite object or aim . . . now with the needs of a young family on my hands, attention to medicine and business occupy every minute, [my] melancholy reflections [are] dispersed." Moses Sheppard answered, expressing his sympathy concerning the arduous duties that now rested on the shoulders of his friend, and continued:

> I am, and have been, a drudge for the old and infirm and the young and helpless . . . in every situation in which I find myself placed, I conceive it to be my duty to do the best I can and leave or meet the consequences with all the magnanimity I can. . . . I have always believed it to be my duty to feel for human suffering and to mitigate it if I could, without reference to cause.[42]

The doctor had moments of discouragement, and mentioned to his friend that life, at times, was dull and monotonous, to which Sheppard replied: "You must draw on your mental resources. I have sent you some means of such enjoyment, and I hope other friends will continue the supply. I know your profession subjects you to constant interruptions." He recalled, however, that when Dr. Benjamin Rush was asked how he could study and write so much while engaged in so extensive a practice, the Philadelphia physician had answered, "By losing no time." [43]

Shortly afterwards, Moses Sheppard asked ten of his personal friends to contribute $10 each to purchase essential articles for the Liberian doctor, who, he declared, "is a man of great talent and great promise, every vessel from Cape Palmas brings evidence of his ability and industry." [44] That Dr. McGill recognized to the full all the humanitarian did for him is shown in his letters of appreciation. After receiving a copy of the life of Elisha Tyson, McGill wrote to Moses:

> I remember him well, and was one of the immense number who followed his remains to their final resting place at Old Town Meeting Burial Ground. . . . Your labors have been principally directed to the removal of one of the causes of defects in the African race, viz slavery. The immediate effects may not be visible, but good results will ultimately come, when your name will be coupled with that of the eminent philanthropist, Elisha Tyson, so deserving equal credit for labors in behalf of the wronged and oppressed.[45]

X

Maryland Quakers and Slavery

In the united states, the feeling between the friends of the colored race who believed that colonization was the ultimate answer to the Negro problem and those who insisted on immediate emancipation grew more intense. The mild tone of the early antislavery papers, such as those edited by the Quakers Elihu Embree and Benjamin Lundy, gave way to William Lloyd Garrison's shrill and vindictive cry against both slavery and slaveowners. Garrison demanded immediate, complete, and unconditional emancipation, but offered no positive program to secure it. He denounced "the popular and pernicious doctrine of gradual emancipation." [1] Like an ancient prophet, his words were harsh and uncompromising: he declared that slavery was a crime and thus slaveholders were criminals. Garrison felt that those who supported the slaveholders in any way, or sought to compromise as Henry Clay and Daniel Webster did, were equally guilty. To Garrison, the Constitution of the United States, on which the slaveowners and State's rights people leaned so heavily, was "no sacred document" but "a covenant with death and an agreement with hell." [2] Garrison, however, did not preach rebellion on the part of the Negro population. The Nat Turner insurrection of 1831 in Southampton,

Virginia, which cost the lives of fifty-seven white people and about a hundred Negroes, was a deterrent to Garrison, but Southerners felt that his inflammatory editorials would result in bloodshed.

Earlier, Moses Sheppard had taken a dislike of Garrison. When the abolitionist first came to Baltimore as an associate of Benjamin Lundy in the publication of *The Genius of Universal Emancipation,* Lundy was writing in favor of gradual emancipation and colonization of the Negroes beyond the bounds of the United States. Garrison wrote in favor of immediate emancipation. When his editorials appeared, many Baltimoreans canceled their subscriptions to the paper, and fiery editorials in rebuttal appeared in Southern papers.[3]

On one occasion, Garrison wrote in the *Genius* that hardly a ship from Baltimore sailed to the South that did not carry a cargo of slaves. He accused Francis Todd, who was from Garrison's hometown of Newburyport, Massachusetts, of engaging in this trade. Mr. Todd instituted and won a suit for libel against Garrison, with the result that the abolitionist was fined $150 and spent seven weeks in jail.[4] Garrison "now became the persecuted leader of the noble cause of abolition."[5] Subsequently, when traveling in England, Garrison declared that he was incarcerated in Baltimore by slave owners who wished to intimidate him. Moses Sheppard determined to find out whether the juries that indicted and tried Garrison were made up of slaveowners. Sheppard hired a lawyer to take affidavits of each member of the Grand Jury that presented Garrison for trial, and of the jurymen who found Garrison guilty.

One juror had no objections to slavery; three owned

slaves at the time of the trial; nine once owned slaves but had sold or manumitted them before the trial; twenty had never owned slaves; and twenty-three were opposed to slavery. One juror said, "I believe slavery to be one of the greatest evils in the world." [6] Another declared, "I would exterminate that evil from our country." A third added, "I would consider it the greatest blessing to our country if there was not a slave in it." And still another said, "It is a sin and disgrace to our country." In addition to refuting Garrison's charges, the affidavits also indicated the general feeling held by many Baltimoreans in 1829.

Justice Arthur, the Chief Judge of the Baltimore City Court, wrote Moses Sheppard that he had manumitted four valuable family slaves, and aided many others to secure their freedom.[7] To most Baltimoreans, slavery was an evil institution—but the problem remained unsolved.

It was during this period that Moses Sheppard wrote to a friend concerning the abolitionists:

> It is the practice not the principle that I object to. Substituting denunciations and declamation instead of remedy. If slavery is a crime, by the laws of Providence, and I apprehend it is, the perpetrators will be punished by these laws soon or late; but that code is too tardy in its operation for the fanatic friends of freedom; they hurl anathemas on the slave holders and seem to think that is the remedy for slavery. I am equidistant from the unyielding slave holder and the uncompromising abolitionists; all that I recommend is to be still.[8]

The northern newspapers pressed their attack upon slavery so vigorously that there was a strong reaction in the South against the entire antislavery movement. The antislavery societies, which had existed south of the Mason and Dixon line since before the Revolutionary War, died out.[9] However, they increased rapidly in the North, and by 1840 numbered more than two thousand, with a membership of one hundred and fifty thousand. They maintained paid lecturers, held mass meetings, issued periodicals, and forwarded petitions to Congress. The movement became a crusade.

Supporters of the antislavery movement had little understanding of the economic conditions that determined the extent and spread of slavery. Cotton, tobacco, indigo, and sugar were the staples of the South, each crop requiring much manual labor. A major divisive issue was the tariff. The manufacturing North favored a high tariff on manufactured goods to protect their factories from foreign competition; the South desired a low tariff on manufactured goods to enable the planters to purchase such articles through the sale of their agricultural products.

Supporters of the antislavery movement also had little knowledge of the problems involved in immediate emancipation of the Negroes. Sharing the laissez-faire philosophy of the era, Northerners assumed that the Negro, once free, could compete on equal terms with white people. Moses Sheppard had in his library a booklet entitled, *A Voice from the South, Comprising Letters from Georgia to Massachusetts,* in which the author asked the abolitionists how Georgia, with nearly 300,000 slaves—a third of whom were children, aged or infirm—could give them their freedom. Georgia could not send the slaves into neighboring States, which would not re-

ceive them; the State did not have the money to send
them abroad nor funds to buy land, houses, and farm
tools if they were freed. The author concluded by saying, "Restricting slave territory does not provide for the
growing population of Negroes and if [Massachusetts]
persists in their approach to the problem they will produce a dissolution of the Union." [10]

Southerners played into the hands of the abolitionists,
where they had power to stifle criticism, by prohibiting
antislavery periodicals from entering the South, and, for
a period, in preventing petitions against slavery from
being read in Congress. As Northerners came to believe
that freedom of speech, of the press, and of petition
were threatened, they reacted even more violently
against both slavery and the South.

Samuel Eliot Morison has summed up the conditions
existing in the later period of Moses Sheppard's life:

> The abolitionists . . . expended so much compassion
> on the slaves that they had no pity left for the owner
> who was equally involved in the system and could see
> no way to get rid of it. But in view of Southern resis-
> tance to any form of gradual, compensated emancipa-
> tion, and of Southern insistence on acquiring more
> slave territory and more Federal protection for slavery,
> violence was the only way left.[11]

In the 1840's, discussion of slavery caused disastrous
breaks in the major religious denominations. As the
antislavery societies were especially strong in the Methodist, Baptist, and Presbyterian denominations, the
leaders of these societies brought pressure on the denominations formally to outlaw those who did not join

in the antislavery position. Southern ministers bolstered their position by quoting Scripture, and denounced the unwarranted interference with the domestic problems of the South. Tension continued to grow, matters coming to a head in the Methodist Church in 1844, when the national convention denied a southern slave-owning Bishop the right to discharge his episcopal duties until he freed his slave. In the following year, the Baptist denomination divided over the question of appointing a slave-owning missionary by the Board of Foreign Missions. After these large denominations split, John C. Calhoun, the most powerful political spokesman for the Southern position, declared, "The cords which bind the states together are not only many but varied in character. Some are spiritual and ecclesiastical, some political, some social." [12] He believed "the strongest are those of a religious nature, and they are beginning to snap." Debate on the antislavery issue was as contentious in the New School Presbyterian churches, although that denomination did not divide until the next decade; the Old School Presbyterians shelved the subject on the grounds that "The Presbyterian Church has stood at an equal remove from the extreme of Abolitionism and Proslaveryism. She has refused to pervert God's word to make it either denounce or sanction slavery."

The Society of Friends was not spared a conflict over slavery; all members opposed the institution, but could not agree how or when to bring it to a conclusion. In addition, the Quakers "felt the restlessness, the novelty, the variety, the diversity which marked all Americans during the turbulent thirties and the roaring forties." [13]

167

There were no major divisions in the East, however. The Meeting Elders refused to countenance intemperate condemnation of slaveholders or to interfere with their legal rights; they closed the Meeting Houses to antislavery lecturers. In Indiana, the Yearly Meeting warned its members against joining antislavery societies, and in 1840 when it closed the Meeting Houses to their lecturers, two thousand members, out of twenty-four thousand, withdrew to establish a new organization. As Drake has written: "What a paradox, that the Society of Friends—the first important group in America to see the evil in slaveholding, and the first to renounce it regardless of cost—the Quakers who had faithfully guarded the antislavery flame in years when it burned low, should now divide over the issue of abolition!" [14]

Small Hicksite groups of antislavery Quakers were formed in New York, Pennsylvania, and four western States. They called themselves "Congregational Friends," or "Progressive Friends." The Congregational Friends of Waterloo, New York, issued a manifesto in which they condemned slavery, war, the inequality with which women were treated, the unequal distribution of wealth, and the iniquity of "prejudice against color." [15]

As the violence of the antislavery attack increased, the Society of Friends drew back. It refused to join with those who advocated violence and tried to replace harsh denunciations with gentle persuasion. The Quakers saw the bitter fruits of Garrison's methods. A mob burned the house of Lewis Tappan in New York, a brother of the Tappan who paid Garrison's fine when he was arrested in Baltimore. A Boston mob tried to lynch Garrison, and in Concord Whittier was splattered with rotten eggs and decayed vegetables. Three Quaker printers had their presses destroyed; Elijah Lovejoy in Alton, Illinois, lost his life defending his press. "What had begun so quietly, as the older Quaker abolitionists had explored the various routes toward freeing the slaves, became a pitched battle, when the American Anti-Slavery Society proclaimed immediate emancipation as the only way." [16]

As early as 1835, Baltimore Yearly Meeting, Moses Sheppard consenting, passed down this advice to its subordinate groups:

> Friends are urged to keep themselves unconnected with the excitement now so generally prevailing in the land, and to be careful in maintaining our principles in the meek and peaceable spirit of the Lamb, and that we avoid compromising ourselves by entering into combinations with those whose motives we do not understand.[17]

Seven years later, the Yearly Meeting again urged its membership not to associate with those whose aims were "inconsistent with the mild and peaceable spirit of the gospel," and added further, "We can rest assured that all attempts to liberate the slaves by coercion will be met with counteracting force, and if persisted in, will finally lead to violence, perhaps bloodshed." [18] The Yearly Meeting declared that "True wisdom leads out of strife, contention and violence. . . . May we study to be quiet, and mind our own business."

Since two thirds of the membership of Baltimore Yearly Meeting lived in Maryland and Virginia and

only one third in central Pennsylvania, the epistle reminded members not to forget the plight of the slaveowners. The Friends were advised to have:

> in an especial manner . . . a benevolent regard to those
> who held the Negroes in slavery. No hostility, or even
> unkindness, was to be entertained towards those who
> claim to be their owners, a large proportion of whom,
> from long established habit and universal example,
> had been very much blinded to the iniquity of the
> system and its awful consequences.[19]

The members of the Anti-Slavery Association of
Pennsgrove, New Jersey, gathered in the Meeting
House as the Clarkson Anti-Slavery Association, took
Baltimore Yearly Meeting to task for another pro-
nouncement, issued in 1842, in which Maryland Friends
urged patience, avoidance of any violence, and trusting
"as did their ancestors . . . to convince the owners of
slaves . . . of the injustice of their practice. . . ." [20] The
Pennsgrove group declared that Baltimore Friends were
mistaken in thinking the Clarkson Association advocated coercive measures, even though a few of their
members had acted without discretion and in an excess
of zeal. Their only aim was "to arouse the conscience of
individuals" in order to "rid the country of the foul
leprosy . . . to clear their skirts of the sin which it involves." [21] They declared further that those who did not
openly and vigorously oppose slavery became partners
in the injustice that existed; and condemned those who
folded their arms and trusted to a "silent testimony."
The Pennsgrove party queried whether Friends in Baltimore might not be more influenced than they would
admit by their commercial and business dealings with

the South, or by owning stock in corporations that owned or employed slaves.

Benjamin Taylor of Virginia, in his correspondence with Moses Sheppard, answered the Pennsgrove assault from a Southerner's point of view. He had finished reading some sermons of Lucretia Mott, who attended Baltimore Yearly Meeting in 1843. Taylor admired the earnestness and intense enthusiasm of Lucretia Mott, as well "as her somewhat impatient desire to see and bring about a moral regeneration of the world." She seemed to desire "the banishment of every evil which is now supposed to retard the progress of mankind to the highest degree of civilization and moral refinement." [22] Taylor hoped that Lucretia would proceed with moral courage and firmness, but felt that this should be linked with meekness and sincerity. He feared she would become like other antislavery lecturers who were characterized by violence, intolerance, and bigotry, without just regard to the feelings of others. The abolitionists, Taylor wrote, in demanding immediate and unconditional abolishment of slavery, did not realize that this might well bring about the destruction of both races in the South.

In a further letter, Taylor said, "The acrimony and violence with which the discussion of the vexed question of slavery is conducted by both sides is rapidly alienating one portion of our people from another." [23] He added, "When a hostile feeling is fully aroused between the North and South, it will not be difficult to dissolve the Constitutional bonds . . . with the inevitable adjunct of internecine war and perpetual commotion."

Thomas Earle sent Sheppard a petition to sign asking

Congress to appropriate the proceeds of public lands to purchase the slaves and give them their freedom. Moses answered, "I am willing to be taxed in this or any other way to do justice to the slave holders and to abolish slavery." [24]

Many Friends, especially those traveling in the ministry, spoke concerning slavery in meetings for worship. Not all members agreed that this was a proper subject to inject into the worship period. Dr. Nathan Shoemaker wrote Moses Sheppard, "When will this vexed question cease to agitate our Society? I had rather not hear it touched upon in our meetings for worship. I do not believe it is a part of gospel ministry. In the Lord's own time this oppressed people will be delivered." [25] Further north, John Greenleaf Whittier and Lucretia Mott kept the Friends agitated concerning the problem of slavery, yet retained their membership in the Society of Friends by diplomatic posture and careful relations with the Quaker Elders. Others were not so successful. The Grimke sisters of Philadelphia; Arnold and Elizabeth Chase Buffum and William Bassett of New England Yearly Meeting; Isaac C. Hopper, Charles M. Merritt, and James Gibbons of New York Yearly Meeting—all active antislavery speakers—were disowned for overenthusiasm. Although Lucretia Mott spoke several times in Baltimore Yearly Meeting, nothing in the records suggests that her message was unacceptable.

Moses Sheppard still believed Colonization was the best solution. He wrote Dr. McGill in 1843 that if two thirds of the free colored people would emigrate with their possessions to Liberia in a short time, the colony would be prosperous and on its way to becoming a real nation. It only required, he considered, ambition and energy on the part of the colonists to give them manhood in the eyes of the world. In Africa they had all to gain and nothing to lose.[26] Dr. McGill answered that the various papers published by the abolitionists were too dangerous to circulate in Liberia. He agreed with his mentor that the best way to better the condition of the American Negro was to secure his transportation to Africa. "What hope can we cherish in the United States of an ultimate elevation to social and political privilege?" he asked; "none whatever." He continued, "We will use every means to elevate our children in Liberia to the rank of whites in the United States, then as strangers we could not fail to receive those marks of respect which are not even allowed the most intelligent and refined colored Americans." [27]

Few Quakers took an active part in politics, where so much of the battle over slavery was fought out. John Jackson of Sharon School declared that Friends should abstain from seeking public office because they would become involved in matters concerning war, the traffic in slaves, and the hiring of chaplains in the armed services." [28] All Baltimoreans, however, followed the fortunes of presidential candidates, since during the first half of the nineteenth century most nominating conventions were held in their city. Andrew Jackson was named in Baltimore to head the Democratic Party in 1832. The Whigs nominated Martin Van Buren in 1836, at the same time adopting a states' rights platform warning that "all efforts of the abolitionists or others to induce Congress to interfere in the question of slavery . . . will have dangerous consequences, diminish the happiness of the people, and endanger the stability and permanence of the Union." [29] General Harrison was selected by the same party in 1840, and Henry Clay in 1844. The Democrats picked a winner in James K. Polk in 1844; and the Whigs did likewise in 1848 when they nominated Zachary Taylor near Baltimore in Ellicott City. When Clay and Polk ran against each other, Sheppard could see little choice between the two, for they were both slaveowners; Polk went further, advocating the extension of slave territory into Texas. Moses entertained several Whig delegates to various conventions, showing some preference for that party. When one of his guests was elected to Congress, Sheppard secured a large number of congressional documents from the Congressman, which he forwarded to Governor Russwurm in Maryland in Liberia.

On February 25, 1845, the Republic of Texas was annexed to the United States by a joint resolution in Congress, and it was certain that war with Mexico would result through this effort to expand slave territory. Moses Sheppard sent word to Thomas Ellicott, "I am in no mood to write, the indications are too warlike, the Democrats are for war." The Quaker not only predicted war with Mexico, but was afraid President Polk would bring about a conflict with Great Britain over the northwest territory. Sheppard was certain the expansionists, whose watch word was "Manifest Destiny," would demand additional territory. "We have Texas," he later wrote, and prophesied, "we shall soon march into Mexico, and finally sweep down the peninsula of South America." [30]

Late in the forties, Moses Sheppard purchased a slave. He related this surprising happening in a letter to Joshua Dugan in Bucks County. Moses awoke one cold morning to find a strange Negro beside his bed. On inquiring how the Negro got there, the man replied that the kitchen help had sent him up, and that he wanted Moses Sheppard to buy him. "Buy you," exclaimed the Quaker, "I don't buy black people; if you knew anything about me, you would know that." [31] But the Negro, Tom Johnson, explained that his master was forced to sell him to meet a debt, and that a slave dealer from Georgia was waiting to take him. Sheppard got dressed, went to the spot where the dealer was waiting, already astride his horse, and verified Tom's story. Moses concluded his account of the event: "The morning was bleak and cold. I was anxious to leave the grounds. No bargaining was necessary. My sympathy was excited, and I turned to the dealer and said to him, 'Come with me and I will give you the money.' The dealer did so, and Tom Johnson became a free man. I paid four hundred dollars for him."

Many Maryland Friends, including Sheppard, took little comfort in the debate over slavery. It seemed doubtful to them that the South would ever give up its slaves, even if properly compensated. If by some miracle emancipation should come, the South would insist on sending the freed Negroes beyond its borders. The North would never receive such an influx of former slaves. African colonization alone seemed to be a feasible solution. But to secure proper leadership among the American Negroes for the task, and to find funds to transport and establish such numbers in Africa, did not seem as possible as when the American Colonization Society began its work. Frustrated, as so many Quakers were, Moses Sheppard wrote to Thomas Ellicott, "After my labors and experience in the cause of blacks, I confess I am surprised to find not only males and . . . ladies, but even little children understand the solution to the case better than I do." [32]

XI

The Vital Fifties

THERE WAS SOMETHING almost miraculous about the vitality of Baltimore in the 1850's, the city was more buoyant than ever." [1] Domestic trade increased as railroads extended further and further into the North, South and West. The Baltimore clipper was again on the high seas rushing men to the Isthmus of Panama or, around Cape Horn, the gold fields of California. The city's tobacco warehouses, fertilizer plants, cotton and iron mills were thriving. The bankers of the Queen City of the Chesapeake had become the credit agents for the South. Coastal freight and passenger ships reached every river emptying into the Bay, picking up the products of farm and forest on local wharves. The Baltimore and Ohio Railroad reached the Ohio River at Wheeling, and connected with Pittsburgh through the McConnellsburg and Pittsburgh Railroad. Vessels of a new line, the Merchant and Miners Transportation Company, steamed between Baltimore and Boston.

In 1850, Baltimore had a population of 169,054—a growth of 67,000 in ten years—of whom twenty-five per cent were foreign born. In the city were 24,937 free men of color and only 2,946 slaves; in the State, however, there were 74,077 free men of color and 90,368 slaves.

To the south, Virginia had 460,000 slaves, and North Carolina 288,000. The total population of the slave states was not quite half that of the free states.

The comfortable little group meeting in Moses Sheppard's parlor was disturbed by events at home and abroad. There was mounting distrust and illwill expressed towards the increasing number of foreign immigrants throughout the country. In Philadelphia, the City of Brotherly Love, fierce riots took the lives of thirty men, wounded one hundred and fifty others, destroyed thirty houses and burned two Catholic Churches. But Baltimore could not boast, for "That lusty, growing city . . . was dominated on the low level by white native American workmen, who were equally hostile to Negroes and the Irish, and intimidated Irish Catholics from voting." [2] The discussion often turned to the uneasy conditions of Europe, where the revolutions in Bohemia, Hungary, Italy, France, and Germany were still being felt, and because of which new immigrants from the educated classes came to America. Sheppard wrote to Thomas Ellicott, "The situation in Europe is awful, the effects of the convulsions there will reach us like the undulations of agitated waters, or like sparks falling on a substance already near combustion." [3] He thought that the three scourges of mankind—war, pestilence, and famine—would take their toll.

Times were good in the United States, however. In 1850, California produced $36 million in gold, and the next year $56 million. With this large addition to the specie of the country, the general level of prices rose, immigration was further stimulated, and the Far West settled much sooner than anyone anticipated. Commercial and industrial expansion took place. Richard Townsend, who was soon to become Moses Sheppard's private secretary, recorded in his diary: "This was a hurrying time in the world's history: Railroads, Atlantic and Pacific steamboats, and telegraph wires were making light of time, space, and gravitation." [4]

Thinking men would have been more optimistic had it not been for the ever-present problem of slavery. Current events continually brought the subject to the fore. An expedition of Southerners, always on the lookout for more slave territory, invaded Cuba. These filibusters were captured by the Spanish government, and fifty were executed.

Taylor wrote his friend that Samuel M. Janney, the Quaker historian of Lincoln, Virginia, was indicted by a Grand Jury for publishing inflammatory and incendiary material on the subject of slavery. "He may not be tactful," wrote Taylor, "but it is a painful fact that he manages some [way] or other to excite a degree of public odium against himself which is unparalleled in our community, and which his goodness of heart, and truly Christian character, does not merit." [5] Taylor reported that the court quashed the proceedings against Janney.

Three Quakers from Chester County, Pennsylvania, came to Baltimore in search of a Negro who had been seized near Kennett Square and brought to the city to be sold. One of the men, George Martin, was held in jail for two nights for his activities in the case. Sheppard wrote to Ellicott: "Martin is an honest farmer and was wrong in coming here, for the black man was, and is, a slave. The trader got possession of him violently and illegally, but no remedy can be had, for the man being a slave, the illegality of his capture must be tried in Pennsylvania, no law of Maryland has been violated." [6] The humanitarian added that if further action were taken, he would help raise a purse to defend the Pennsylvania Friends. After the case was dismissed, Martin and his companions, Samuel and Moulton Pennock, had tea with their fellow Quaker. Sheppard commented to Ellicott: "Martin is a plain farmer, reasonable and moderate. I formed a good opinion of him; if thee sees him, tell him so; if he should come here again on a like occasion, he shan't go to jail. The Pennocks are noisy, declamatory abolitionists, the very kind of men to injure such a cause here." [7]

Benjamin Taylor commented that there were "incendiary spirits both in the North and South who would dissolve the Confederacy to remove some evil, real or imaginary, not remembering that while this catastrophe would certainly fail to produce the particular object sought for, it would certainly bring upon us other evils and calamities." [8] Such a separation of the states, Taylor felt, would not settle the question of slavery or enlarge the area of freedom. "If the Union were shattered," he commented, "Virginia and Maryland . . . would be a Flanders in Europe, the battlefield ground where the fragments of the Union would struggle for supremacy and power . . . misery resulting." He said further, "Dissolution would mean insult and violence, civil war, rapine and plunder, and the political slavery of the whole continent."

The famous Compromise of 1850, which was advocated in Congress by Henry Clay and which fixed the boundaries of Texas, admitted California as a free state, organized the Southwest without reference to slavery, and abolished slavery in the District of Columbia, preserved the Union for another eleven years. It shattered the Whig party, however, and ended its political power. Richard Townsend expressed the relief felt by all Friends in his Diary, "The hour of disunion, by the wisdom of Providence had not yet come. It was now thought that all cause for sectional dissatisfaction had been removed." [9]

The item in the great Compromise that "stuck in the craw" of most Northerners, as well as all Quakers, was the strengthening of the Fugitive Slave Law. Riots took place in many Northern areas. Edward Gorsuch of Baltimore was murdered in Christiana, Lancaster County, Pennsylvania, when he attempted to remove his runaway slave. In Syracuse, a mob violently freed a slave taken by the officers of the law. In Boston it took "a battalion of United States artillery and four platoons of marines," plus twenty-two companies of state militia to return a slave to his master.[10] This was the last slave sent South from Massachusetts. When Dr. McGill asked his Baltimore friend what he thought about the Fugitive Slave Law, Sheppard replied, "A law made by a community is binding on every member of the community provided it does not compel him to *act* contrary to his judgment and conscience. A law to compel me to own slaves, or to arrest fugitive slaves I would not consider obligatory." [11]

Quakers, active in the Underground Railroad since 1800, doubled their efforts. But it is impossible to estimate the extent to which Friends engaged in assisting Negroes to flee to the North, but no doubt "it was a noble minority" of the members of the Society. Their efforts were less effective, however, than those of the Free Negroes, who never received the credit they deserved.[12]

With tension increasing between the North and South, Sheppard was gratified by the *Report of the Managers of the Maryland Colonization Society,* issued in 1850. He was pleased with the references to his own work as a manager of the Society in its early days. He noted that between 1832 and 1850, the Colonization Society sent twenty-five ships to West Africa, transporting 977 immigrants. Expenditures for these journeys and settlement of the colonists were $285,964.43, of which $171,139.91 was provided by the State Legislature of Maryland. The government at Cape Palmas seemed firmly established, all officials except the governor and his assistant were elected by the community, and the Chief Justice was an immigrant who had received his law training in Baltimore. It seemed to the founders, including Moses Sheppard, that the day might not be distant when a new nation would be acknowledged on the west coast of Africa. The 1850 report looked forward to the day when there would be a "mighty exodus from amongst us of people that can never be of us,—that can never be bone of our bone and flesh of our flesh . . . to assimilate with [those] in Liberia raising them up to their standard of excellence, redeeming, regenerating, and disenthralling them." [13]

Meanwhile, Sheppard continued to aid his friends in Cape Palmas. He congratulated Joshua Stewart on having "six head of horned cattle, fine hogs and goats, a comfortable garden and an industrious wife." [14] He reminded Joshua, who wanted to be a teacher of the native children, that the best instruction was not necessarily done in the classroom, but was performed "by showing industry and the habits of civilized life . . . to the natives." In the same vein, the humanitarian told Anthony Wood: "Industry and economy will make you comfortable, and your being comfortable will make your friends here feel comfortable. . . . Several people who saw Anthony Wood here, expect him to act the part of prudence and energy." [15] The Baltimorean accompanied this letter with a gift of shoes, five dollars worth of lead for seining nets, and a grindstone. James Hall, one of the teachers, thanked Moses for sending 161 New York State school readers, graded for different classes. An organization of Baltimore women was paying the support of Hall's school.

Moses Sheppard had word that Dr. McGill had now remarried, and hastened to send him a box of books for the new Mrs. McGill, with other gifts for the doctor. He thanked the physician for several long letters telling of events at the Cape, and added that he "could not answer them all, since writing by candlelight hurt his eyes." [16] He added, "In the various scenes and conflicting opinions which present themselves and arise, you will have my good wishes and goodwill."

The philanthropist received gratifying news from West Africa. Dempsey R. Fletcher, whom Dr. McGill had been training for some years as an assistant, was coming to the United States to receive a formal medical education. The Liberian doctor wrote that this young man was the only person in the colony capable of succeeding him. Sheppard secured admission for Dempsey Fletcher to Dartmouth College, helped establish him there, and assisted him in many other ways, as he had aided Dr. McGill years before. Dempsey Fletcher finished his work at Dartmouth in two years, and received the degree of MD. After Fletcher's return to Africa, Moses Sheppard had a second correspondent who could keep him informed concerning the state of the colony.

Many improvements took place in Maryland in Liberia during the absence of Dr. Fletcher. A lyceum was established, and, as usual, Moses Sheppard shipped off several boxes of books to begin a library. The Quaker received a request from A. Simpson for a set of tools, which he sent, with the word, "We are strangers. You may be lazy and good for nothing. I hope not, what money I have I worked hard for, and I don't like to give it to the idle. I shall inquire, let me hear a good account of your industry." [17] To Thomas Ellicott, Moses wrote, describing his African collection: "I now have snakes and king and queen bugabugs in spirits." [18] Dr. Fletcher added the skin of a boa constrictor and several small deadly snakes to the developing museum in the Brick House on Pratt Street. Dr. McGill sent a large leopard's skin similar to those worn by African kings. From the Baltimore Quaker, seeds, books, chemicals, and tools were sent regularly to the two doctors.

There was a severe drought in Liberia at the turn of the decade, and the colonies came to the very verge of starvation. Dr. McGill reported that conditions were due to lack of industry, lack of foresight, and dependence on the home society. Sheppard had always feared that such a condition might arise, in spite of all his sermons to the colonists about industry and providence. He told them that this incident "would *feelingly* convince the colonists that they must work." [19] To Anthony Wood he wrote: "The crop failed and you were short of provisions . . . it will teach you a lesson not to depend on living from hand to mouth. Rice will keep, raise it yourself and lay it by, don't depend upon natives for it. . . . I send you a grindstone, use it to sharpen your tools." [20] To Thomas H. Gross, Moses wrote, "I want the citizens of Liberia to demonstrate the fact that knowledge, prudence, and worth of character does not belong to any color exclusively." [21]

During the time of the famine, Dr. McGill was acting Governor of Maryland in Liberia. Governor Russwurm went to England with a delegation asking for recognition of Liberia as a separate nation. In this the Governor was successful. Dr. McGill favored joining the Maryland colony in Liberia to the larger unit of Liberia in some type of federation, but this did not come about for several years. The doctor thought his fellow colonists would not develop a responsible government until they ceased to be dependent on the Maryland Colonization Society. "If they were citizens of a free nation," he declared, "it would give the colored men a field whereon to put in full play every faculty with which he is endowed by our Creator, by the judicious exercise of which, he can not only promote his own, but be instrumental in contributing to the happiness of an entire people." [22] The doctor said further, that the colony at Cape Palmas was considerably behind conditions in Liberia proper, "there are not enough well informed among us to leaven the mass of ignorance; for the rapid and positive improvement of this Colony we must have among us a few educated men, as well as some with money." The doctor especially lamented the ignorance and shiftless attitude of Negro immigrants from "the low counties of Maryland."

Dr. McGill reported that the mercantile business, which he started some years before with the assistance of his brothers and the advice of Moses Sheppard, was prospering. He received from it at least two thousand dollars a year, while his position as colonial physician paid him only five hundred dollars. He was able to purchase a schooner, which he named the *Moses Sheppard*. In this boat his helpers carried goods from the warehouse up the coastal rivers. Dr. McGill was thinking seriously of moving to Monrovia, where he had spent his youth, in order to enlarge his business as well as the opportunities for his children. He reported that he took time to read the newspapers, magazines, and the books that the humanitarian sent him.

Sheppard wrote that he would not give advice on a possible move to Monrovia, nor on the wisdom of independence for Liberia. "I have no doubt the Republic of Liberia will be treated as an independent country, but whether the Liberians have the intelligence to sustain an independent government, or whether any nation has, is a problem yet to be solved." [23] He added, "The original design to establish a colony in Africa was benevolent, not commercial,—the colonists were free to choose any type of government they desired, or attach themselves to any nation which they believed would be most beneficial to them." In the next few letters that passed between the two men, Sheppard made several pertinent observations. In one letter, he wrote, "I agree with you that the civilization and Christianization of

Africa must be accomplished by colored agents." [24] In another, he said, "The United States has not recognized the Negro Republic of Haiti, nor will it recognize Liberia; a black Minister Plenipotentiary could not be received as such in Washington." [25] Later, Moses wrote, "Don't forget for a moment that American Negro slavery is not the only kind of slavery. Slavery is a tree with many branches proceeding from the same trunk, and assuming different aspects." [26]

In July of 1851, Governor Russwurm died, and Dr. Samuel McGill became Governor of Maryland in Liberia. He was forced to postpone his move to Monrovia, much as he desired "to live under the flag of his youth." [27] The governorship was an office to which he did not aspire. He sent word to his Quaker friend: "Since the Declaration of Independence of Liberia, I have felt convinced that Liberia is the only true home of the civilized man of color, elsewhere we are sought only as 'hewers of wood and drawers of water,' my aspirations from my youth have been for a more exalted position." [28] He concluded by adding regretfully, "My time is so thoroughly occupied with my own and the government's affairs, and my business correspondence is so engrossing, that I have been under the necessity of neglecting my most valued friend. I feel it, but I cannot help it."

At this time, Moses Sheppard also corresponded frequently with Joshua Dugan of Bucks County, Pennsylvania. This new acquaintance was an ardent Whig, a man of means, known as the "Gentleman Farmer." [29] He was energetic, younger than Moses Sheppard, and would have no part in the collectivist ideas then current, whether expressed in the Utopian socialism of Fourier or such attempts as that of Robert Owens at New Harmony. Dugan wrote his Baltimore friend: "Society should always encourage honest ambition. This preaching against adding field to field, and house to house, if it is done by honest enterprise and industry, is all nonsense." [30] Moses informed Dugan that he owned a farm at the head of tidewater, [where] much of the land was so marshy that even the frogs got attacks of ague "and became so transparent that it took two of them to make a shadow!" [31] At another time he told Dugan that he had another farm, well supplied with crabs and catfish, which he desired to sell.[32]

The philanthropist might not be adding field to field, but his investments were steadily increasing. He conducted his counting house in a very business-like manner, as his account books indicate. To N. C. Brooks he wrote: "the transaction between us is of a business character only and involves no other consideration. I find it would derange my arrangements . . . to let interest accumulate. I therefore [expect] that you will meet the case the 1st of July." [33] To another borrower he sent word, "I must request you to call me before the first of the month. I have not been pressed heretofore." [34] A man who rented one of Sheppard's houses wished to take advantage of the philanthropist's known charitable nature. The Quaker answered, "In your letter of January 24th you inform me you are educating your children with the money you owe me. Most of the rent was due a year ago. I have no objection to your giving your children a good education, but would a correct man do it at the cost of another, unauthorized? Your notes are in the hands of [my lawyer]. Please settle with him." [35] At the same time Moses instructed his lawyer to collect the money, but he added, "if the renter would secure the payments, even in twelve months, accept it." [36] B. M. High, who owed the Quaker $200 interest on a mortgage, asked for an extension of time, and Sheppard said "he would renew for one year . . . the amount to be given to such charitable institution as I may designate." [37] Benjamin Price of West Chester, Pennsylvania, told Sheppard about a young man off to the gold rush who needed money to help him on his way. Moses loaned him $100, and reported to Benjamin Price that he was "willing to adventure twenty dollars more on him." [38] Later, Moses said that he did not expect to collect interest on this loan. The Quaker businessman was certainly not a hard-driving money lender.

Oliver Evans often acted as the third party for the Baltimore Quaker when the latter sent funds to pay the expenses of the young people he supported in one of the Pennsylvania schools. On several occasions, Moses wrote, "I enclose a check . . . send no account, I want none." [39] In the late 1840's and early 1850's, Moses Sheppard was supporting five young people in boarding schools, two of whom were related to him. Nathan S. Tyson, a second cousin, became a ward of the philanthropist and received his education through Moses' generosity. When he came to Baltimore he "was a bundle of rags infested with vermin . . . having been neglected and mistreated by his father and step-mother." [40] Arrangements were made to enter Nathan at Prospect Hill Boarding School in West Chester, Pennsylvania, where the cost was $35 a term. The boy took with him a note from his guardian in which the older man wrote: "The boy has not been with me long enough to know much about him, but from the manner in which he was treated it is probable his habits will require revision, and I leave him to your paternal and maternal care." [41]

After a few months Benjamin Price, the principal, reported, "It will take a long and vigilant course of training to make a useful and agreeable man of him. . . . Nathan seems in pretty good temper, but is rough and noisy in his play, and if there is any mischief afoot he is in it." [42] After a second year's schooling, Nathan was placed as an apprentice in a Philadelphia store. Moses agreed to pay all of his expenses, including $3.50 a week for boarding, room, washing, and mending. The store owner was to pay the boy $25 for the first year's work, $37 for the second, and $50 for the third; at the conclusion of his apprenticeship he was to be taken on at $300 a year. The Baltimore Quaker declared that he wanted Nathan "to have every advantage." [43] Moses paid a fee for the boy to attend an apprentice's library, offered to send him to night school, and gave him $1.00 a month as an allowance. Nathan made a good start in the store, then fell into bad company. Moses wrote to Oliver Evans, "Time and experience has furnished me with no system in cases like this . . . much depends on the company the boy or man keeps." [44] Eventually Nathan was discharged and returned to his parents. There he made a better adjustment, and after a time wrote his second cousin, "I now keep books in my father's counting house . . . I have everything I want, and do all I can to please my friends here." [45]

Another of Sheppard's proteges was Nathan Sheppard, Junior, a great-nephew, whom Moses offered to educate after the early death of his father. This lad had an excellent mind, and was sent to Joseph Foulke's boarding school in Gwynedd, where he excelled. Once, writing to ask his great-uncle if he would pay an extra tuition for him to take French, Moses reminded Nathan that unless he was to be among people who spoke that language it would do him little good—but he paid the cost. On being asked the meaning of education, the philanthropist replied, "If education is an end in itself it terminates in a circle . . . the scholar then lives with the ancients, breathing in the 19th century, but living in the sixteenth . . . If education is a means, [education] leads to an active energetic life which sustains the human family in their onward course of progress." [46] He admitted that some people limited education to literature, while others thought a man well educated if he was instructed in the efficient and essential pursuits of life, though possessing but little "school learning." Moses added that if an individual had both, he was well fitted to enter upon the stage of action, especially if to his acquirements he added industry. Nathan, who had joined the church of his mother, went on through Attleborough College and Rochester Theological Seminary. The two men remained companionable, Nathan often visiting in Baltimore, and was at his great-uncle's bedside during his last illness. [47]

On one occasion, the businessman had reason to feel that his nephew, Oliver, was in need of funds himself and sent word, "Enclosed is a check on the Bank of the Republic, New York, for three thousand dollars. If thee

. . . wants it, send me a note at such time as suits thy convenience. If thee does not want it, return." [48] Shortly afterwards the note came back, properly signed. When a first cousin, Samuel C. Sheppard of Philadelphia, was in financial difficulty, the philanthropist sent word to Oliver Evans, "I want to do something for Samuel Sheppard, but I want to know what to do. I want to benefit him and his family, I do not want to pay his creditors." When the needed information was at hand, Moses directed his nephew to "Tell Samuel C. Sheppard I will relieve him from the mortgage on his house . . . tell him it is a donation, not a loan." [49] The Baltimorean dropped a note to Samuel Sheppard, saying, "Thy creditors may take their medicine, but they cannot take thy house. I hope thee will get on now." [50]

After visiting a female orphanage, Sheppard gave the director a check for fifty dollars "with the requirement that nothing ever be printed about it." [51] Visiting the House of Refuge, he noted that the steep steps had no railings. He sent a check for $500 to the Superintendent to remedy the situation, "for the assistance of the aged and infirm," adding, "this was to be clearly understood . . . nothing was to be said about the gift." [51] On a visit to the Brick House, Oliver Evans commented on a certain comfortable chair that he had earlier purchased at the direction of his uncle. Later, Moses wrote, "I still have the chair thee bought for me, it is most of the time out in the service of some invalid. I don't want to part with it. I want [another] one for a female charitable institution . . . purchase and send the bill to me." [52]

But the humanitarian did not answer every appeal that he received. He told Thomas Ellicott that he was

besieged with "begging ladies." [53] "The Old English
law," he wrote, "makes a man's house his castle, but I
find that I am liable to be besieged . . . not by men at
arms, but by 'heaven's best gift to man.' " He related
that a very attractive young lady asked for a gift to purchase a silver chalice for the baptismal font of her
church. Sheppard asked how long she had been married,
and when she told him for only three months, he remarked, "Then you have no baptising to do in the family yet, I presume. Excuse me till you have."

Personal sorrow touched Moses Sheppard in the death
of his favorite brother, Thomas, who, with his wife
Nancy and their son Nathan, lived in the Brick House
with him for many years.[54] Nancy and Nathan continued to stay on with Moses, but Nancy became an
invalid. A fellow Quaker, Dr. William Riley, often attended her, though her illness was of such a nature that
he could do little for her. "But if she was not attended
by a physician," Moses wrote to Thomas Ellicott, "it
might be supposed to be owing to my parsimony." [55]
His sister-in-law was often in bed for long spells at a
time, once for an entire year. Moses found it difficult
to secure adequate help to care for Nancy. He tried local
assistance but "the young men kept hanging around." [56]
He imported a niece from Ohio, but she remained for
only a few months. After Nancy's death which followed
several years of suffering, Thomas Ellicott wrote from
Avalon asking Moses how he was situated. Sheppard replied that he was "fixed" with three colored citizens,
"Eveline who was raised in the family as housekeeper
was a good one, though her health was feeble, "and the
other woman does the heavy work." George Barton con-

tinued to run errands and keep up the garden. "I have a good deal of jobbing," he continued, "which employs the main part of my time. I never was so comfortable. I did not know till now how great a sacrifice I had made of my own comfort for the comfort of others. The house is as well kept as it ever was, everything is clean and in good order, and I have a choice of company." [57]

Sheppard discussed with Thomas Ellicott what he should do after the death of his sister-in-law, for he preferred to have a companion, yet knew a suitable one would be difficult to find. "Men at the age that would suit me," he declared, "would have fixed habits, and so have I. . . . I am very plain in my mode of living, and might not accord with the state of another." There was also the possibility that if he secured another housekeeper, she might not agree with the cook Eveline. "I have got out of the frying pan," he wrote, "and I don't plan to jump into the fire." [58] In the end, the problem was solved when Isaac Tyson, a son of Moses' honored friend Elisha Tyson, took up his residence in the Brick House on Pratt Street.[59] The two Quakers were congenial, sharing common interests, as they both served as directors of several institutions.

As he entered his seventieth year, the Quaker was more at ease in female society than he was in his younger days. John H. B. Latrobe twitted him on this: "I hear of your gallantry—calling on the ladies. . . ." [60] Yearly Meeting was still a festival time, though Moses sent word to Benjamin Taylor, "I [will] entertain but few this year [only] Henry Taylor, Elisha Janney, Thomas Sheppard, Jonathan Seaver, and thyself." He added, "Come a few days before Yearly Meeting, it is a crowded and hurried time, and stay a few days afterwards." [61] Taylor formed the habit of spending some days with his Baltimore friend at the close of each school term. After one Christmas visit, he thanked his friend for the pleasant time they had as "they sat around the open fire discussing religion and the Negro situation." [62]

It was the custom for three to five friends to gather in the back parlor of the Brick House for an evening's conversation; to them apples and crab apple cider were served when in season. A newcomer to the group was a young man, Richard H. Townsend, son of Joseph Townsend, a "weighty" member of the Aisquith Street Meeting. Richard Townsend had known Moses Sheppard for many years, since he was an employee of the Union Manufacturing Company for nearly a quarter-century, during a period when Sheppard was a director of the corporation. Richard contributed much correct information to the older group. Over the years he kept a detailed diary concerning the major events of the day, which later was a valuable source for historians interested in Baltimore affairs.

The humanitarian accepted the fact that he was now "a looker on in Venice . . . and that it would be imprudent . . . amidst the obscurity of the evening to venture far on unknown ground." [63] Dr. Shoemaker made occasional trips to Baltimore and, on returning home, wrote, "I often think of thee and Isaac T., and imagine I can see you seated in the spacious room with a basket of apples, discoursing on some abstract subject of philosophy or metaphysics. How I should enjoy the occasion, for I am not too old to learn." [64]

Moses remained in excellent health, sending word to

his friend Thomas Elliott at Avondale, "I never was so comfortable, but I am withering fast, with the effect of time. It is said, 'An old man in good health is like a tower which is being undermined.' " [65] More than seventy years had whitened Moses Sheppard's hair, and he desired to arrange his affairs to achieve greater leisure. He hoped to spend more time with his books and his friends. In the last decade of his life, many friends came to visit him, usually spending several days at a time. Businessmen sought his advice, those engaged in Meeting affairs and Quaker concerns asked for his suggestions and his money, and letters came from and went to Liberia. Chiefs of the Iroquoian Indian tribes lodged with him on their way to Washington, black men still turned to him for assistance, and itinerant Quaker ministers from his own and other Yearly Meetings were housed in the dwelling on Pratt Street. Yet, in 1850, that "concern" for which he was to be best remembered had not unfolded in his mind.

A New Concern

As he sat among his friends in quiet meetings for worship, Moses Sheppard's thoughts turned to the disposal of the fortune he had accumulated through diligence and sagacity. He was fond of his nephew Nathan, and there were other nephews and nieces and several very close friends; but Moses felt no obligation to any of them. He wrote: "I have had very little intercourse with the greater part of my relatives. They are strangers. To some of them, I have been liberal: by others, I have lost heavily, amounting, together with my donations, to a larger sum than I ever expected to acquire." [1] He added: "No person has a claim on me, either for pecuniary favors that I have received, or from consanguinity: I, therefore, have the right to dispose of my Estate, according to my judgment."

Like many rich people of his day, Moses Sheppard considered that he was a trustee for his wealth. This was an era when there was no more honorable name than "philanthropist." The name carried no hint of condescension, but it was the expression of a deep concern for one's fellowmen coupled with a desire to ameliorate the conditions surrounding many often less fortunate. "Within a generation, Baltimore found itself the object of a veritable avalanche of philanthropy such as it had never seen before, nor has it seen since." [2] Sheppard's contribution was the first major gift, and in a few decades "Baltimore was richer by a university, a modern hospital, a superb scholar's library and conservatory of music, a free public library, and an art gallery that for quality compares favorably with any in the country." [3] The manner in which Sheppard gave his gift, and the direction he left for its management, were copied by some later philanthropists.

As early as 1846, Moses Sheppard discussed with John H. B. Latrobe the ultimate use to which he should put his estate. At that time, Moses had thought of endowing a Mercantile Library Association, to be housed in a large house that he owned on Lombard Street, especially for the use of young mechanics. Latrobe commented on this plan, "You wish to aid those whom Fortune has not aided, in the contest which is ever going on, in our Free Country, between those who are at the bottom, and those who are at the top of the ladder of Society." [4] The lawyer felt that "in this never-ending contest, knowledge—education—is the great weapon, and with this you [can] arm those who have not the means to purchase it." He declared, "This wish on your part, does equal honor to your forecast and your liberality. Upon the education of the classes, to which you are looking, depends everything morally or politically valuable to our institutions."

Latrobe did not think, however, that a Mercantile Library should be housed on Lombard Street, since it was out of the usual path of business. He made an alternate suggestion, which was that the Quaker endow a lectureship, or a professorship, in a local University. "Why should not the Sheppard lectures of Baltimore be as well received as the Dane lectures of Cambridge?" he queried. Or "Why not a Sheppard professor . . . to give lectures on the application of science to the arts?" [5] "The example thus set by you," Latrobe added, "would probably be followed by others, and the good which you proposed to do, would cease to be bound by your means of doing good." Moses Sheppard considered his lawyer's ideas, but, cautious man that he was, was not yet ready to act.

He desired to invest his estate "in such a way as to meet some need that would not otherwise be met," and to see that "the money would be so carefully managed that it would continue to be a blessing to men and women on down through many generations." [6] Moses Sheppard was well acquainted with the needs of the poor, from serving on committees appointed to see to the needs of indigent Friends, and from his experience as warden in the Second Precinct. He took literally the biblical statement, "Ye have the poor with you always." He believed that the various denominations should look after their own unfortunates, and the city fathers should meet the needs of the rest.

Sheppard's interest in the education of youth was demonstrated by the assistance he gave in the establishment of the Fairhill Boarding School, and by his willingness to pay the cost of boys and girls in attendance at several out-of-town schools. However, the public school system was growing stronger, and might be expected before long to meet the educational needs of most young people. Moses did not wish to found a second institution similar to McKim's Free School, and, following the advice of John H. B. Latrobe, he gave up the idea of establishing a library for apprentices, clerks, and mechanics.

Sheppard was still interested in the progress of the American Indians, but was skeptical concerning the red man's desire to accept the civilization of the white man. Now more sympathetic to the needs of its Indian wards, the legislature of New York State was establishing free public schools on the reservations and looking after the rights of the Senecas. Sheppard felt it was time for private organizations to withdraw their aid.

For a time, the Baltimorean considered giving his fortune for the building of schools in Maryland in Liberia.[7] But after Dr. McGill assured him that the Maryland colony would soon unite with the larger Republic of Liberia, Sheppard decided that the education of youth in West Africa should be taken over by the Republic. None of these concerns for which the philanthropist had given time and money in the past—the poor, the education of youth, the Indians, Colonization—seemed now to meet his desire for an altruistic use of his fortune.

Moses Sheppard lived to an age well beyond that of most men in his day; in letters to Thomas Ellicott, Benjamin Taylor, and Dr. Shoemaker, throughout the late 1840's and 1850's, Moses frequently referred to the mental conditions of men slightly older than himself or those of his own generation. It saddened him to see these acquaintances suddenly lose their minds or slowly approach senility. In a series of letters, for example, he traced the decline of Henry Payson, a man with whom he had been connected on a public service for several years. He first mentioned that Payson enjoyed tolerably good health and a serene mind; then he commented that Henry had become an object of pity, incapable of rising from his chair; still later described his old friend as having but a remnant of body and mind; and finally, that "Payson's mind was gone, he does not know me, though I was one of the last he recognized." [8] During the next few years Moses mentioned that several of his old time friends were in various stages of senility.[9] Comments such as these seem to represent an awakening interest in mental illness, as Moses wondered if senility could be delayed, treated, cured, or made easier to bear.

Tradition has it that a daughter of Joseph Lafettre, watchmaker and eloquent minister of Old Town meeting, became ill, and it was necessary to place her in the public hospital.[10] Sheppard visited the young lady, and was struck by the deplorable conditions existing in the hospital. Gerard T. Hopkins, a long time friend of Moses Sheppard, believed it was the death of two of Sheppard's acquaintances in the public hospital that aroused his interest in the subject of mental derangement.[11] These events may have quickened Moses' concern in this field, but the cause was a more extended one.

Through his work as a member of the prison board in his younger years, and from serving as a caretaker of the poor in the Second Precinct, the Quaker already knew of conditions existing in the public and private institutions for the insane in Baltimore. It was said that such treatment was no worse or any better than in most states, but the lot of the mentally deranged was a tragic one. "Over-crowded conditions were the rule in almost all institutions where the insane were kept," comments

Lavens Thomas, "and the treatment accorded them was atrocious." [12] A contemporary wrote:

> Sheppard was horrified at sight of the treatment extended to insane paupers. Men and women were crowded into narrow cells, stripped of every comfort, chained to the floor or braced to the miserable apologies for beds, and literally forced to wallow in filth. Their coarse and insufficient food was grudgingly meted out to them, and scantily clad they were exhibited like wild animals to the morbid gaze of those whose gorge did not revolt at the spectacle. Many whose mild maladies, which might have been cured by timely and proper treatment, were transformed into raving maniacs, and instances were not rare of patients tortured to death by the use of scourge or the lack of decent food. They were treated as though they were incarcerated for heinous crimes rather than confined as a security to themselves, with the hope of ameliorating conditions. Custom had deadened the sensibilities of the public, and its very antiquity was a sufficient excuse for brutality.[13]

These conditions were found in many places outside of Maryland. In 1842, Charles Dickens visited a newly opened lunatic asylum on Blackwell's Island, New York, and wrote in his *American Notes for General Circulation:*

> I cannot say I derived much comfort from the inspection of this charity . . . I saw nothing of that salutary system which had impressed me favorably elsewhere; and everything had a lounging, listless, madhouse air which was very painful. The moping idiot, cowering down with long disheveled hair; the gibbering maniac, with his hideous laugh and pointing finger, the vacant eye, the fierce wild face, the gloomy picking of hands and lips, with the munching of nails; there they were all, without disguise, in naked ugliness and horror. In

the dining room, a large bare, dull, dreary place, with nothing for the eye to rest on but the empty walls, a woman was locked up alone. She was bent, they told me, on committing suicide. If anything could have strengthened her in her resolution, it would certainly have been the unsupportable monotony of such an existence.[14]

Most Maryland counties had their alms and work houses where paupers, disorderly persons, vagrants, and the insane were placed. If physically able, all inmates were put to the labor of maintaining the buildings and grounds. At the Baltimore almshouse, the cost per inmate in 1826 was $37.63 per year; by 1840, those counties that sent their insane paupers to the Baltimore Hospital were charged $100 annually. By 1849, half of those cared for in the Baltimore Hospital were foreign born. A menu, which has survived from that date, is as follows: *breakfast,* rye bread and coffee; *dinner,* beef and soup, mush and molasses; Friday's herring was served with hominy; on Sunday there were pork and vegetables.[15] Some insane paupers were reported to be chained in damp basement rooms.

In 1840, Alexander C. Robinson, an attending physician, mentioned various improvements, which made the mentally ill more comfortable. The white and colored inmates were separated, more light and air had been introduced, and the inmates were no longer crowded together in unclassified conditions; but the doctor appealed for better physical equipment, some form of activities for the patients, and more professional skill in their treatment. The attendants, who were drawn from the pauper class, "did not possess the qualities of mind required in a nurse . . . and hence the coercive system

[had] become necessary." [16] He said further, that twelve of the forty insane women were in chains, two to a cell, and he found four mentally ill patients in one cell, three of whom were in chains.

Conditions were not much better in the Maryland Hospital, an institution in which two of Moses Sheppard's friends had died in 1850. This hospital was an outgrowth of an act of the legislature, which established it in 1797, erected on grounds later occupied by the Johns Hopkins Hospital. The Maryland Hospital, called at various times the Public, City, or Baltimore Hospital, was opened in 1800, but there never were sufficient funds to operate or keep it in proper repair. It was leased to two doctors for twenty-five years, until conditions grew so bad that the city took it over and appointed a Board of Visitors, headed by Dr. Richard S. Steuart. This Board included John H. B. Latrobe, Evan T. Matthews, and Johns Hopkins. The first report of the Visitors stated that they did not approve of "the method, order, invention, or energy displayed in the operation of the institution." [17] The city granted $30,000 for repairs, and placed the Sisters of Charity in charge to upgrade conditions.

The Board could soon report that "the horror . . . of the former mode of treating the miserable victims confined to cells and loaded with chains . . . with stripes and various kinds of severity employed to subdue this malady of mind disease, was a thing of the past." [18] Neatness, order, and good feeling soon prevailed. The Board of Visitors urged the State to build a new institution for the insane, where, with modern treatment, "under happy auspices, the dull eye of the lunatic may kindle again." [19] But nothing was done.

In 1849, the Board reported that the cost per patient had risen to $130 per year, although the counties still paid only $100. The number of patients was 120, which again overcrowded all rooms, and some men and women were placed in basement areas. The heating plant was defective and unfit for use. Private patients were admitted, and that year, "twelve individuals recovered, seven were discharged greatly improved, and five discharged unimproved." [20]

In 1842, the Sisters of Charity withdrew to found their own hospital, first on Front Street next to St. Vincent's Church, then on North Avenue, and still later on the Reisterstown Road. Dr. William H. Stokes reported in 1845 that there was a marked change in public opinion toward the insane. The insane were no longer considered to be witches or possessed by an evil spirit. "It would gladden the heart of every true philanthropist," he stated, "to see the evidence everwhere apparent throughout the country, of a growing interest in everything pertaining to well being of the insane." [21]

Moses Sheppard visited the Pennsylvania Hospital for the Insane in West Philadelphia. Established in 1751 under the stimulus of Benjamin Franklin and Dr. Benjamin Rush, the original hospital was financially assisted by wealthy Quaker merchants, and admitted the mentally ill from the beginning. It is the oldest private hospital for the insane in America. In Sheppard's time, it was treating an average of 125 mentally ill a year. Although Dr. Rush was a student of the great French reformer, Dr. Philippe Pinel, and is called "the first American psychiatrist," he yet advocated a program of frequent bleedings, purgings, and blistering to be rid of bad blood.[22] The conditions in the Pennsylvania Hospital, however, must have been far different from those in Maryland. The Steward of the northern hospital, a Quaker named Samuel Mason, wrote in 1818:

> I have not the most distant doubt but kindness in every instance has a more happy effect than contrary treatment, and when coercion is resorted to, still to impress on their minds that it is for their own good and not to gratify any resentment that punishment is inflicted. . . . Their memory is generally acute, and kindness is remembered, also an unkind image is not forgotten.[23]

Sheppard was well acquainted with Dr. Thomas S. Kirkbride, Superintendent of the new Pennsylvania Hospital. He studied the reports of the doctor, some of which he had in his library. He also sent copies to Dr. McGill in Liberia. Moses noted Dr. Kirkbride's suggestions concerning better treatment of insanity, and incorporated them in his own directions to the Trustees of the institution he later founded. Dr. Kirkbride wrote: "Insanity is curable in proportion to the early period at which a [patient] is placed under treatment, and a prompt removal from familiar scenes is commonly desired."[24] He stated at another time, "If prompt treatment is given . . . at least eighty per cent will probably recover; and yet the records of most of our institutions show that of all those discharged only a little more than fifty per cent are considered well."[25] Conversely, the doctor felt, "A large proportion of the permanent population, from the long duration of their disease, present but a feeble prospect for their recovery." [26] He admitted, however, that recovery took place among some after a prolonged period, and wrote, "every case should be considered under treatment—if not to cure, at least to keep from becoming worse [we will] treat all as though there was a hope of recovery." [27]

Sheppard was impressed by Dr. Kirkbride's statement that "it is [among] the lowest class of patients, that attention should be most steadily directed; it is amongst these that will yet be found the widest sphere for benevolent labor, and from which results will occasionally flow, that will reward any one who engaged in this work in the true spirit." [28] Sheppard also mulled over the doctor's statements that to witness a mind that seemed lost, "completely restored to health and usefulness, is of no ordinary gratification, [and] to see minds that cannot be restored, kept from losing all their powers, and . . . becoming wretched" is a blessing.[29]

Moses Sheppard knew the Asylum for the Relief of Persons Deprived of Their Reason, or The Friends Hospital, in Frankford, even better than the Pennyslvania Hospital. He visited the establishment a number of times in company with Dr. Nathan S. Shoemaker, one of the six Consulting Physicians. The Asylum was founded by Quakers in 1811, and patterned after the York Retreat in England. The latter was the creation of William Tuke and his associates, who in 1796 created the first institution for the *moral treatment* of the insane.

In his copy of the *Description of the Retreat, an Institution near York for Insane Persons of the Society of Friends,* Moses Sheppard read that York Friends decided they needed an establishment, under their own care, "in which a mild and more appropriate system of treatment, than that usually practiced, might be adopted; and where, during lucid intervals, or the state of convalescence, the patient might enjoy the society of those who were of similar habits and opinions." [30] No noxious drugs, so often used at the time, were given to patients, but a schedule of warm baths, a liberal diet, suitable amusements, occupations, reading and walking were substituted. Bleedings, blisterings, or the giving of large doses of salts were taboo; mechanical restraints were seldom used. Patients able to leave the hospital grounds attended Quaker meetings for worship in the city, and religious services were held in the buildings. As much fresh air as possible was advocated, and those able to walk about had available well-kept gardens. Attendants were courteous, kindly, and firm. "Such was the moral treatment of the insane, found in this place." [31] A statement in the history of The Retreat remained firmly entrenched in Moses Sheppard's mind, "The comfort of the patient is therefore considered of the highest importance in a curative point of view." [32]

The lessons learned at The Retreat were duplicated in the Friends Asylum, opened in 1817. The prospectus said, "Beside the requisite medical aid, such tender sympathy and religious oversight, as may sooth the agitated minds [will be used] and thereby, under divine blessing, facilitate their restoration to the enjoyment of their reasons." [33]

From an experience that Moses Sheppard had in his middle years, he quite understood why a schedule of activities, working in the hospital gardens, about the grounds, or within the establishment, were beneficial to the patients in The Retreat. For seven years, Moses was a member of the twelve-man Board of Inspectors of the Baltimore City jail. This experience he found neither pleasing nor satisfying. He decided that organized society knew little about the treatment of offenders and had little success in reforming their characters. He felt that punishments were unequal and arbitrary. He wrote at the time:

> When I was connected with the penitentiary, I had several small or silent cells constructed in which I made experiments with criminals. I gained information, but it only served to convince me that there was no knowledge by which to graduate punishment. The information I secured was analogous to that portion of light which makes darkness visible; to some silence and solitude is torture, to others the suffering is small, and to some no punishment at all.[34]

Sheppard noted that some Negroes "would lie in their cells like terrapin with philosophic composure."

While serving as Inspector, Sheppard introduced a plan that was helpful to the prisoners and saved the State a sum of money. He had read an earlier report of the prison officials in which they said that one of the major difficulties in handling the inmates was that there was no employment for them of a productive nature. Moses suggested to the board that they erect a suitable shop to manufacture felt hats, for which there was a ready market. This would bring a small return to the inmates, keep them usefully occupied, and return a sum to the State. His idea was approved, a shop was established, and the prisoners were enthusiastic. A marked change was seen in their conduct.[35]

Sheppard noted at both York and Frankford, forethought was given in taking care of indigent Friends. The original cost of patients at The Retreat varied from four to fifteen shillings per week, set according to the ability of the family to pay. This rate was raised to six shillings as a minimum in 1854. Costs at the Friends Asylum were comparable.

In the winter of 1851-1852, Dorothy Lynde Dix came to Maryland to visit the jails and almshouses. Miss Dix had studied social conditions in England, taught school in Boston, and for a period lived in the home of Dr. William Ellery Channing, the famous liberal much admired by Moses Sheppard. Miss Dix visited The Retreat in York under the guidance of Dr. William Tuke, and learned from him the techniques of moral treatment for the mentally deranged. She later was horrified by conditions found in the almshouses and jails of Massachusetts where the indigent insane were placed. She found mental inmates, "forgotten by their families, confined in cages, closets, stalls, and pens . . . chained, beaten, and lashed into obedience." [36] When she had collected sufficient facts, Dorothy Dix placed before the legislature of Massachusetts a memorial describing what she had seen, and asked for funds to remedy the situation. She was bitterly attacked, both in print and by word of mouth. But an investigating committee verified all her findings, and in the end funds were provided to build a new State Hospital, the Worcester State Hospital in Massachusetts for the Insane.

Before coming to Maryland, Miss Dix conducted investigations in seventeen states, all of which did take steps to improve the treatment of the insane. The reformer found conditions in Maryland to be as disgraceful as those elsewhere, and clearly set forth these facts in her Memorial to the Legislature, which "had the support of the *Baltimore Sun,* and humanitarian minded persons such as Moses Sheppard." [37] Again she was successful, and a liberal appropriation was approved to found a new institution for the treatment of the insane, although this was not opened until a year after the death of Moses Sheppard.

Sheppard enjoyed his contacts with Dorothy Dix. She visited him in his home on Pratt Street, and they corresponded freqently. The Quaker especially appreciated the careful manner in which Miss Dix gathered and correlated her material, and the fact that she did not attack or condemn any individuals, but placed the blame for existing conditions on ignorance and the lack of funds to provide proper care for the mentally ill. He was a sponsor of her Memorial to the legislature.

Dr. Steuart, well known to the humanitarian because of their joint work over the years in the Maryland Colonization Society, was named chairman of the commission appointed to create the new establishment. The two men visited each other, and corresponded concerning the mentally ill. Through the encouragement of Dr. Steuart and Miss Dix, Moses Sheppard was led to formulate his plan to leave his fortune "to establish a small, well-built, and wisely conducted asylum." [38] His Quaker belief "that *all* men are children of a common father," [39] his lifelong training received in the Society of

Friends, his knowledge of the appalling need for better care of the insane, combined to center his belief that this concern was one not met by others, and one to which his fortune could minister through the future. As recorded by the *Baltimore Sun,* "He could not have chosen an object more truly benevolent and Christian; of all the subjects of sympathy and compassion, a human being deprived of reason, is the most pitiable and helpless." [39]

XIII

The Developing Concern

My attention has long been directed to the case of the insane," wrote Moses Sheppard to Dr. Shoemaker.[1] The humanitarian knew from observation the miserable conditions found in most Maryland institutions in which the mentally ill were hidden and forgotten. He had also observed the improved treatment offered the fortunate few at Mt. Hope, The Friends Asylum, Pennsylvania Hospital, and the Bloomingdale Hospital in New York City. Sheppard knew that moral treatment was practiced at the McLean Hospital near Boston and in the Hartford Retreat in Connecticut. Of the state hospitals for the insane, Moses was especially interested in learning of the Worcester State Hospital in Massachusetts, founded in 1833, "which served as a proving ground for the moral treatment and demonstrated beyond doubt that recovery was the rule." [2] From the statistics published by this hospital, he was convinced that in a small establishment, with sympathetic and understanding treatment, the rate of cure would be high.

In a twenty-year period, out of 2,267 patients who came to the hospital whose illness had only recently begun, 1,618 were discharged as recovered or improved (66% recovered, 5% improved); of a total admission of

19. 3 mo 53

Dr. Shoemaker ; — Thy letter of 2nd mo. 20th was received and ought to have been answered sooner ; — my fall has disturbed my nerves, and writing occasions a cramp in my hand. I also have a letter from Franklin, to which I have not responded, owing to the cause I have mentioned. Thee remarks that thee is afflicted with the Bronchitis ; — we hear of old friends with new faces ; and this I suppose is an old disease with a new name. I have observed that the regular clergy are more subject to this disorder than any other class of public speakers. We have a member in our gallery, a lawyer suffering from it. We have a new member in our gallery, whose exhortations are frequent and earnest, she generally speaks twice in a Session, and speaks as one having authority, and not as a scribe. She visited Francis Cochran, and he has been much more depressed since — There is a strong movement here, to complete a juvenile house of reformation, and erect two Hospitals for the insane ; one for white, and one for black patients. My attention has long been directed to the case of the insane ; — and I expect what I may leave, will take that direction, and not to individuals. It has been stated in England, that more of the Society of Friends become insane, in proportion, than of any other Society or class. — I don't know if it is so, or not ; but there is several here, and more of us, half-crazy. I notice thy remarks on the future world, and coming judgment ; — whatever was the original design of the creating power must and will be accomplished —

Moses Sheppard

Letter, Moses Sheppard to Dr. Nathan Shoemaker

4,119 the per cent discharged as recovered was 45%, and of improved 14%.[3] Similar high rates of cures were reported in other hospitals such as McLean and Hartford. The state hospitals for the insane, such as at Williamsburg, Virginia, Utica, New York, and Lexington, Kentucky, also sustained high ratios of cures, since at this time they practiced the same type of sympathetic treatment. In this period, most state institutions accepted patients who could pay the cost of their treatment, as well as indigents whose expense was paid from public funds.

Dr. William H. Stokes, physician in charge at the Baltimore Mt. Hope Institute, wrote in 1844: "At least ninety out of every hundred cases can be cured, and instead of being the most untreatable, insanity is the most curable of all diseases . . . that is to say, in cases of a less duration than one year." [4] The newly formed Association of Medical Superintendents for the Insane, meeting in Philadelphia in 1844, stressed the fact that insanity was a curable disease, "if the afflicted individuals could only be given proper institutional care at an early stage. Quick recovery is certain for such." [5]

Sheppard had read the summary of an article printed in *The Lancet,* a medical journal issued in London, in which a Dr. Jacobi stated that there was a greater number of insane among English Quakers than among the general population. Dr. Jacobi thought this was due to several factors existing among this comparatively small denomination. "Quakers had a greater liveliness of conscience," the doctor wrote, "rather easily leading to despair." [6] Since at this period English Quakers were exempted from politics and positions in the State church, "they were more or less limited to trade and commerce where the inward feelings of discrepancy brought on by a harsh, competitive business life, brings on its pernicious fruits." The fact that "in securing for themselves an independent livelihood [Quakers] marry late, or not at all, with the resulting loneliness oftentimes unfortunate in its results for mental health," also increased the proportion of mental illness. Dr. Jacobi considered the high rate of intermarrying among the Friends an additional consideration.

Dr. Tuke, at The York Retreat, denied the validity of the article printed in *The Lancet*. He said that at The Retreat there were practically no patients suffering from "religious madness," prevalent in other asylums in England, and practically no alcoholics, because of the testimony of the Society against the use of spirituous liquors. "Extreme poverty, and distress from want," which caused so many to go to public foundations for the mentally ill, "simply did not exist among Friends," wrote Dr. Tuke.[7] Few non-Friends were admitted to The Retreat at this period in its history, and the Quakers who were there came chiefly because of "disappointment of the affections, domestic affliction, or failure in business." [8]

Moses Sheppard was not able to judge between the two doctors, and wrote to Dr. Nathan Shoemaker: "It has been stated in England, that more of the Society of Friends became insane, in proportion, than of any other Society or class. I don't know if it is so or not, but there are several here; and more of us half-crazy." [9]

The philanthropist was now ready to set in motion the machinery by which his concern could be carried out. In the spring of 1853, he approached David M. Perine, for many years Register of Wills in Baltimore, concerning the proper procedure. The lawyer has left an account of what took place:

Some years before his death, he came to my office and requested me to give my opinion in relation to his will, which he had with him. I read it carefully, and then told him that I thought it would not accomplish the object he desired. By this will all his property was devised to certain gentlemen as trustees, for a benevolent purpose; that purpose, however, was not clearly stated, and was too indefinite; the second objection was, that there was no accountability of the trustees, and too much unlimited and undefined power was given them; the third, and principal, objection was, that in the course of time all the trustees named in the will would pass away, and then, even if the object of his benevolence was expressed with sufficient clearness in his will, it would necessitate the application of a Court of Equity to appoint trustees in the place of those named in the will. Upon my stating these objections, he was much worried, and said that his will, having been drawn up by a prominent member of the bar, he had supposed it was all right.[10]

David Perine wrote that Sheppard then explained the purpose he had in mind, and something of the details of his plan. "He said that he had visited many hospitals, and had endeavored to get some of them to make the experiment he desired, but had been informed by the managers that his plan was expensive, that with their means, they could not undertake it." [11] He asked Perine to redraw his will to cover the objections and, with the lawyer's advice, decided that a Charter would be more suitable for his purpose. This Perine was commissioned to secure.

The Quaker wanted this final gift to be anonymous, but the lawyer insisted that attaching the name of Moses Sheppard to the document would assure its approval by the Maryland General Assembly. While awaiting action, Moses wrote to Philip Perine, who was commissioned to present the Charter to the Assembly: "As we only ask sanction to spend our own money to mitigate the suffering of the forlorn and wretched, I suppose there can be no objection to giving us the privilege to do so. It is very desirable that it pass at this session." [12] The Act of Incorporation was first read and approved in the House of Delegates and the Senate on May 24, and received final approval by the House on May 27, and the Senate May 28, 1853.

The Charter stated: "That the object and design of the said Corporation is hereby declared to be, the founding and maintaining an Asylum for the Insane; the entire management of which shall be vested in the said Trustees." [13] The Trustees were empowered "to make by-laws and rules and regulations for the management and government of the Asylum, and the persons residing therein, whether officers, servants, or patients, the same not to be inconsistent with the public laws of the State." [14] As a "Body Politic and Corporate," the Trustees, were to be "capable in law, to acquire property, real, personal, and mixed, by gift, devise or purchase; and to hold, sell, dispose of, and convey the same; and to sue and be sued, plead and be impleaded, answer and be answered, defend and be defended, in any Court of Law or Equity, or other place whatsoever . . . and to receive and to make all deeds, transfers, contracts, covenants, conveyances, and grants . . . necessary to carry into effect the provisions of this Act, and to promote the object and design of said Corporation." [15]

The Trustees were charged with the duty of removing any of their number "who in the opinion of the majority, may be negligent of his duty, or otherwise conduct himself improperly: to fill all vacancies occasioned by removal or otherwise; to elect annually a President and Secretary who shall perform the duties usually incumbent on such officers; . . . and to remove them at pleasure; to appoint and employ all such officers and servants as they may deem necessary or proper; to dismiss them at their pleasure; to fix their duties and compensations; and generally to exercise all the powers conferred on the said Corporation by this Act." [16]

The Charter specified that the number of Trustees should be "not less than five nor more than seven," and all vacancies should be filled by the Trustees within sixty days; if, at any time, three vacancies existed, the President, "under a penalty of five hundred dollars," was required to notify the Governor of the State, who would then fill the vacancies himself." [17]

On the first of January of each year, the Trustees were required to file with the Governor a full report in writing "of their proceedings during the year, and of the State of the Asylum; sending the number and condition of the inmates, and all matters necessary to the full understanding of the affairs and situation of the Corporation . . . [also] showing the receipts and expenditures for the year, and the assets and pecuniary condition of the Corporation . . . copies [by the Governor] to be laid before the General Assembly at its then or next session." [18] The Trustee's funds were further protected by a section of the Charter giving the General Assembly or the Court of Justice the right at any time to inquire into the affairs of the Corporation, and to remove one or all of the Trustees "who may be guilty of fraud, embezzlement, or misapplication of the funds of the Corporation," and to "replace one or all." [19]

The first Trustees (picked by Moses Sheppard) were named in the Charter, in order: Moses Sheppard, David

M. Perine, Dr. William Riley, Archibald Stirling, Charles Howard, William M. Metcalfe, and Richard H. Townsend.

David M. Perine (1796-1882) who served as Trustee until 1878, was a birthright member of the Society of Friends, but was disowned from membership in July, 1814, for military service.[20] He joined the Episcopal Church. "He was of a grave and dignified bearing, upright, just and of sound judgment, with great knowledge of testamentary matters . . . he was sought as advisor and man of business by many." [21] Perine was the attorney for Charles Carroll of Carrollton, and concluded the details of the arrangements by which land owned by Robert Oliver became Greenmount Cemetery. He also drew the Charter for the Samuel Ready School for Female Orphans.[22]

Dr. William Riley (1807-1887) was Moses Sheppard's personal physician, well acquainted with the Brick House on Pratt Street, and often a member of the interesting gatherings held there. Born in Baltimore and an active member of the Lombard Street Meeting, he was graduated from the University of Pennsylvania Medical School in 1832. Dr. Riley served thirty-four years on the Board of Trustees of the Sheppard Asylum, the last four as President.

Archibald Stirling (1798-1878?) was a native Baltimorean, born July 13, 1798. Associated with the shipping firm of William Lorman, he at twenty-one took charge of his father's large estate. He served as director, and later President of the Savings Bank of Baltimore. He was a Presbyterian. It was written of Archibald Stirling that "he was one of our representative men, whose valuable and venerable life, is alone an occasion of admiration to his friends and citizens, and an inspiring example." [23]

Charles Howard (1802-1869), was a younger son of Colonel John Eager Howard, one of the most public-minded citizens of Baltimore during the first quarter of the eighteenth century. It was said of Charles, "his tastes and favorite pursuits were altogether those of a private gentleman," but there was scarcely an enterprise or an Institution of public benevolence or usefulness to which at some time or other he did not give his personal aid and labor." [24] As President of the Maryland Colonization Society, he worked with Moses Sheppard for many years in that philanthropy. He was as interested as Sheppard in the development of railroads, and held the office of President of the Susquehanna Railroad.

William M. Medcalfe was a member of the Baltimore Monthly Meeting of Friends, associated with Moses Sheppard in business affairs and perhaps in the colonization movement.

Richard H. Townsend (1804-1879) was a birthright Friend, attended Friends School in Baltimore and the Quaker Boarding School at Nine Partners, New York.[25] Throughout his life he was a member of Aisquith Street Meeting. Townsend was associated with the Equitable Fire Insurance Company, and for twenty-seven years with the Union Manufacturing Company. He became private secretary to Moses Sheppard in January 1853, at a salary of $1,200.00.[26]

The first meeting of the Board of Trustees of the Sheppard Asylum was held at the Union Bank of Baltimore on June 23, 1853, all Trustees present. The

Founder presented the Act of Incorporation approved by the Maryland Legislature, and "after it was read and duly considered, it was upon the motion of Moses Sheppard, unanimously Resolved, and ordered, by the persons present . . . and named in the Charter as Trustees . . . that they adopted the aforesaid Charter . . . with all the provisions and conditions imposed." [27] The Founder was then elected President of the Board, and Richard H. Townsend was elected Secretary.

No further meetings of the Board were held for the next three years, when five of their number again gathered in the Union Bank of Maryland to receive the resignations of Archibald Stirling and William M. Medcalfe. On nomination of Moses Sheppard, J. Saurin Norris and Gerald H. Reese were elected to fill the two vacancies. Some months later, a third session of the Board was convened to receive the resignation of Charles Howard. His place was filled by the election of Gerard T. Hopkins. The Board now remained intact for many years, with the exception of Sheppard himself. No explanation was ever given why three members of the original Board resigned, unless it was knowledge of a clause in Moses' will that postponed the immediate construction of asylum buildings.

J. Saurin Norris (1813-1882), the second President of the Asylum, served for twenty-two years, during the most critical period in the institution's history. He was born in Baltimore, the son of a "substantial and capable citizen." [29] He was Secretary to the Merchants Fire Insurance Company and Treasurer of the Savings Bank of Baltimore. When the First National Bank was organized at a later date, Norris became in turn Cashier, Vice

President, and President. He was "well and favorably known to [the] community, as a gentleman possessing integrity and thorough business qualities. . . . He held the esteem of all who knew him, and possessed both practical experience and great financial ability." Like his friend on Pratt Street, Norris was a wide reader, and contributed several papers to the Maryland Historical Society's journal.

Gerard H. Reese (1818-1879), was a birthright Friend, Senior partner in the firm of G. A. Reese & Co., wholesale grocers, and later associated with Gerard T. Hopkins. He became a Director of the Union Bank of Baltimore and of the Third National Bank. "He gave much time and thought to the erection and completion of the Sheppard Asylum for the Insane. He spent many days visiting similar Institutions, noting and studying their practices and arrangements, so that the best and most approved methods of treatment found [could] be adopted." [30]

Gerard T. Hopkins (18??-1900), a successful merchant, was an uncle of Johns Hopkins. He was a member of Lombard Street Meeting, but left it to join the Orthodox Friends at the time of the Separation. He was a Recorded Minister and traveled widely in that service. With his appointment, the Board consisted of five members of the Society of Friends and two non-Friends, both of whom, however, had Quaker connections.

Until the death of Moses Sheppard, the Trustees of the Asylum had no funds to spend, and thus rarely met as a Board. The Founder, however, "surrounded himself with plans, examined carefully the designs of the most advanced asylums in this country and abroad, and stud-

ied the various systems adopted for treatment of luna-
tics." [31] Before his death, Sheppard developed his ideas
for an institution where courteous treatment and the
comfort of all patients would be given first consideration in the plans for buildings and grounds, and in the
medical treatment given. From time to time, he passed
directives and suggestions on to members of his Trustees.

Sheppard desired that the asylum should "be kept
separate and distinct from any one of a similar character, now being or hereafter to be erected by the State, or
in any other way." [32] That he wanted it "free from political domination and control" [33] was shown conclu-
sively when Sheppard refused a plea made to him by
Dorothy Dix, while she was seeking funds from the
General Assembly for a new hospital. She wrote:

> Not hearing from you and singularly impressed with
> your ability, I stand forward in this time of need, to
> aid a good cause, the cause of the weak infirm human-
> ity. I write to say that should you, as I hope you will,
> determine to give a liberal sum for the purchase of a
> farm for the State Hospital for the Insane, I think it
> will assure the passage of the bill at this session, which
> would place the question beyond all danger of long
> delay or final failure.[34]

Dr. Richard S. Steuart wrote, in *The Baltimore
American,* that the reason why the Legislature had
voted only $10,000 to draw up plans for a new hospital
was "the impression created in the House of Delegates,
as well as in the Senate, that a gentleman of this city was
about to give, for the purpose of establishing a large
Lunatic Asylum, the sum of $200,000." [35] Moses took

some pains to dispel this idea with a letter to Dr. Steuart
—also published in the newspaper—in which he said that
"his means had been greatly exaggerated, and his intentions misunderstood." [36] He wrote:

> I never mentioned, or authorized any person to men-
> tion any sum, that I designed appropriating to it. It
> was intended in the first instance, for the members of
> the Society of Friends to which I belong. Quakers are
> never found in Almshouses; and they have been com-
> pelled, for want of an Insane Asylum of their own, to
> send their patients to such Institutions abroad. They
> have but one institution for the Insane; a small one,
> near Philadelphia. My object is to establish a similar
> one here. Although the Insane of that Society have
> been sent to public Institutions, I never knew an in-
> stance in which the Society did not pay their expenses
> in the cases where the family of such was not in pecu-
> niary circumstances to do it." [37]

Sheppard added that he had no intention of interfering
with the State of Maryland in its erection of an asylum.
He did not believe that his securing a charter for a small
establishment in which to treat mental illness would, in
any way, relieve the State of a much larger responsibility.

During the next few years, he wrote out several instructions, which he hoped the Trustees of the Asylum
would follow. "My desire is, an Institution, similar to
the one near Philadelphia, belonging to the Society of
Friends, known as "The Asylum" and, like that, under
the direction of that description of persons, principally;
by the term "Quaker," I mean to include the different
parts or divisions of the Society." [38] Again he wrote,
"My desire is all for use, nothing for ornament; the

farm house style; fireproof as far as practical, a small and expensive institution; an experimental establishment; first, for the poor of the Society [of Friends]; secondly, for such of the Society as are able to pay; and then, for the poor indiscriminately; afterwards, the Trustees will use their discretion."[39] "My leading purpose is, to found an Institution, to carry forward, and improve, the ameliorated system of treatment of the Insane, irrespective of expense." [40]

To the Secretary of the Board, Sheppard wrote:

> The Trustees will bear in mind, that it is the Income, not the Principal of the Estate, that is to sustain the Institution. They will, therefore, see the necessity of diminishing the income as little as is consistent with true economy, by avoiding all unnecessary expenditures of the principal, in the purchase of land, and the erection of buildings for the Asylum: Let all that is done, be for *Use,* and not for *show*. . . . One thing I will mention particularly: let all the cells and rooms for the patients be *above ground,* and let there be a window, communication from each room, into each adjoining room so that a person in any room, can see into the rooms on each side of him.[41]

In later years, Gerard Reese wrote that Moses Sheppard mentioned to him that he wanted "to devote his wealth to ameliorate the treatment of the insane," founding an "experimental asylum," which would be "small and expensive, to increase the ratio of cures, that if through his means five persons were restored to health and reason, or even one, he would feel satisfied." [42] On one occasion, Reese remarked to Moses Sheppard, "it was [his] impression, the asylum was only for the comfortable maintenance of insane people till they died," and Moses replied, "It was to be a curative institution, a hospital to increase the rate of cure. A patient removed, to make room for another who might be restored to reason." [43]

David Perine, who drew up Moses Sheppard's will, wrote on January 16, 1855:

> He then explained what the object of his bounty was. He said he had long been impressed with the belief that many persons were made permanently insane for the want of kind treatment and proper attendance in the incipiency of their disease, and that he was willing to devote the whole of his fortune to making an experiment to test his belief upon this subject, by establishing an institution of a curative kind. His plan, he said, would be expensive, and therefore could accommodate but few persons; it was thus: that the buildings for the purpose should resemble, as far as the nature of the case would admit, a private residence, that two rooms of some size, communicating with each other, should be assigned to each patient, one for the patient, and the other for a companion of intelligence and of a kindly disposition. [44]

Gerard H. Reese related that he held a conversation with Sheppard, in which Moses said:

> I desire to found a hospital . . . for about seventy-five men and seventy-five women. No patient to be confined below ground, but all of them to have privacy, sunlight and fresh air. Every patient to have an attendant or companion. I wish everything done for the comfort of the patient, that the rate of cures may be increased. On inquiry if he had any particular plans for the Hospital, he answered, that may be left to the trustees . . . and that the income from the Estate, and from persons who were able to pay, should support it. [45]

Later, John Saurin Norris recalled that "the Estate was given unshackled into the keeping of the Trustees, relying on their prudence and discretion, yet holding them to a strict and frequent accountability to the authorities of the State of Maryland, and providing remedies for remissions or perverted action." [46] He said that "the views of the Testator are stated in general terms, sufficient to indicate them clearly, but not binding the Trustees by detailed instructions, which might hereafter prove impolitic or impractical." Norris also recalled that privately the Founder told him more in regard to his dream. Sheppard wanted the institution "to combine every feature that science and experience might indicate as requisite or desirable to minister to the greatest possible advantage to the patients." [47] "Moses expressed the wish," Norris wrote, "that the experiment might be tried, to ascertain how much goodwill would result from the unlimited amount of attention to everything, that could possibly alleviate the condition of the Insane." [48]

When Dr. Steuart heard of the plans his friend was projecting, he was alarmed, feeling that Moses was "not proceeding in the right manner to do the most individuals the greatest good." [49] He urged the Quaker not to found a private asylum. "I beg you to reflect well on the step you are taking," the doctor wrote, "and ask yourself whether the noble sum you have at your command . . . could not be more judiciously expended than as proposed." With more than one thousand insane individuals in the State of Maryland, the doctor felt the need "was not to give a few extraordinary advantages, but to provide suitable accommodations for a larger number." From his experience Dr. Steuart stated:

> For the interest on $100,000, say $6,000 a year, I could
> guarantee to keep fifty patients in the best possible
> condition, thus in a house of 250 patients of all classes,
> less than half the money you propose to expend, would
> support three times as many as your present plan aims
> at.[50]

Dr. Steuart also indicated that to provide every patient
with an attendant was a waste of money, and that the
patients would become like spoiled children with too
many servants waiting on them. He urged Moses Sheppard to build a large hospital, *without* endowment, ex-
pecting private patients to be paid for by relatives, and
the cost of the indigent to be met by contributions from
city and county.[51]

Dr. Thomas Kirkbride, Superintendent of the Pennsylvania Hospital for the Insane, also felt Moses Sheppard was on the wrong track. He wrote that for $5,000
one could endow a bed in his hospital, and suggested
that Sheppard give a gift to the Pennsylvania Hospital
of $50,000 which would endow ten beds. He also stated
the hospital would name certain wards, or a wing, after
the Baltimorean.[52]

Sheppard admired Dr. Richard S. Steuart for all he
accomplished for the mentally ill of Maryland; and he
appreciated the labors of Dr. Thomas Story Kirkbride
when he served as resident physician at Friends Hospital
and later as Superintendent of the Pennsylvania Hospital. Yet Sheppard determined to continue with his plans
for a small, experimental institution.

XIV

The Closing Months

No sooner were Moses Sheppard's benevolent intentions made public than he began to receive letters of advice and congratulation as well as letters soliciting aid or contributions to various charitable institutions." [1] Dr. John N. Galt, medical superintendent of Eastern Lunatic Asylum, Williamsburg, Virginia, sent his warm felicitations.[2] Dr. Shoemaker wrote, "I rejoice in the scheme and am proud of my relative for the noble act." [3] Joshua Dugan and other old acquaintances added notes of appreciation.

But there were also unexpected results following the securing of the charter. Moses Sheppard told of these in letters to his friends. "The whole subject of the Hospital is in the incipient state," he wrote John Bigelow; "all the notoriety has been produced by letter writers, and scribblers of newspaper paragraphs, it is mortifying. I want no such 'chroniclers of mine living honor.'" He added, "I thought I could proceed unnoticed, without a Law; I was advised not to do so. I am not pleased with the course the affair has taken." [4] To Benjamin F. Taylor, Moses declared that his intentions had been greatly exaggerated by the press, and that as a result he was flooded with requests for donations. "I anticipated," he stated, "I should be exempt from applications for donations for other charitable purposes. I supposed that would not be expected for any other charity . . . but I was mistaken . . . more requires more." [5]

The first begging letter came from Barnstable, Massachusetts, from a man who had been in a lunatic asylum for a time, now released, who asked for "a small sum, five hundred dollars." He was in debt and had a family to support. Such a gift "would secure for me a home, and make us happy, wife and family could together dwell." [6] A young woman in the same state, who was passionately fond of music, asked for a gift of $300 or $400 to purchase a piano. "Oh, do not refuse my request," she begged, "you would not, if you knew, how wildly my hopes are fashioned upon the result of this message." [7] A cripple in Hallowell, Maine, asked for $1,000 that he might purchase a horse and carriage, and so drive around the countryside as an itinerant salesman.[8]

Sometimes the letters were pathetic. A woman, forced to leave Germany with her husband and eight children when the Revolution of 1848 failed, mailed a request from Rochester, New York, in which she said that they "own no home, and I can scarce clothe my children; and I know of no greater charity than to assist persons in distress who have been reared as we have; and who fall into misfortune through no vice or fault of their own. . . . Pray hear my petition," she added, "and if God should inspire you to act kindly towards me, may He, in His Infinite goodness and mercy, reward you here and hereafter." [9]

A nineteen year old girl in New Brunswick, New

Jersey, asked for a loan to pay the debts of a deceased
father, and concluded, "Oh Sir! I have heard that you
are a good man, and a charitable one; will you refuse an
orphan's prayer?" [10] A country doctor, who had practiced medicine for forty years in rural Michigan, wrote
that he was now 65 years of age, and had "a horror at the
thought of being transported to a Poor House . . . soon
to be [his] destiny." He asked for $1,000 to enable him
to purchase a small farm.[11]

A woman who had read of Moses Sheppard's plans in
the *New York Evangelist,* and who had been "struggling
with poverty and ill health" for years, needed a loan of
$400 or $500 to buy a lot and build a small house.[12] A
widow in Philadelphia needed a loan of $30 for six
months to start a small business by which she could support her child [13]; a boy of nineteen, who had a blind
sister, requested $500 to build a cabin, have a garden,
and so take care of his sister.[14] Another woman, in
Corning, New York, read in the *New York Observer*
that Moses Sheppard was making a donation of $300,-
000. She praised his "magnificent and exalted liberality," and asked for "such aid as your generous heart may
lead you." [15] A girl in New York State, told by her
physician she must go to Saratoga or Ballston Springs for
her health, sent an urgent letter stating that she had no
money to make the trip or to stay in a sanitarium. She
asked for Moses' assistance.[16]

During this period, Richard Townsend, who took
dictation from his employer, copied the correspondence
in a letter book; but few of the answers to these "begging" letters are recorded. Moses was concerned about a
young boy who was a pupil in Emerson Lamb's school at

Sparks, Maryland, and he helped the boy with his education.[17] A Sheppard cousin who lived in Greenwich, Connecticut, wrote about a settlement of fifty free people of color, who "were sunk in ignorance and indolence, with too much wretchedness and wickedness."[18] This cousin, Clarkson C. Sheppard, desired Moses' help in establishing a Friends School for the benefit of the children in the group. He suggested his city relative give $5,000, the interest of which would pay for a teacher. Not knowing this correspondent, Moses wrote to his old friend, Samuel C. Sheppard, for information about Clarkson. Moses was especially interested because Clarkson lived in "the residence of [his] forefathers." In the end the Baltimore Quaker declined the request, commenting, "If they cannot rise by their own efforts, by their own exertions, they cannot be kept up. . . . A piece of lead may be held on the surface, but without the hand to sustain it, it sinks to the bottom whence it was raised."[19] Moses invited this new-found cousin to visit him in Baltimore, but added, "I have already done as much for this race as duty requires and inclination prompts me to do."[20]

Among the unusual letters that came to the Quaker batchelor was one from a young woman in Chambersburg, Pennsylvania:

> I have seen you frequently, as I often visit the city; and I have tried my utmost to get an introduction to you, but could not. I came home and thought I would try to forget you, but found it useless to try, for I never could forget thee, no, never. . . . If my wish is accomplished, and I receive a letter from you, I will tell you more; I will then tell you where to inquire of me. The reason I have taken this bold step I cannot tell, but as

my birthday has just passed and I was seventeen, and am determined not to lead a single life, and you are the only one I have chosen; I hope you will not take an offence from the above, but answer it immediately; your admirer.[21]

Occasionally the philanthropist did make a donation in answer to one of the many requests that came. He sent $50 to the Ashman Institute, in Oxford, Pennsylvania, accompanying his gift with a set of African mats received from Dr. McGill, and, as usual, a supply of books.[22] Something about the frankness of a letter from Portsmouth, New Hampshire, must have pleased him, for he did not refuse the request. Elmira Stowe wrote:

I am a poor woman, with two children, one an invalid, and I have tried hard to get along. . . . I take in sewing, and do what I can to earn something, and I make a living after a fashion. As it is coming cold weather, I thought if I could raise a small loan to buy wood and other things for the winter, it would be a great help to me . . . do you think if you was to send me $5 out of your riches, you would miss it? But think what a fortune it would be to me and mine . . . he that giveth to the poor lendeth to the Lord.[23]

Moses sent the money, and in February there came another letter, in which Elmira Stowe said:

I received your gift three months ago, and should have returned my thanks before now for your kindness, but was taken sick with the rheumatism in my arms. . . . If the rich only knew how much a few dollars helps a poor person, they would not be so loath to give. You don't know in how many ways we poor folks can make five dollars go. We have had a severe winter . . . if at any time you have anything to spare, remember me and my invalid child, among the rest of your pensioners.[24]

234

More help came from Baltimore, and was received as "a godsend."

Although Sheppard did not accept many new financial responsibilities at his age, he did not forget his old philanthropies. His interest in John Jackson's school at Darby, Pennsylvania, was as keen as ever. His Secretary, Richard Townsend, made inquiry at Sharon about a young woman Moses was helping, and passed on interesting information. E. H. S. was "the youngest daughter of an excellent widow who was raising four daughters and one son." [25] Jackson had already given four years of free instruction to the older daughter; another left Sharon to begin her teaching. The daughter whom Moses was supporting was "an earnest child," determined to render herself independent. The principal was sorry to say that "the son is at a trade, separated from the restraining hand of his mother . . . adding much to her anxiety. To be bereaved of a husband and a father is a great sorrow, but a rebellious son must be a living torment."

In 1852, John Jackson wrote thanking Moses for $150 which was "for thy ward, Mary Reese," who was "now amply provided for till the end of the term." [26] The following year, Moses explained to Jackson how he happened to be assisting some of the young women:

> Cathy was employed in the kitchen; her amiableness and capacity deserved patronage, she was sent to boarding school; Jane took her place. Jane was as deserving as Cathy, she was too smart and promising for the kitchen, and was placed in school also; Mary succeeded Jane. Mary was as capable and meritorious as her predecessors, and equal justice required justice for her, and she followed Cathy and Jane to school. There

was no one to occupy her place; the kitchen was vacant, all were worthy of a higher sphere. I enclose one hundred and fifty dollars for the benefit of either, or all three, or for one of the 'freshman' class. I want no account.[27]

When Mary Reese was ready to leave Sharon, Moses wrote "thee may take another in her place. I will pay one hundred and fifty dollars." [28] The philanthropist continued to pay for the education of pupil after pupil until the death of the principal in the spring of 1855. There had been no year in which the Quaker did not pay for the education of some boy or girl.

Sheppard did not cease to maintain contact with those colonists he had assisted in emigrating to Liberia. With the many letters that passed between Dr. McGill and his patron, there went from Baltimore "seeds, tools, and books [29];" and now and then a special gift for one of the doctor's growing family. McGill wrote, "For your continued kindness in supplying my wants, and for your very acceptable presents to my little girls, you have my warmest thanks." [30]

Clothing, seeds, books, newspapers, grindstones, agricultural implements, articles of tin to resist the attack of insects, went to many colonists.[31] Of cotton twine, long stored since the days when the Baltimore merchant manufactured it, $200 worth was sent to James McGill. Seeds of the cassada plant came to Sheppard from Liberia, and Emily made cakes stuffed with them for Moses' friends.

Doubtful as he was at times over the ability of some of the colonists to "shake off the laziness so common in warm climates," [32] Sheppard still considered that emigration to Africa, was the only practical solution to the problem of slavery in the United States. At the annual gathering of the American Colonization Society, in 1853, John H. B. Latrobe was elected President to succeed Henry Clay. Moses, who was at the convention, was delighted, and wrote Isaac Tyson, "he considered Latrobe [was] better qualified to carry forward the cause than any other man." [33] The Quaker sent Latrobe a letter of congratulations and the promise of aid. He forwarded $100 to the Treasurer of the Society, and volunteered to ask each of the other eighty-four national Vice Presidents to match his gift. To Dr. McGill, Moses sent word of Latrobe's election, adding that he was "the first having a practical knowledge of the subject, and I hope his characteristic energy will enable him to give a new impulse to the cause." [34]

Latrobe summed up the aims of the Colonization Society: "The early advocates of African Colonization looked to it as a means of improving the condition of free people of color, morally and politically; of separating them from contact with the slaves, that was prejudicial to both parties; and of civilizing and Christianizing Africa." [35] He pointed out that "the two races, between whom amalgamation by intermarriage was impossible, could never occupy the same land in peace, on terms of social and political equality." He stated that the great plan of colonization had become a political necessity, and as the only solution to the problem that, more than once, threatened the existence of the Americans as a united people. As European immigration continued, Latrobe said the free Negro found it harder to find employment, and the bitterness, engendered by the Abolitionists, caused the Southern States to tighten their laws against the free men of color.[36]

In an article in the *Colonization Herald,* Sheppard wrote, "The question is not whether slavery ought to be abolished, but how to abolish it, and how it can be done properly in the slave states." [37] He continued, "A right thing can be done in a wrong way . . . slaves may be made wretched . . . and the holders of slaves ruined." Moses felt that "It is a right of the slave to be prepared for freedom, before he is thrown on the world. Those who [have] brutalized him are bound to raise him to the condition of man."

Summing up his continued belief in Colonization, the philanthropist wrote: "The Negro can never obtain what he has a right [to] which is perfect liberty here. He may be made equal by statute law, [which is] now the case in some States; but there is a conventional statute that nullified the State Law. He cannot exercise the rights the Statute Law allows him." [38] Because of this, Moses wrote, "the only place the Negro can secure the elevated position amongst men and nations that he is entitled to" was Liberia.

The name of Moses Sheppard was still carried on the lists of the Indian Affairs Committee. Although he was no longer active in its concerns, his interest continued. He enjoyed the visits of Philip Thomas who related his 1855 journey to the reservations in New York. Thomas went, at the request of the tribes, to attend the dedication of the Philip E. Thomas Orphanage. The Federal Government and the State of New York built the structure at a cost of $4,000, and Baltimore Friends paid $500 for its furnishings. The Baltimore Committee also agreed to pay the cost of educating five Indian children at the Orphanage. [39] The Indians, who still considered Philip Thomas their Ambassador to Washington, thought highly of him, and when he left for home an aged Sachem spoke for the Senecas:

> May the Great Spirit safely protect you and yours on your homeward journey, and when your sun shall set beyond the western hills, and darkness shall shroud the mounds which cover you, may the moon, when she shall rise above the trees in the east, look down upon your grave in peace.[40]

Baltimore became acquainted with the bigotry and activism of the Know-Nothing party throughout the 1850's. "In the beginning the Know-Nothing Party was pressure politics," [41] then it combined terrorism and brutal force to achieve its aims. It supported the short lived American Party.[42] Know-Nothing members organized clubs in Baltimore known as the Black Snakes, the Rough Skins, the Thunderbolts, and the Plug Uglies, whose members engaged in open fights with members of the Democratic Party, in an effort to keep them from voting. In 1853, the Know-Nothings held many mass meetings at which Catholics and foreigners were denounced, and the Know-Nothings were able to elect a Mayor and to control the City Council. The following year they gained a majority in the House of Delegates at Annapolis, two years later they carried the national election in Maryland, one of two States in which they were successful. Four men were killed and several hundred wounded in the battles at the polls during this period of upheaval.[43] The old term "Mobtown" could again be applied to Baltimore.

239

Added to the political turmoil was the ever-present problem of slavery. Townsend wrote in his diary: "slavery was the all engrossing topic, and its existence was shaking the Republic to its very center. It seemed to be doubtful at times, if the North would consent to remain in the Union permanently and forever, with the curse of slavery always hanging about it." [44] The Compromise of 1850 brought an uneasy peace to the United States; but the Fugitive Slave Law made the North gag, and could not be enforced in many States. In the South, fear of abolition, with its implication of Negro equality, was binding the plantation owner and poor whites more closely to the slaveholding neighbors.[45] In rapid succession came the Kansas-Nebraska Bill, which restored the old doctrine of popular sovereignty and repealed the Missouri Compromise of 1820. This "was explosive enough to blow up the Union." [46] "Bleeding" Kansas and John Brown's raid followed, and was capped by the Dred Scott Decision of the Supreme Court. That decision came a month after Moses Sheppard's death. During these years, Benjamin F. Taylor of Virginia wrote frequently to his Baltimore friend concerning his fears that the Union was about to break up and be shattered by a civil war beyond repair.

New York Yearly Meeting, Orthodox, declared, "Kansas closed the way for any attempt to plead the cause of suffering humanity, or to allay the agitation so fearfully prevalent." [47] *The Friend*, published in Philadelphia, was optimistic:

> The great object to be attained should ever be to convince and convert the slaveholder. . . . If sectional jealousy and ambition could be allayed, the clamor of

selfish politicians hushed, and a calm obtained in which the voice of reason and human kindness would be allowed to make itself heard, we think a great change in the condition of the slaves and slaveholding states would soon be apparent.[48]

Baltimore Yearly Meeting of 1854 advised: "We are constrained against mingling in political affairs, that we may, with clean hands, bear a faithful testimony against violence and oppression in all its forms, few of which require a more constant unceasing testimony than slavery." [49] The situation worsened; "agitation could not be hushed, nor calm contained . . . nothing seemed to have effect." Two young Quakers marched with John Brown to Harpers Ferry, one disappeared during the conflict at the river, and one was hanged with his leader. They represented those young Quakers who "compromised one Quaker principle to fight for another." [50]

Most Americans were at a loss concering the best way to end the problem of slavery, and few had a better answer than the Quakers to "convince and convert" or to colonize in Liberia. Abraham Lincoln believed that slavery was "founded on both injustice and bad policy," but in his speech at Peoria in 1854—published in the Baltimore papers—he declared, "If all earthly power were given to me, I should not know what to do with the existing institution of slavery." [51]

Moses Sheppard was busy with his books and papers. He discovered some interesting facts about Benjamin Banneker, the talented Negro who helped lay out the District of Columbia. A friend of Thomas Jefferson, Banneker authored a series of almanacs that had wide circulation. Sheppard had some of Banneker's works published and distributed them among his friends. Moses also made a study of the condition of the former slaves freed by Great Britain in Jamaica. Out of this research came a booklet, *African Slave Trade in Jamaica and Comparative Treatment of Slaves,* which he read before the Maryland Historical Society.

Dr. McGill found the office of Governor of Maryland in Liberia a taxing one. He wrote to the humanitarian "I am worn down with my official duties and mercantile affairs, anxious too for the success of schemes that are hardly mature yet. . . . they occupy my mind to the exclusion of everything else." [52] These schemes were the pending union between the colony and the larger Republic. Dr. McGill was not sure the people of the Maryland settlement were ready for union, and quite sure that Liberia would not accept a union unless Maryland entered the Republic as a country or state. At one point the doctor wrote, "Although reared in the midst of republican institutions, the American colored people have no reason to be particularly attached to such a form of government; they hear of the superior advantages of democratic institutions, of equal rights, equality, but these are only for the Caucasian race." [53] In the end, the doctor decided to follow his original plan to move to Monrovia, take up the practice of medicine there, and continue the mercantile business of his family. In both, he was eminently successful. In 1856, Dr. McGill sent $6,000 to Dr. Hall in Baltimore to have a schooner built for the African trade. When it was completed, McGill named it *Moses Sheppard.*

During the last few years of his life, the philanthropist had several portraits painted, a charcoal drawing made, and a daguerreotype. One went to Dr. McGill, who was most grateful to have an oil portrait of the man who did so much for him, making possible "the comforts with which [he] was surrounded." [54] A second likeness went to Rachel Jackson, and a third to Benjamin Taylor. Taylor wrote, "I scarcely can express my deep and earnest appreciation of this act of kindness and considerate regard," [55] and added, "I shall carefully preserve it, as a precious memorial to our friendship, which I have ever looked upon as among the most pleasing recollections . . . of my life."

In several long letters of reminiscence, Dr. McGill recalled how, as a young boy in Baltimore, he knew of the efforts of Elisha Tyson in behalf of his race, and how he used to stand on the pavement in front of Tyson's house, patiently waiting to catch a glimpse of the aged Quaker. "I felt happy in the distant admiration of the friend of my race," the doctor wrote, "he was too exalted in my boyish opinion for any near approach." [56] Thinking of what Moses Sheppard had done to continue the work of Elisha Tyson, Dr. McGill wrote:

> If the grateful acknowledgement of one of the African race who feels that he is indebted to your kind patronage, for whatever comfort and respectability he now enjoys, and for his opening prospects of future usefulness to his fellowmen in Africa be accepted; and if the efforts he has so far made to prove himself worthy of that patronage he received as a proof, I would say that your labors have been served.[57]

A few months before Sheppard's death, Dr. McGill sent word again that "a single day of my life does not pass that I do not think of my Patron, every step toward prosperity, my power of being serviceable to my fellow men is in some way referrable to and afforded me through your instrumentality. Your patronage has been a stimulus to my exertions. I have striven to be worthy of it." [58] In one of his last letters to Moses Sheppard, the doctor wrote: "I am sorry to learn you feel your strength diminishing, I would vain escape from all reflection on the probable effect of time on distant friends." [59] From Dr. Fletcher came notes of appreciation for many books and packages of seeds received, and the message: "I regret I cannot thank you for your kindness and the favors constantly meeting with by every vessel arriving [in Liberia]." [60] He spoke cheerfully of the arrival of new emigrants, this time mostly from Georgia, and expressed the wish, "that your life may be spared to witness favorable results in Maryland in Liberia is [my] sincere prayer."

When in 1855 Benjamin Taylor spent the week of Yearly Meeting with his friend, as was his custom, he felt that Moses had failed a good deal. In December of 1856, Sheppard resigned from the Board of Trustees of the Sheppard Asylum, requesting that John Saurin Norris fill the vacancy and be named President.[61] For about nine months before his death, when age and infirmity prevented his leaving the house, Moses could not attend meetings for worship at Lombard Street Meeting. In November of that year, Benjamin Taylor noted that Sheppard was forced to miss his first Yearly Meeting since coming to live in Baltimore. "Drop me a line," Taylor wrote to Townsend. "His friendship, ever since our first acquaintance, has been invaluable to me. I feel

244

the deepest solicitude and anxiety. . . . Present my love to him, and assure him of my hopes and prayers." [62]

Nathan Sheppard came to visit his uncle in January of 1857. He jotted down some of their last conversations. The older man said, "I was always diffident and of a retiring nature, avoiding society, and two lamentable results followed. I obtained no powers of conversation, and no wife, both of which were great mistakes." [63] Nathan remarked, "I too am diffident by nature," and Moses continued, "I know it, and I want to advise thee on this point. Push thyself forward, mingle in company, talk, talk, whether thee feels an inclination or not. Conversational powers are of incalculable importance. And marry, by all means marry." Moses added, "It is a matter of fact that many eminent literary men were great bunglers in conversation. I have often been out generaled by a loquacious fool, because his tongue was loose and mine was tight." [64]

Nathan commented on his uncle's work for Liberia, and Moses answered, "That is an experiment. They are chiefly mulattos who have gone. The hope is that they will infuse their energy into the natives, but it will require more than an age to make the experiment." [65] During these conversations, the older man remarked, "Old age is not desirable, patience and obedience is what we want then. I ought to be grateful to the common Benefactor for his comfort and mercies." [66] About two weeks before his death, after months of confinement to his bed, Moses "asked for pen and paper to test his ability to write. After ruling three distinct lines, he wrote these words, 'The law of progression is probably a law of nature, of slow development.' He then dropped the pen with the remark, 'I could add more, but it is too late.' " [67]

Isaac Tyson was constantly near, and to him his long-time friend said, "I trust to my creator for forgiveness and a more comfortable home than this. Oh! Lord, I trust, I abide in thy covenant." Emily, Eveline, and George, Moses' faithful servants, were attentive at all times. It meant much to the aged Friend to have Isaac Tyson, Nathan Sheppard, and Richard Townsend with him every day. To Nathan, his uncle said: "The world retreats farther and farther in the distance, and its possessions gradually diminish in value. I have been fortunate and accumulated something. I have made others, as well as myself, comfortable with it, now I leave it to take its course." [68]

Richard Townsend wrote of the last evening: "His reason came and went, like the sun struggling through a sky of clouds. His last words he said slowly and distinctly, 'Thou wilt keep him in perfect peace, whose mind is stayed on thee.' The long life of struggle, achievement, and helpfulness to others closed at 6:30 AM, First-day morning, February 1, 1857." [69] Moses Sheppard was eighty-two years of age.

The funeral service took place in the Brick House, February 4.

A large gathering of members of the Society of Friends, as well as others were present. This group was addressed by Samuel Townsend, a minister of the Friends Society, after which the remains were taken to the burial grounds attached to the meeting house on the corner of Fayette and Aisquith Streets in Old

Town. The six Trustees of the Sheppard Asylum placed his body in the vault there.[70]

The following week, the body was removed to the plot he had purchased years before in the Greenmount Cemetery.[71]

Richard Townsend wrote in his diary that day: "To me, he was always kind, confiding, and relying . . . He had a sound and discriminating mind, with some strong prejudices. He was honest, straight-forward, and punctual . . . Quiet and unostentatious . . . He was very kind and benevolent to others." The Secretary continued, "He was a deep thinker, and a close concise writer . . . his style tight and compact, intermingling with a spice of quiet raillery and sarcasm." [72]

The newspapers of Baltimore were prompt to record the death and accomplishments of Moses Sheppard, with special reference to his plans to establish a mental asylum. *The Baltimore Patriot* called him, "a wealthy, well known, and highly respected citizen of Baltimore." [73] *The Baltimore American* recounted many of Sheppard's activities and benevolences, classifying him as "our venerable and highly esteemed fellow citizen . . . the unwavering friend of the black man, in all that could protect him in his legal rights, or ameliorate and better his condition . . . he was for many years, a prominent, active, and useful member of the Colonization Society." [74] A few weeks later, *the Baltimore Sun,* in recounting Sheppard's plans for an institution to serve the mentally ill, concluded, "His charities, which we learn were numerous, were unostentatiously given, and rarely alluded to himself." And of the institution Shep-

247

pard founded, the editor wrote, "No tongue can tell, no mind can conceive, the amount of human woe, which this Institution may be instrumental in relieving. Unborn generations will have reason to bless the name of Moses Sheppard." [75]

Thus a quiet, energetic humanitarian passed from the Brick House, the commercial activities of Baltimore, and the Lombard Street Friends Meeting. He made his religion a practical guide through life. Having experienced many hardships in his youth, by diligence and the use of a keen intellect he acquired the means to live comfortably, within the bounds of Quaker simplicity. He took practical steps to eliminate, as far as he was able, the injustices he saw in his city and nation, and left his fortune to alleviate tragic conditions among the mentally afflicted.

XV

Epilogue
The Shadow Cast Before

THE TRUSTEES OF THE SHEPPARD ASYLUM met in the
Brick House on Pratt Street, which now became their
headquarters, on February 21, 1857. The President, J.
Saurin Norris, announced the death of Moses Sheppard,
and presented the following Resolution, which was
endorsed:

> That the members of this Board have heard, with deep
> regret, of the decease of Moses Sheppard, the first
> President of this Asylum; and we consider it due to his
> memory, to place upon the Minutes of the Board, our
> united testimony, derived from a long and intimate
> personal acquaintance with him, of his moral worth as
> a man, his uprightness and usefulness as a citizen, his
> spotless character through all the varieties of an active
> and long life, and his kind and benevolent disposition
> to all.[1]

The will of Moses Sheppard was then read with ac-
companying memoranda. The philanthropist left $500
to a niece in Philadelphia, a like amount to Nathan
Sheppard, and $1,000 to Isaac Tyson. Monthly pay-
ments of $10 per month for life were left to three dis-
tant relatives. His grandfather clock was given to Oliver

Evans in Philadelphia, and his "watch, and guard and seal" were to be sent to Dr. Samuel F. McGill." [2] There was a notation that the Trustees were to care for Eveline Scott, " a colored woman brought up in the family," and to see to the needs of George Barton, his houseman.[3]

The will directed that Moses' books, papers, maps, pictures, and furniture go to the Trustees, to be kept in the Brick House until transferred to the Asylum where they were to be used "and not kept for show." [4] The Library, which meant so much to the Quaker, and which he considered "large and well selected," was "intended for the officers and patients of the Asylum." He directed "as great care [had] been taken, to have the books bound, and put in good order, a like care [should] also be exercised for [their] preservation." The donor requested that the books were not to be taken from the premises, "as by this means, they are frequently scattered and lost."

Richard Townsend was directed to take charge of all the papers of the Corporation, purchase proper office furniture and account books, and see that a Corporation seal was made. On the rim the seal was to read, "Seal of the Trustees of the Sheppard Asylum, Maryland." [5] In the center of the seal there was to be a shield, with the words, "Founded by Moses Sheppard, of Baltimore, 1853."

By the next spring, the Trustees knew the amount of money with which they could proceed to carry out the wishes of the Founder. The Executors submitted their accounts to the Board and to the Governor, giving the value of the estate[6]:

Library, pictures, etc.	$ 657.63
Sundry stocks	252,599.95
Leasehold properties	32,300.00
Ground rents	20,000.00
Notes and mortgages	53,833.33
Cash	17,626.55
	377,017.46
Real estate which went directly to the trustees	186,396.00
Net revenue from real estate to 4/14/58	8,026.95
	$571,440.41

The Trustees recorded their opinion that they "deem it prudent to postpone the erection of buildings for the Asylum." [7] From the beginning, the Trustees determined to abide by a strict interpretation of Moses Sheppard's instruction—that they spend only the interest derived from the income of the estate. They told the Governor that they were "early impressed with the serious nature and responsibilities of the duties which devolved upon them, and they were desirous to avoid such errors as frequently arise from too hasty action . . . they would give every matter due deliberation before proceeding to act." [8]

Meanwhile, David Perine secured action by the State Legislature that exempted the Corporation from the payment of the collateral inheritance tax. He had not asked for this at the time the Charter was secured, for fear that it might imperil the passage of the bill. The Act of the Legislature saved the estate $14,000. [9]

Late in his life, Moses Sheppard, for sentimental reasons, purchased the old farm and mill at Jericho Mills, where he had spent his boyhood. [10] Considering this

251

location unsuitable for the Asylum, the Trustees adver-
tised in the Baltimore papers for a site. Many farms
offered for sale were visited by the Trustees. Mt. Airy,
six miles north of Baltimore on the York Turnpike, was
purchased at a cost of $60,000 in 1858. The farm con-
tained 341 acres.[11] Since an outlet was also desirable on
the newly constructed Charles Street Extension, the
Trustees purchased additional land to the west, making
a total of 375 acres.[12]

Prizes of $300, $200, and $100 were offered for the
best design for the Asylum, and twenty-one sets of plans
were received. The first prize went to Thomas and
James Dixon of Baltimore, the second to Samuel Sloan
of Philadelphia, and the third jointly to the Richard
Upjohn Corporation in conjunction with Dr. D. Tilden
Brown of the Bloomingdale Hospital in New York.[13] It
was specified that the buildings should accommodate
200 patients, be durable, safe, utilitarian, and without
architectural display. The Trustees suggested a central
building, with two wings, and that "Particular attention
be given to providing ample and suitable apartments,
either within or without the principal structure, for
exercise and enjoyment of the patients in such occupations and amusements as may be conducive to their
benefit." [14]

In December, 1859, it was decided to lay off roads
with the help of engineers, and to landscape the grounds.
Trees were planted about the area on which the buildings were to be constructed, and, since it was anticipated
that the farm would provide vegetables and fruit, arrangements were made to plant 334 apple trees. No
meeting of the Trustees was held without some atten-

tion being given to the investments, the sale or purchase of stocks, bonds, and ground rents. The first of several projected railroads from Towsontown to Baltimore was organized and the Corporation asked permission to cross the Sheppard grounds. A route was granted under certain restrictions.[15]

A quarry was opened on the grounds from which granite blocks were cut for the foundations of the future Asylum, and a quantity of brick-clay discovered. Kilns were erected, a yoke of oxen and a cart secured, and a first order of 500,000 bricks baked. The President was instructed to build a stone Gate House on the western side of the property by the terminus of Charles Street Extended, the stone to be quarried on Mt. Airy.[16]

A few months after the Battle of Bull Run, the Board reported to the Governor, "The committee . . . had labored diligently . . . and had made much progress [but] their operations were suspended by the extraordinary revulsions which have taken place in the community." [17] Mr. Charles Vaux of New York was appointed architect, and was directed to cooperate with Dr. Brown. Unsettled conditions, however, prevented Mr. Vaux from coming to Baltimore because of "impeded travel, and the existing excitement in the country." [18] Various members of the Board inspected twelve mental institutions in several States; an appropriation of $700 was voted to send Dr. Brown on an exploring expedition to England and the Continent to visit mental institutions.

In 1861, the Trustees reported to the Governor, "disturbed conditions of public affairs has been such, that common prudence required them to refrain from making . . . such contracts as will be necessary for the Hospital buildings." [19] In spite of the War, foundations were dug and bricks were baked. On May 25, 1862, the cornerstone of the Western Division, as it was called, was laid. A barn was constructed with various outbuildings—stables, granaries, poultry houses, carriage and wagon sheds. One million bricks were baked.[20] The next year a crew of men worked on the basement of the western building, and bricks were laid for the first floor.

In spite of the high cost of labor and materials, the work pushed forward; in 1865 a new farm house was constructed, and as many as fifteen bricklayers were employed, as well as several stonecutters.[21] The walls slowly rose along the 365 foot length of the western building, and soon work was begun on the Eastern Division. The two buildings were built exactly alike. By 1878, both main buildings were nearly completed, and several million bricks had been baked on the grounds.[22] Now and then, work slowed for a time because of lack of income, "but the quality of the material used, and that of the workmanship [continued], as from the beginning, to be the best and most desirable." [23] The Trustees reported that the buildings, "though devoid of lavish adornments, present an agreeable appearance. The object of divesting the buildings of all appearance of confinement and physical restraint has been as nearly obtained as is possible in a structure of this kind." [24]

The panic and subsequent deflation of 1878 did not embarrass the Trustees of the Asylum, as "the Corporation suffered a very small decrease in income." [25] They did mention, however, a change in the tax structure of the State of Maryland, which "detracted largely from

[their] ability to progress rapidly with construction."
The County and City tax rose from $136.50 to $4,584.10.

After a quarter-century from the time the Charter was granted, death began to make inroads on the Board. David M. Perine, who suggested the Charter to Moses Sheppard, resigned in April of 1878, having reached the age of eighty-three.[26] Richard H. Townsend, private secretary of Moses Sheppard and Executor of his will, died on April 10, 1879.[27] Gerard H. Reese died the following August.[28] The heaviest loss came with the death of J. Saurin Norris, on December 29, 1882. As stated in the Trustee's minutes, Saurin Norris had been chosen by Moses Sheppard himself as the one to whom "he wished to commit the management of the Charity." [29] Norris continued to his death "as an esteemed, active, and useful member of the trust committed to [his] case, and one who, in a period of twenty-six years . . . faithfully and wisely discharged the difficult and responsible duties that devolved on him as President of the Board." Dr. William Riley, an original member of the Board and one time physician of Moses Sheppard, was elected the third President, and served until his death on April 15, 1887. He was succeeded by Benjamin A. Pope, a member of Lombard Street Meeting.

By 1882, both Western and Eastern Divisions of the Asylum were under roof. On hand were "552 panel doors, 354 sets of shutters, and 2,100 light window sashes." [30] Work was begun on the laundry building and steam power plant. Various springs were connected with a small lake from which water was pumped to the tower of the power plant. Water for laundry purposes was secured from large cisterns, which caught rain water

Sheppard and Enoch Pratt Hospital 1966

from the roofs of the Eastern and Western Divisions. For flooring, 100,000 feet of prime yellow pine was purchased.[31]

In 1890, the Trustees began a search for a qualified doctor to serve as Superintendent of the Asylum, to build a suitable staff, and to organize the future work of the Asylum. The choice fell upon Dr. Edward N. Brush, assistant at the Pennsylvania State Hospital for the Insane.[32] Dr. Brush took up residency at the Sheppard Asylum February 9, 1891, and the Asylum received patients in the next December. The first patients were two women and one man.[33]

Several times, letters to local papers inquired why the Sheppard Asylum was not opened, it not being generally known that the Trustees built only as they had funds in hand.[34] By the time the Asylum was open, the Trustees had spent $917,940.00 for the farm and buildings, and the value of the original trust had increased meanwhile by $100,000, to a total of $666,930.00.[35]

Patients were admitted to the Asylum as fast as they could be accommodated. Under care in 1895 were 154 men and women; the next year, 164. The Board reported to the Governor that "The benevolent results were limited in extent only by lack of means to broaden [the] work, and not by scarcity of cases it might have cared for." [36] This condition was shortly remedied, and the work of the Trustees enlarged.

In 1881, when the Trustees were considering an arrangement by which they would purchase 5,000 first mortgage notes of the Baltimore and Delta Railroad to assist that corporation in completing its line through the grounds, the Board asked Enoch Pratt to advise them on the proposition.[37] Enoch Pratt then became interested in the Asylum and frequently visited it. Pratt had come to Baltimore in 1831 at the age of twenty-two and shortly afterwards established a hardware store. He was an active Unitarian and, like Moses Sheppard, a great friend of Rev. George W. Burnap. He was associated with Sheppard in the work of the American Colonization Society and the Baltimore Library Company.[38] In 1894, George A. Pope, President of the Trustees of the Asylum, asked Dr. Brush, "under a seal of confidence," to give him, in writing, a statement of what could be done with an increased endowment in promoting the original objects of the institution, and advancing the knowledge and treatment of mental disorders.[39] Dr. Brush prepared such a statement, stressing the charitable work already carried on at the Asylum, the growing cost of treating mental patients, the prolonged duration of many types of mental illness, and the need for scientific study of all forms of mental disturbance. This statement was passed on to Enoch Pratt.

On September 17, 1896, Enoch Pratt, then President of the Farmers' and Planters' Bank, and recent founder of the Baltimore Free Library, died; his will made the Trustees of the Sheppard Asylum his residuary legatee. Enoch Pratt had told George Pope that "in his opinion the trustees [of the Sheppard Asylum] had more closely adhered to the wishes of the founder than any similar body of which he had knowledge." [40] The will was contested in the courts, but in each case decided in favor of the Sheppard Trustees, who, in 1898, received the estate of Enoch Pratt. The estate, after deducting all charges and expenses of litigation, amounted to $1,069,300.41.

The only stipulation in the new donor's will was that the name of the Sheppard Asylum be changed to The Sheppard and Enoch Pratt Hospital. Enoch Pratt indicated that he did not desire any changes made in the management of the Hospital, but desired that it accommodate additional patients, mainly the "indigent insane in the most advisable manner, at very low charges or absolutely free . . . the Trustees [were] to exercise their best judgment as to the rate to be charged." [41]

Certain that Moses Sheppard was so indifferent to "having the Institution bear his name that he had not thought of it," [42] the Trustees accepted the bequest of Enoch Pratt, and asked the Legislature to change the name of the Asylum as required. One Trustee, E. Glenn Perine, son of the lawyer who named the original Corporation in the Charter, resigned from the Board, fearing that the change in name would detract from the honor due Moses Sheppard as the originator and founder of the Institution.[43] The remaining members of the Board considered that the memory of the Founder would be enhanced, rather than curtailed, by the enlarged work made possible at the Hospital. They believed that "the memory of a good man, who had devoted the labors of a long life to the benefit of the most afflicted of all God's creatures," [44] would be recalled with gratitude through future decades.

Notes on Sources

THIS BIOGRAPHY of Moses Sheppard rests primarily on manuscript material located as follows: At Friends Historical Library, Swarthmore College (FHL), are letters of Sheppard from 1804 to the time of his death in 1857; letters to him from his friends in the United States and West Africa; and essays written by him. In FHL are found manuscript minutes of Baltimore Preparative, Baltimore Monthly, Baltimore Quarterly, and Baltimore Yearly Meetings of the Society of Friends; as well as the record books of the Fairhill Boarding School, the Indian Affairs Committee, the records of the Yearly Meeting for Sufferings; and of the firm of John Mitchell and the firm of Mitchell and Sheppard.

The records of the Trustees of the Sheppard Asylum and of the Sheppard and Enoch Pratt Hospital (SEPH) are at the hospital at Towson, Maryland.

Books, newspapers, and other materials covering the history of Baltimore Town and City and of Maryland are easily available at the Maryland Room of the Enoch Pratt Free Library, Baltimore. Materials on the history of the Society of Friends are found in the Friends Historical Library, Swarthmore College (FHL); those in relation to slavery and the Quakers are in the Forbush Collection of Morgan State College, Baltimore.

ABBREVIATIONS AND SHORT TITLES

MS BPM   Records of Baltimore Preparative Meeting of the Religious Society of Friends.

MS BMM   Records of Baltimore Monthly Meeting, to which Baltimore Preparative Meeting was subordinate.

MS BQM   Records of Baltimore Quarterly Meeting, to which the Monthly Meeting was subordinate.

MS BYM   Records of Baltimore Yearly Meeting, to which all Quarterly Meetings in Maryland, Virginia, and south-central Pennsylvania were subordinate.

MS Disc BYM   Manuscript Book of Discipline of Baltimore Yearly Meeting of the Religious Society of Friends.

Disc BYM   Printed books of Discipline of Baltimore Yearly Meeting, issued about every twenty years.

MS Min   Handwritten minutes of the transactions of all Quaker business meetings, or of Quaker committees, such as Indian Affairs or Fairhill Boarding School were carefully kept and preserved.

SEPH   Sheppard and Enoch Pratt Hospital.

MS   Moses Sheppard.

NOTES AND REFERENCES

PREFACE

1. *Discipline of the Yearly Meeting of Friends, Held in Baltimore for the Western Shore of Maryland, and the Adjacent Parts of Pennsylvania and Virginia, as Revised and Adopted 1821* (Baltimore, 1821), p. 70.

2. *Ibid.,* p. 67.

3. Moses Sheppard (MS) to Dr. Samuel F. McGill, November 12, 1844, FHL.

4. MS to Thomas Ellicott, June 28, 1847, FHL.

I: THE FORMATIVE YEARS

1. Thomas W. Griffith, *Sketches of the Early History of Maryland* (Baltimore, 1821), p. 54.

2. Hamilton Owens, *Baltimore on the Chesapeake* (Garden City, New York, 1941), p. 1.

3. One Hundred and Fiftieth Anniversary, 1730-1880, Supplement, *The Baltimore Sun,* January 10, 1880.

4. *Ibid.* The Federal Census of 1790 gave the town a population of 13,503; this included 11,925 whites, 1,255 slaves, and 323 free Negroes.

5. The block that included the Meeting House, burial ground, and school house, was bounded on the south by the Great York Road, now Baltimore Street; on the east by Harford Road, now Central Avenue; on the north by Pitt Street, now Fayette Street; and on the west by Smock Alley, now Aisquith Street.

6. Moses Sheppard (MS) to Charles Sheppard, March 14, 1831, FHL.

7. Thomas Sheppard, the great-grandfather of MS, settled in Cumberland County, New Jersey, in 1683. He was a large land owner, member of the Assembly, who died in 1721. MS Lavens M. Thomas, 2nd, MS, 1775-1857, Humanitarian, A Short Biography (Baltimore, 1941), p. 2. Sheppard and Enoch

Notes and References

Pratt Hospital, Towson, Maryland. Moses, the grandfather, was born in 1698; he was a member of the Fourteenth Assembly in 1744. He died in 1753. MS Thomas, *MS*, p. 2.

8. MS Thomas, p. 3, Nathan Sheppard joined the Society of Friends when he was twenty-five years of age, but was later disowned for a violation of the Discipline—taking a dispute with a neighbor to court.

9. The couple had eleven children; five died while young.

10. MS Thomas, MS, pp. 4, 5.

11. *Ibid.,* p. 6.

12. The peace testimony was expressed in all Quaker Books of Discipline. The Baltimore Discipline of the period said, "Believing . . . it is our earnest concern, that Friends may adhere faithfully to our ancient testimony against wars and fightings, either offensive or defensive. . . ." Disc BYM, 1821, p. 85.

13. Nathan Sheppard was already acquainted with Nova Scotia, since he was an agent of the Philadelphia Company, which received a grant of land in Nova Scotia.

14. In 1780 Nathan Sheppard appeared before a Notary Public to make a declaration that he found a stray horse. His will was made in March, 1783, and in 1785 he secured a lease of land in Baltimore County. MS Thomas, pp. 7-8.

15. By transfer from Gwynedd Monthly Meeting, MS Min, pp. 473-74, FHL.

16. MS List of Births and Deaths of Members of Baltimore Monthly Meeting . . . from 3rd of Eleventh Month, 1773, p. 6, FHL.

17. *The Baltimore American,* February 2, 1857. There is some uncertainty concerning the year in which Moses Sheppard was born. The Quaker records, which usually are very accurate, give the date as May, 1775. His tombstone in Greenmount Cemetery, Baltimore, first carried the date 1773, which was later changed by order of the Trustees to 1775.

18. MS John Saurin Norris, Biographical Sketch of the Late MS. Trustees Records, SEPH.

19. *The Baltimore Patriot,* March 7, 1857.

20. *The Baltimore Sun,* March 6, 1857.

21. *The Biographical Cyclopedia of Representative Men of Maryland and the District of Columbia* (Baltimore, 1879), p. 214. *The Baltimore Sun* of March 6, 1857, added, "Like many self-educated men he was a profound and vigorous thinker, and

a writer of more than ordinary talents. He was a man of considerable literary culture, and displayed special interest in theology, psychology, and intellectual philosophy. He read the best works he could obtain on these subjects, and such was his proficiency in them that there were few minds so deeply versed in those departments of inquiry as not to be enlightened by his clear and logical discussions of them."

22. Isaac Weld, *Travel Through the States of North America* (Philadelphia, 1800), p. 47.

23. MS Thomas, p. 10.

24. *The Baltimore Sun,* March 6, 1857.

25. *The Baltimore Patriot,* February 12, 1857.

26. MS to William Poke, November, 18, 1837, reprinted in *The Liberian Herald,* November, 1838, p. 1, FHL.

27. *Ibid.,* November 21, 1837, FHL.

28. MS Indenture between John Mitchell and MS, 1794, FHL.

29. *Baltimore City Directory 1796,* "Mitchell and Sheppard, grocery store, 20 Cheapside . . . Running North and South from Water Street to the Basin."

30. Copy of the will of John Mitchell. Trustee's Papers, SEPH.

31. Ernest L. Bogart, *Economic History of the American People* (New York and London, 1939), p. 361.

32. Hamilton Owens, Baltimore historian, writes of this period in the City: "there was a whole group of honest merchants, many of them Quakers, to whose simple and ascetic souls the extravagance of the more flamboyant spenders and showoffs made no appeal. These men loved the town for its own sake, and their names are found in the lists of subscribers to benevolent undertakings."

33. Frederick B. Tolles, *Quakers and the Atlantic Culture* (New York, 1960), p. 60.

34. *The Revised Discipline, Approved by the Yearly Meeting of Friends for the Western-Shore of Maryland and the adjacent parts of Pennsylvania and Virginia, in the Year One Thousand Seven Hundred and Ninety-Three* (Baltimore, 1794), pp. 9, 10, 26, 27, 32, 34.

35. See chapters 33 and 5 of *Meeting House and Counting House: The Quaker Merchants of Colonial Philadelphia, 1682-1763,* by Frederick B. Tolles (Chapel Hill, 1948); and his *Quakers and the Atlantic Culture,* chapters 3 and 4.

36. MS John Saurin Norris, A Biographical Sketch of the Life of MS, Trustees' Papers.

37. The Quakers did not use the days of the week or the names of the months of the year in common usage, because they were named, in most cases, after heathen gods and goddesses.

38. Howard H. Brinton, *Friends for Three Hundred Years* (Harper and Brothers, 1952), p. xiii.

39. 1 Corinthians 12:4-11. Quakers used many terms to express the word Spirit; it was synonymous with the Inner Light, the Indwelling Christ, the Christ Within; they delighted in using the Johannine phrase, "The true light that enlightens every man that cometh into the world."

40. *Book of Discipline . . . of Maryland, 1794,* p. 26.

41. MS Min Baltimore MM. "Testimony of Baltimore Monthly Meeting, held the 11th of 8th month, 1796, Against Anne Alleson (formerly Sheppard) who hath had a right of Membership with us the people called Quakers. But she having so far given way to the vanity of this world, as to attend publick plays, and hath had her Marriage accomplished by the assistance of a Hireling, which practices we Testify against, and disown her from being any longer a Member of our Society, until her further conduct may recommend her to be worthy, which is what we desire."

42. MS Min BMM, Oct. 6, 1807.

II: THE MAN OF BUSINESS

1. Ernest L. Bogart, *Economic History of the American People* (New York, 1939), p. 234.

2. Hamilton Owens, *Baltimore on the Chesapeake* (Garden City, 1921), p. 142.

3. *Ibid.,* p. 72.

4. MS Lavens M. Thomas, 2nd, Moses Sheppard (MS), 1775-1857: Humanitarian, A Short Biography (Baltimore, 1941), p. 12.

5. MS's Papers, Trustees SEPH, Towson, Maryland.

6. MS Gerard Reese, Reminiscences of MS, Trustees, SEPH.

7. Sheppard Papers, Trustees.

8. Notices of repeated elections to the Board of Directors, and to attend special meetings, MS's Papers, FHL.

9. Francis F. Beirne, *The Amiable Baltimoreans* (New York, 1951), p. 146-47.

10. MS Min, BMM, April 13, 1808, FHL.

11. *Disc BYM,* 1794, p. 34; *Disc BYM,* 1821, p. 86.

12. Thomas W. Griffith, *The Annals of Baltimore* (Baltimore, 1833), p. 228.

13. MS Thomas, MS, p. 14; *The Baltimore Patriot,* March 7, 1857.

14. The Act of Legislature allowed Sheppard to build a warehouse upon ground facing Light Street, eighty-two feet six inches, and on 314 feet of Conway Street.

15. MS Financial Papers, 1820-1827, FHL.

16. *Ibid.*

17. John Worthington to MS, May 4, 1825, FHL.

18. Owens, *Baltimore,* p. 262.

19. MS Thomas, MS, p. 24.

20. MS Financial Papers, FHL.

21. *Ibid.*

22. MS List of properties made by the Executors of MS's will, Trustee's Records.

23. MS MS's Instructions to the Trustees, Trustees' Records.

24. MS Thomas, MS, p. 17.

25. *Ibid.*

III: MOSES SHEPPARD AND QUAKER CONCERNS

1. *Disc* BYM, 1821, p. 67.

2. Though the individual sums spent for the poor were not large, $437 were subscribed for the purpose in 1821; and almost as large amounts in 1823 and 1824. In the latter year, the Committee reported: "they have paid much attention to the object of their appointment . . . to affect the benevolent views of the Society. Although they have endeavored to observe frugal economy . . . yet the age, infirmity and distressing indigence of the objects of their care, has made it necessary . . . for them to draw on the funds of the Meeting to amounts, that have to some, who have not been engaged in this concern, appear large." MS Min, BMM, May 7, 1824, FHL.

3. MS Treasurer's Book, Baltimore Monthly Meeting, 1857-1861, FHL.

Notes and References

4. *A Collection of Epistles of London Yearly Meeting* . . . (Baltimore, 1806), p. 92.

5. The McKim School, housed in one of the architectural gems of Baltimore, has continued its usefulness into modern times.

6. The Friends School in Portsmouth, Rhode Island, began in 1784; that at Westtown, Pennsylvania in 1789; the Nine Partners Boarding School at Millville, New York, in 1796.

7. A copy of the rules of the Nine Partners Boarding School was sent to the Fairhill School. Boys were to bring from home four shirts, four pocket handkerchiefs, three pairs of stockings, two pairs of shoes, and two suits consisting of coat, waistcoat and trousers. Girls were to bring four frocks, four shifts, four to six pairs of stockings, two pairs of shoes, four aprons, six handkerchiefs, four nightcaps, two bed gowns, and four towels. Bliss Forbush Papers, Baltimore.

8. MS Records Fairhill Boarding School, FHL.

9. *Proceedings of Baltimore Yearly Meeting of Friends, 1850* (Baltimore, 1850), Report of the Educational Committee. The fund is still in existence.

10. MS Thomas, MS, p. 17.

11. *The Baltimore Patriot,* February 7, 1857.

12. John Jackson to MS, March 10, 1833, FHL.

13. *Ibid.,* March 3, 1953, FHL.

14. MS to Oliver Evans, April 16, 1852, FHL.

15. MS MS's Papers, 1840, FHL.

16. MS to John Jackson, September 18, 1851, FHL.

17. MS to Rachel Jackson, February 16, 1855, FHL.

18. *Disc BYM, 1821* p. 54.

19. *Rev Disc BYM, 1794* p. 34. Johns Hopkins, founder of the famous university and medical school that bear his name, was disowned for vending liquor by Baltimore Monthly Meeting. MS Min BMM, November 15, 1826; December 8, 1826. In later years, Hopkins told his nephew Joseph that he now thought it wrong that he had sold liquor. Helen Hopkins Thom, *Johns Hopkins: A Silhouette* (Baltimore, 1929), pp. 30-31.

20. *Rev Disc BYM, 1794,* p. 18.

21. Rufus M. Jones, *The Quakers in the American Colonies* (London, 1911), p. 568.

22. MS Richard H. Townsend Diary, vol. I, pp. 60-64.

23. MS Min, BMM, August 12, 1813; September 7, 1814; October 10, 12, 1813, FHL.

24. Onas was the name given to William Penn by the Indians. The Quaker delegation spoke to the Indians in the name of "the sons of peace, the Quakers who live on the other side of the mountain towards the rising sun"; they desired to instruct the tribes "in those things which make for smooth waters and clear skys . . . that [you] may rest at ease under the shade of the great tree of peace." Congress appropriated $15,000 to purchase agricultural tools and domestic animals for these tribes. Congress asked the Friends to establish a trading post at Fort Wayne, Indiana. MS Indian Affairs Committee BYM, May 22, 1796; October 10, 1797; October 15, 1799; May 24, 1802; October 10, 1803. FHL.

25. MS Indian Affairs Committee, BYM, October 15, 1799; May 24, 1802, FHL.

26. *Ibid.*, pp. 92-94.

27. Thomas E. Drake, *Quakers and Slavery in America* (New Haven, 1950), p. 9.

28. *Ibid.*, p. 82.

29. *Ibid.*, p. 120. Another 160 years went by before Baltimore Monthly Meeting welcomed a Negro into membership.

30. The visits of Elias Hicks began in 1798 and extended through 1828. Bliss Forbush, *Elias Hicks: Quaker Liberal* (New York, 1956), pp. 290-93.

31. Drake, *Quakers and Slavery*, p. 113.

32. *Life of Elisha Tyson the Philanthropist.* By a Citizen of Baltimore (Baltimore, 1825), pp. 24-33. Some writers hold that MS both wrote and paid for the publication of this biography of his friend. Many copies were given away by MS and many remained in his library. The book was printed by Benjamin Lundy after he moved to Baltimore.

33. *Ibid.*, pp. 80-83. There is evidence that some of the jailers were in league with the kidnappers, and were paid for informing them when a Negro was confined.

34. Drake, *Quakers and Slavery*, p. 120.

35. The Protective Society of Maryland, *Maryland Historical Magazine,* vol. 1, No. 4, December 1906, pp. 358-60.

36. MS Lavens M. Thomas, 2nd, MS, 1775-1857, Humanitarian, p. 24. Trustee's Records.

Notes and References

1. MS John Saurin Norris, Trustees' Records, SEPH.
2. The Brick House was purchased by Moses Sheppard (MS), May 1, 1831. Liber W. G. 163, Folio 537, Baltimore, Maryland. MS Lavens M. Thomas, 2nd, MS. 1775-1857, Humanitarian, p. 17. Trustees' Records.
3. Frederick B. Tolles, *George Logan of Philadelphia* (New York, 1953), p. 4, from which the quotation is taken.
4. MS gave the clock to Oliver Evans of Philadelphia; later it came to the Trustees of SEPH. On a card inside the clock it is noted that MS owned it "for nearly sixty years."
5. Pictures and descriptions of some of the Sheppard furniture are found in Edward C. Miller's two volumes, *American Antique Furniture* (Baltimore, 1937).
6. MS willed his library to the institution he founded.
7. Books sent to Benjamin F. Taylor were varied, and included sermons, biography, travel, history, and Quaker works. Sheppard kept lists of books and pamphlets sent to others. For example, he sent 33 copies of Rev. Burnap's *The Position of the Unitarians Defined* to 22 individuals. He gave away 50 copies of Martineau's *The Bible and the Child.*
8. These were sent to Dr. Samuel S. McGill. Sheppard also stocked the local lyceum in Harper, Liberia.
9. Published in October, 1854.
10. "Nothwithstanding his chief attention was given to the accumulation of wealth, he never neglected the cultivation of the mind, but was a studious and thoughtful man to the last." *The Baltimore Sun*, March 6, 1857.
11. Receipted bill among Sheppard's financial papers, FHL.
12. These included the works of Robert Burns, Samuel Coleridge, Oliver Goldsmith, Alexander Pope (six volumes), and John Greenleaf Whittier.
13. Sheppard said, "I wrote this index in 1796, and now after an elapse of sixty years, I add my name, Moses Sheppard, 1856." MS Thomas, MS, p. 113.
14. *Baltimore Patriot*, March 7, 1857.
15. Dr. E. N. Brush, Moses Sheppard, *in The Institutional Care of the Insane in the United States and Canada* (Baltimore, 1917), vol. IV, p. 498.

16. MS Thomas, MS, p. 115.

17. *Ibid.,* p. 111.

18. Benjamin F. Taylor to MS, January, 1851, FHL.

19. Dr. Nathan Shoemaker to MS, October 26, 1854 FHL.

20. MS Thomas, MS, p. 112.

21. *Ibid.,* p. 107.

22. MS to Dr. Nathan Shoemaker, December 1, 1851, FHL.

23. John Sheppard to MS, September 30, 1830, FHL.

24. *Ibid.,* November 5, 1830, FHL.

25. MS Thomas, MS, p. 27.

26. *Ibid.,* p. 30. In 1835 Hallowell had students in his school from 14 states and territories, South America, Cuba, and England. In 1859 he drew up the plans for the first agricultural college, and was named President, but because of ill health served only a few months. *The Autobiography of Benjamin Hallowell* (Philadelphia, 1884), pp. 144-48, 162-66.

27. MS to Thomas Ellicott, April 16, 1884, FHL.

28. Benjamin Hallowell to MS, May 23, 1847, FHL.

29. MS to Benjamin Hallowell, May 15, 1847, FHL.

30. *Ibid.,* August 8, 1846, FHL. When Samuel Morse explained his telegraph to Louis Lane, then President of the Baltimore and Ohio Railroad, Lane told Latrobe "that he had interviewed a crazy man." Latrobe answered, "The day when you and I are dead and forgotten this man will be remembered." Francis Beirne, *The Amiable Baltimoreans* (New York, 1951), p. 303.

31. Benjamin Hallowell on occasions illustrated his lectures with mechanical aids, which he constructed.

32. Dr. Nathan Shoemaker to MS, July 13, 1846, FHL.

33. MS to Dr. Nathan Shoemaker, July 26, 1842, FHL.

34. MS to Thomas Ellicott, December 25, 1843, FHL.

35. MS Thomas, MS, p. 28.

36. MS to Nathan Shoemaker, Dec. 12, 1843, FHL.

37. Thomas Ellicott to MS, June 1844, FHL.

38. MS to Thomas Ellicott, June 1844, FHL.

39. *Ibid.,* January 11, 1849, FHL.

40. Edward Hungerford, *The Story of the Baltimore and Ohio Railroad* (Baltimore, 1928), p. 185.

41. *Ibid.,* pp. 185-186. "Thomas had often been remarked in Baltimore for his self-possession, his energy, his clearness of perception, and his rare judgment; of the Quaker faith, he had

the calm serenity of this religion. . . ." "Never thrown off his balance, quiet in speech, laborious in his search for facts. . . ."

42. G. W. Howard, *The Monumental City* (Baltimore, 1873), p. 571; Thomas W. Griffith, *Annals of Baltimore* (Baltimore, 1833), p. 254.

43. John E. Semmes, *John H. B. Latrobe and His Times: 1803-1891* (Baltimore, 1917), pp. 44-45, 60-66. Francis F. Beirne, *The Amiable Baltimoreans* (Baltimore, 1951), pp. 270, 302, 358-359, 374-375.

44. Semmes, *John H. B. Latrobe,* p. 285.

45. John H. B. Latrobe to MS, May 27, 1847. MS 1402 Maryland Historical Society.

V: RELIGIOUS FERMENT

1. Most of the Anglican clergy returned to England when the Revolutionary War began, and parishes were deserted. Conferences held at Chestertown, and at Annapolis, Maryland, in 1780 and 1783 started the church anew. The Methodist Episcopal Church began in 1784, and the United Brethren in 1800. John Carroll, of the well-known Maryland Carrolls, was the first Catholic Bishop in the United States.

2. Rufus M. Jones, *The Later Periods of Quakerism* (London, 1921).

3. John Sykes, *The Quakers: A New Look at Their Place in Society* (Philadelphia, 1959), pp. 164-68.

4. MS Essay, Moses Sheppard (MS), "Nothing Can be More Certain," FHL.

5. MS to Dr. Nathan Shoemaker, December 20, 1843, FHL.

6. MS to Thomas Ellicott, June, 1845, FHL.

7. Revised Discipline . . . Yearly Meeting of Friends. . . . (Baltimore, 1794), pp. 15, 16.

8. *Discipline . . . 1821,* p. 2. Jesus was also referred to as "the head of the church," "the blessed Shepherd," and "our Holy Head."

9. *Ibid.,* p. 22.

10. MS to Benjamin Hallowell, August 8, 1845, FHL.

11. Benjamin Hallowell to MS, July 20, 1846, FHL.

12. MS to Dr. Nathan Shoemaker, September 2, 1846, FHL.

13. Elias Hicks of Long Island came to Baltimore in 1797, 1801, 1813, 1817, 1819, 1822, 1824, and 1828.

14. MS Lavens M. Thomas, 2nd, MS, 1775-1857, Humanitarian, p. 42, Trustees Room, SEPH.

15. Thomas, MS, p. 42.

16. MS Letter William Foster, Box 51, Library, Friends House, London.

17. MS Diary, Richard H. Townsend, Enoch Pratt Free Library.

18. *Ibid.*

19. Anna B. Thomas, *The Story of Baltimore Yearly Meeting from 1672-1938* (Baltimore, nd), pp. 52-55.

20. Of the eight Yearly Meetings in America, five divided—Philadelphia, New York, Baltimore, Ohio, and Indiana. A sixth Hicksite Yearly Meeting was established in Illinois during Sheppard's lifetime.

21. MS to Thomas Ellicott, December 25, 1843, FHL.

22. Dr. Nathan Shoemaker to MS.

23. MS to Thomas Ellicott, June 13, 1846, FHL.

24. MS Min BYM, 1854, FHL.

25. William W. Sweet, *The Story of Religions in America* (New York, 1930), p. 397.

26. MS to Thomas Ellicott, April 15, 1844, FHL.

27. MS to Benjamin F. Taylor, August, 1844, FHL.

28. MS Min BMM, February 24, 1844, FHL; MS to Benjamin P. Moore, February 24, 1844, FHL.

29. MS to Dr. Nathan Shoemaker, March 19, 1853, FHL.

30. MS to Thomas Ellicott, September 14, 1849, FHL.

31. Bliss Forbush, *Elias Hicks Quaker Liberal* (New York, 1956), p. 202.

32. *The Baltimore Sun*, March 6, 1857. "He was most interested in theology, psychology, and intellectual philosophy. He read the best books he could procure on these most important and interesting subjects, and such was his proficiency in them, that there were few minds, so deeply versed in these spheres of inquiry, as not to be enlightened by intercourse with him."

33. Nathan Shoemaker to MS, December 9, 1848, FHL.

34. Benjamin Taylor to MS, March 4, 1848, FHL.

35. MS to Benjamin Taylor, October 10, 1850, FHL.

36. MS to Nathan Shoemaker, December, 1847, FHL.

37. *Ibid.,* February 25, 1847, FHL.

38. *Ibid.,* January 1, 1847, FHL.

39. MS to Thomas Ellicott, March 26, 1846, FHL. A young theological student once asked MS, "What does Quakerism

teach?" Sheppard replied, "It teaches that wherever man is, there is Christ to teach him." MS to Dr. Nathan Shoemaker, December 12, 1851, FHL.

40. *Ibid.*, May 10, 1843, FHL. Sheppard wrote to Dr. Shoemaker, May 21, 1845, "When I was absent one of my old acquaintances left us, as the Chinese say, to wander with the immortals."

41. MS, Fragment, Trustees' Papers.

VI: THE EXCITING THIRTIES

1. Raphael Semmes, "Baltimore as Seen by Visitors, 1783-1860," *Studies in Maryland History*, Number 2, Maryland Historical Society (Baltimore, 1853).

2. William Wirt to Catherine Wirt, November 24, 1822, quoted by Hamilton Owens in *Baltimore on the Chesapeake* (Garden City, New York, 1941), pp. 228-30.

3. Thomas W. Griffith, *Annals of Baltimore* (Baltimore, 1833), Appendix.

4. Owens, *Baltimore*, p. 251.

5. William Edmundson, a prominent Quaker of the Eastern Shore, began to build ships about the same time William Fell started his shipyard.

6. Owens, *Baltimore*, pp. 50, 56.

7. *Ibid.*, pp. 59-64.

8. *Ibid.*, pp. 253-254.

9. *Ibid.*, p. 209. Owens said that few Baltimore ship owners went willingly into the slave trade, "and there is evidence that a few of them found themselves involved against their wills . . . and found it easier to continue than to quit."

10. *Ibid.*, p. 210. They lay in spoon fashion during the entire voyage, often rough and stormy, across the Atlantic. Many died.

11. Notice of the meeting of the Managers, FHL.

12. Robert G. Albion, *The Rise of New York Port*, 1815-1850 (New York, 1939), p. 29.

13. *Ibid.*, p. 38.

14. *Ibid.*, pp. 390-391. 1840 was a bad year commercially; in 1839 imports to New York were $99 million, to Philadelphia $16 million, and to Baltimore $6 million.

15. The project of the Chesapeake and Ohio Canal was strongly supported by George Washington, when first proposed.

He held extensive lands in the territory of Ohio. The canal company was reorganized in 1824.

16. Owens, *Baltimore,* p. 234.

17. Shortly afterwards, another group of Baltimoreans organized the Baltimore and Susquehanna Railroad to go from the city to York and Harrisburg, Pennsylvania. The State of Maryland, for seventy years, provided large sums of money for the B&O RR (*Atlantic Monthly,* vol. 157, March 1936, p. 305.) It is surprising how many Quakers were involved in the B&O RR. There were four Quaker directors; and Jonathan Knight and Casper Wever first surveyed the roadway. Wever was the first Superintendent of construction. Samuel Brown of Winchester, Virginia, suggested the Point of Rocks route; Gideon Davis of Georgetown suggested using cross sills resting on stone slabs. Phineas Davis of York, built the first successful engine. ("Sidelights on the Baltimore and Ohio Railroad," *Maryland Historical Magazine,* vol. xlviii, 1953, pp. 267-309.)

18. Sheppard's papers, FHL.

19. The *Tom Thumb,* the first locomotive used on the B&O, could not negotiate the curves. The railroad reached Cumberland, Maryland, in 1842, and Wheeling, Virginia (now West Virginia), in 1852.

20. Owens, *Baltimore,* p. 242.

21. Moses Sheppard (MS) to Thomas Ellicott, March 26, 1841, FHL.

22. MS was elected a director of the Bank of Maryland on February 9, 1820. He was a director of the Savings Bank of Baltimore in 1827, and evidently was President or Acting President from February 5 to July 27.

23. Owens, *Baltimore,* 245.

24. *Ibid.,* p. 247.

25. *Ibid.,* p. 249.

26. Ernest L. Bogart, *Economic History of the American People* (New York, 1939), p. 330.

27. John E. Semmes, *John H. B. Latrobe and His Times, 1803-1891* (Baltimore, 1917), p. 359.

28. Bliss Forbush, *Elias Hicks Quaker Liberal* (New York, 1956), p. 281.

29. Edward Hungerford, *The Story of the Baltimore and Ohio Railroad* (New York, 1928), pp. 185-186.

30. Semmes, *Latrobe,* p. 361.

31. MS to Thomas Ellicott, September 11, 1848, FHL.
32. *Ibid.,* December 14, 1842, FHL.
33. *Ibid.,* September 11, 1849; October 25, 1848, FHL.
34. *Ibid.,* September 19, 1849, FHL.
35. Bogart, *Economic History,* pp. 333-334.
36. MS to Thomas Ellicott, October 25, 1849, FHL.
37. Owens, *Baltimore,* pp. 220-221.

VII: CARE FOR THE INDIANS

1. Benjamin F. Taylor to Moses Sheppard (MS), December 4, 1848, FHL.
2. MS to Samuel F. McGill, January 18, 1850, FHL. Philadelphia Friends had worked in the area since 1796.
3. Benjamin F. Taylor to MS, December 24, 1848, FHL.
4. The Six Nations comprised the Senecas, Oneidas, Mohawks, Cayugas, Onondagas, and the Tuscaroras. The Tuscaroras from North Carolina joined the federation of the Five Nations in 1712.
5. John Snow, a Seneca Chief, was paid $2,000 and given a lease of fifty acres of land provided he would vote to give up the New York Reservations; likewise, Chief Halftown was given $500 in cash and a lease on sixty acres of land, Chief Bigdeer $10,000 and a ten-year lease. It was later proved that eight additional chiefs were promised $21,600 if they would agree to move West. *Proceedings of the Joint Committee . . . of Friends from the Yearly Meetings of Genesee, New York, Philadelphia and Baltimore, For Promoting the Civilization and Improving the Conditions of the Seneca Nation of Indians* (Baltimore, 1847), pp. 19-22.
6. *Ibid.,* p. 31.
7. *Ibid.,* p. 48.
8. *Ibid.,* p. 49. MS Minutes and Proceedings of the Committee on Indian Concerns Appointed by the Yearly Meeting of Baltimore, from 10th month 1815 to 2nd Month, 1847, p. 164, FHL.
9. *Ibid.,* pp. 164-166.
10. *Proceedings of the Joint Committee . . . 1847,* p. 60.
11. *Proceedings of the Indian Council held at Buffalo Reservation, State of New York, Fourth Month, 1842* (Baltimore, 1842), pp. 82-83.

12. *Ibid.*, p. 14; *Proceedings of the Joint Committee* . . . *1847*, p. 96.

13. MS Min Indian Concerns, pp. 169-70.

14. *Ibid.*, p. 172.

15. The canal packet was 80 to 100 feet long, and eleven feet wide.

16. The aqueduct over the Mohawk River was 1,184 feet long, that over the Genesee River 748 feet long. Madeline S. Waggoner, *The Long Haul West: The Canal Era 1817-1850* (New York, 1958), pp. 79, 80, 109-37.

17. *Proceedings of the Indian Council . . . 1842*, pp. 11, 12.

18. *Ibid.*, p. 27.

19. *Ibid.*, p. 32-33.

20. MS Min Indian Concerns, p. 178.

21. *Proceedings of the Indian Council* . . . 1842, p. 72.

22. *Ibid.*, pp. 63-65.

23. *Ibid.*, p. 75.

24. *Proceedings of the Joint Committee* . . . *1847* (Baltimore, 1847), p. 106.

25. MS Min Proceedings of the Indian Affairs Committee . . .

26. *Proceedings of the Joint Committee* . . . *1847*, p. 105.

27. *Ibid.*, p. 106.

28. MS Min Proceedings, pp. 179-185.

29. *Ibid.*, pp. 190-205.

30. *Proceedings of the Joint Committee*, pp. 123-124.

31. MS Min Proceedings, p. 209. Baltimore Friends corresponded with Friends in Great Britain concerning the work of the united Yearly Meetings for the Indians. Early in their efforts, Friends in England contributed $8,000 towards their efforts, and Friends in Ireland added one hundred pounds. Eventually the Quakers in Great Britain gave $31,500. Of this amount, $6,000 went to New York Yearly Meeting, and the rest was divided between Philadelphia and Baltimore Yearly Meetings. Rayner W. Kelsey, *Friends and the Indians, 1655 to 1917* (Philadelphia, 1917), pp. 138-140.

32. *Ibid.*, pp. 314-315. Chief Two-Guns had visited MS in Baltimore as early as 1842. He gave the latter a pair of moccasins, which Sheppard passed on to John Sheppard's daughter.

33. MS Min Proceedings, pp. 218-225, 361-371.

34. *Ibid.*, pp. 222-223.

35. *Ibid.*, pp. 223-233, 236.

Notes and References

36. *Further Proceedings of the Joint Committee* . . . *for Promoting the Civilization of the Seneca Indians, from 1847 to the Year 1850* (Baltimore, 1850), pp. 57, 58.

37. MS Min Proceedings, Book C, May, 1849.

38. Philip Thomas' "citation" read, "You are hereby nominated, constituted, and appointed an Ambassador, Envoy Extraordinary, and Minister Plenipotentiary to the seat of Government of the United States of America, by the constitutional Convention and Government of the Seneca Nation of Indians . . . to represent them in their name and behalf, with full powers . . . and whatever you may do in our names and behalf will be binding upon us. . . ." Kelsey, *Friends and the Indians,* pp. 224-25.

39. MS Min Proceedings, Book C, p. 238.

40. The tribes were receiving $3,000 a year in annuities from the Federal Government, and $500 a year from New York State. By this time the Seneca nation owned $100,000 in United States Bank stock, and $75,000 in trust with the United States Treasury, plus $45,000 in the Ontario Bank. (MS Min Proceedings, Book C, p. 93.) Between 1807 and 1828, the Baltimore Indian Affairs Committee spent $22,212.75 for the Indians. (MS Min Report of the Indian Affairs Committee, Book C. 1850.) Only the interest of the money received from Great Britain to aid the Indians was spent by the Committee. A large proportion of the fund is still in possession of Baltimore Yearly Meetings, and is used to aid Indians west of the Mississippi River.

VIII: A NEW MANDATE

1. *Report of the Board of Managers of the Maryland Colonization Society* (Baltimore, 1850), p. 5.

2. *African Repository and Colonial Journal* (Washington, 1827), vol. II, 110-119.

3. Lawrence A. Marinelli, *The New Liberia* (New York, 1964), p. 8.

4. MS Lavens M. Thomas, 2nd, Moses Sheppard (MS), 1775-1857, Humanitarian, 1941, p. 50. Trustees' Papers, SEPH.

5. *African Repository,* vol. III, pp. 31, 224-228, 322-324, 355-356.

6. *Report of the* . . . *Maryland Colonization Society,* pp. 2, 3.

7. *Ibid.,* p. 6.

8. *African Repository,* vol. II, pp. 254-255.

9. MS John H. B. Latrobe, Address before Maryland Colonization Society, April 30, 1832, FHL.

10. *African Repository,* vol. II, pp. 188-189.

11. *Ibid.,* p. 296.

12. MS to Henry Gassett, April 22, 1852, FHL.

13. Samuel E. Morison, *The Oxford History of the American People* (New York, 1965), p. 553.

14. Joseph Bringhurst to MS, February 7, 1832, FHL.

15. MS Thomas, MS, p. 51.

16. *Ibid.,* p. 52.

17. John E. Semmes, *John H. B. Latrobe. . . .* (Baltimore, 1917), p. 143.

18. The Board of Managers of the State Fund were selected from the membership of the Maryland State Colonization Society, affiliated with the American Colonization Society. The State society had funds enough from private contributions to cover all its expenses, so the State contribution could go directly to "preparation of a place for the reception of emigrants, and their removal thereto. . . ." *Report . . . Maryland Colonization Society,* p. 4. The chief town of the Cape Palmas colony was Harper, named after the General.

19. MS Maryland Colonization, written by MS, August 1833, FHL.

20. MS to Robert Finley, June 12, 1833, FHL.

21. MS Thomas, MS p. 51.

22. MS to Willoughby White, June 11, 1833, FHL.

23. MS to Stephen Tippet, May 6, 1833, FHL.

24. MS to Willoughby White, June 15, 1833, FHL.

25. MS to James Reese, June 10, 1833, FHL.

26. MS to Samuel Sheppard, June 8, 1833, FHL. He added, "I forbade to mention it to Uncle John . . . he could not have known that in one instance the family changed its color."

27. MS to R. R. Gurly, April 16, 1833, FHL.

28. MS to Susan Hyman, June 10, 1833, FHL.

29. MS to Henry Hyman, June 10, 1833, FHL.

30. MS to Thomas Jackson, June 10, 1833, FHL. The Maryland State Colonization Society sent thirty-one emigrants on the schooner *Orion* to Monrovia in November 1831; it sent 146 emigrants on the ship *Lafayette* to Monrovia in December, 1832. The first ship for Cape Palmas carried only seventeen emigrants; but going south from Monrovia it picked up enough other earlier emigrants to

make a total of fifty-four settlers to begin the new colony. *Report of . . . the Maryland Colonization Society,* pp. 8, 9.

31. MS to Nathan Neilson, December 1, 1933, FHL.
32. MS to Henry Hyman, May 30, 1834, FHL.
33. MS to Ann Polk, June 2, 1834, FHL.
34. MS to Dr. Theodore E. Bond, May 1, 1833, FHL.
35. MS to Rev. George McGill, June 10, 1833, FHL.
36. MS to Jacob Prout, October 10, 1833, FHL. Moses Sheppard at this time asked Prout if it might be profitable to establish a warehouse with an assortment of goods for trading purposes. George McGill had already begun this in a small way.

IX: SHEPPARD AND MARYLAND IN LIBERIA

1. Six hundred and twenty-four colonists were transported. *Report of the Board of Managers of the Maryland State Colonization Society* (Baltimore, 1850), p. 33. The settlement at Grand Basa was between Monrovia and Cape Palmas. Sheppard wrote to its founders: "It is past, and I would rather applaud the exertions to retrieve the disaster than investigate the causes and censure the error that produced it." Moses Sheppard (MS) to Elliott Cresson, February, 1836, FHL. Sheppard believed a chain of colonies would stop the slave trade from the interior.

2. Samuel F. McGill was the son of Rev. George McGill, Assistant Governor of the Maryland colony. Samuel was brought up in Baltimore, and wrote to Sheppard, "With all the disasters we are subject to, I would not give up Africa for any other place of permanent residence under existing conditions." Samuel F. McGill to MS, October 9, 1835, FHL.

3. MS to Samuel F. McGill, January 12, 1836, FHL. John H. B. Latrobe wrote McGill, "Our mutual and esteemed friend, Moses Sheppard, has shown me [your letters], and I fully accord with him in the views expressed. It would be unfortunate if you entertained notions on your arrival here which subsequent experience would disappoint; but you will be kindly treated. . . . keep before your eyes that Africa . . . is the best and happiest home for descendants of her sons in America." John H. B. Latrobe to Rev. George McGill, July 4, 1836, FHL. Sheppard's last message to young McGill before he left West Africa was, "You must not land at any port south of Norfolk,

the laws would subject you to imprisonment." MS to Samuel F. McGill, January 12, 1836, FHL.

4. MS to Rev. George McGill, July 4, 1836, FHL. Washington College was on the site of the present Church Home and Hospital on Broadway. While the correspondence was in process, Samuel McGill worked in the colony's warehouse to secure money for his passage, and Sheppard offered to make up the balance that was needed.

5. Students to the Faculty of Washington College, December 13, 1836, FHL.

6. MS Ira A. Easter to the Board of the Maryland Colonization Society, reporting the opinions of the Students of Washington College, December 26, 1836, FHL.

7. Dr. Edward Phelps to Ira A. Easter, January 9, 1837, FHL. Lavens M. Thomas writes: "The steps Sheppard had taken to get the young African protege located and started to work reads almost like a fairy tale. He tried to get him admitted into the Medical School of the University of Pennsylvania . . . students drove him off." MS Lavens M. Thomas, 2nd, MS, 1775-1857 (1941), p. 56. Trustees of SEPH.

8. MS to Matthew and Hopkins, January 18, 1837, FHL. Sheppard also wrote to George W. Light in Boston about Samuel McGill: "He is an intelligent young man, and it may be gratifying to you and other friends of Colonization to see him and converse with him. Perhaps you may be useful to him, in directing him on the best way to pursue his journey. . . ." MS to George W. Light, January 28, 1837, FHL. Ira Easter wrote young McGill, "Whatever may be your sense of equality with your fellowmen, remember it is dangerous to show it. Prudence dictates that we submit to prejudice when neither reason, humanity, nor religion could control." Ira A. Easter to Rev. George McGill, February 8, 1837, FHL.

9. Ira A. Easter to McGill, February 18, 1837, FHL.

10. MS Notebook, Correspondence Relating to Samuel F. McGill, January 20, 1837, FHL. Sheppard asked Dr. Keener of Baltimore to secure a copy of Ainsworth's *Medical Dictionary;* from three other doctors he secured a three volume set of Mackel's *Anatomy,* Leannee *On the Chest,* and *Mackentosh's Practice of Medicine.* MS to Dr. Keener, January 26, 1838, FHL.

11. Samuel F. McGill to MS, May 29, 1837, FHL.

12. MS to Samuel McGill, May 29, 1837, FHL.

13. This was mentioned several times by Sheppard to Joshua Dugan in 1846; to Thomas Ellicott in June, 1848; to Samuel F. McGill, May 29, 1837, FHL.

14. MS to Rev. George McGill, May 29, 1837, FHL. MS Lavens Thomas, *Moses Sheppard*, p. 57.

15. Samuel F. McGill to MS, June 15, 1837, FHL.

16. *Ibid.*

17. *Ibid.*, November 28, 1837, FHL.

18. MS to Rev. George McGill, May 15, 1837, FHL. Sheppard received a letter from T. A. Whan in Elkton, Maryland, about a free Negro boy who was in danger of being sold South, and replied, "I will see that justice is done." Sheppard kept an abstract of manumissions in the State of Maryland, and the dates when they would take effect. In 1831 there were seven; 1832 there were two hundred and forty-three; in the next five years there were thirty-one. Between 1838 and 1860 they averaged five manumissions a year. In this period there were two hundred and seventy-five manumissions in the City of Baltimore; forty-three in Frederick County and the same number in Ann Arundel County; fifteen in Kent; fourteen in Cecil; twelve in Sumerset; eleven in Montgomery and ten in Talbot. There were no manumissions in Charles or Calvert Counties between 1831 and 1860 in this list; from three to nine in the other counties. MS Collection Manumissions, Maryland Colonization Society, MS's papers, FHL.

19. MS to William Polk, May 1, 1837, FHL.

20. MS to Henry Hyman, November 27, 1834, FHL.

21. *Ibid.*, October 17, 1835, FHL. Sheppard sent to Hyman at this time eight yards of heavy Russian linen, six yards of muslin, two pairs of trousers, six tin plates, fifteen pounds of white sugar in a tin, twenty pounds of brown sugar in a tin teakettle, a pound of tea in a canister, and ten pounds of coffee. For Rev. George McGill he sent plates, clothing, paper, seeds; to Elizabeth Cresson went eighteen handkerchiefs, and eight yards of cloth.

22. *Ibid.*, December 10, 1835, FHL.

23. *Ibid.*

24. *Ibid.*, November 25, 1836, FHL.

25. Joshua Stewart to Dr. Macauley, February 16, 1834, FHL.

26. MS to Sarah Russwurm, November 22, 1837, FHL.

27. MS to Joshua Stewart, May 11, 1837, FHL; MS to William Polk, May 1, 1837, FHL; Sheppard wrote Polk, "I know you had a hard time when you arrived in Liberia . . . but your reward is your freedom . . . freedom is worth the price . . . Freedom is worth a big price, but freedom in poverty loses much of its value. You must try to raise yourself above poverty. You have it in your power to do so."

28. MS to Dr. Samuel F. McGill, April 24, 1838, FHL.

29. R. D. Mussey to MS, October 29, 1838, FHL; Samuel F. McGill to MS, April 24, 1838, and June 3, 1838, FHL; MS to Samuel F. McGill, May, 1839, FHL. The fee for McGill's senior year at Dartmouth College was: tuition $50.00; special classes and laboratory $15.00; graduation fee $18.00; board and washing $28.00; wood and light $18.00; total $129.00. Samuel F. McGill to MS, August 11, 1838, FHL.

30. MS to Rev. George McGill, November 21, 1838, FHL.

31. MS to Samuel F. McGill, November 30, 1838, FHL. In one of his last letters before Dr. Samuel McGill sailed home, MS warned the colonists that if they planned to visit the United States they must be acquainted with the laws of the various slave states. He had found it necessary to come to the assistance of several Liberians who had fallen into difficulty through neglecting to become acquainted with the laws. Rev. Ephraim Titler, a missionary returning to Cape Palmas, was to take a boat from Norfolk, Virginia, but no captain in Baltimore would transport him to Norfolk for fear of being fined $500 for bringing a Negro into that state. Sheppard solved the problem by directing the Baltimore captain to take Rev. Titler to Norfolk, and without landing him, have him rowed to the waiting ship bound for Liberia. MS to William Polk, May 10, 1837, FHL.

32. Samuel F. McGill to MS, December 21, 1839, FHL.

33. Also spelled in Dr. McGill's letters "sausey," "sausy," and "saucy."

34. Named for the Baltimore philanthropist.

35. MS to Samuel F. McGill, June 29, 1841, FHL.

36. MS Lavens, *Moses Sheppard*, p. 52.

37. MS to Samuel F. McGill, December 6, 1839, FHL. MS wrote to Dr. McGill, "When I began my colonization career I did not expect to write a single letter on the subject. Writing is not my department, I have always referred it to my associates, but I wrote one letter after another, until I found myself en-

gaged in a correspondence with the colonists . . . that would occupy half my time . . . writing is not a pleasant employment for me, so far from [it] that it is irksome." MS to Samuel F. McGill, December 6, 1839, FHL. Sheppard disliked the new steel pen points just coming into fashion; he and Thomas Ellicott often referred to their difficulty in using them, and now and then went back to the quill.

38. MS to Dr. Samuel F. McGill, July 5, 1852, FHL.

39. MS to (perhaps Thomas Ellicott), December 14, 1842, FHL.

40. MS to Samuel F. McGill, October 25, 1843, FHL.

41. Samuel F. McGill to MS, May 7, 1844, FHL. Rev. George McGill had been paid $300 a year by a group of Baltimoreans to teach the school in Maryland in Liberia for children of emigrants. In 1843 he had forty pupils, who had progressed to the point where they "were writing the letters and keeping the accounts of their parents." George R. McGill to Mrs. M. S. Duncan, June 27, 1843, FHL. Rev. McGill was also Assistant Governor in Maryland of Liberia for the home Board in Baltimore.

42. MS to Samuel F. McGill, November, 1844, FHL.

43. MS to Samuel F. McGill, November 20, 1842, FHL. Dr. McGill acknowledged his patron's advice with appreciation, "Your admonitions, your censure, and your advice will be taken kindly and thoughtfully. Have I not steadily prospered by an adherence to rules prescribed by you, and can I now from a feeling of self-sufficiency relinquish the experienced and friendly advice, which yet points me to still higher and nobler pursuits? . . . I must pray the continuation of your kind solicitude." Samuel F. McGill to MS, February 10, 1842, FHL.

44. MS to Franklin Anderson, January 9, 1841, FHL. In this letter Sheppard told Anderson that Samuel McGill came to the United States as the ward of the Maryland Colonization Society to secure his education, but that Moses "relieved the directors by taking on myself the principal care and attention which his education required." In the same letter Sheppard stated, "Liberia afforded the only asylum for the free colored race in this country, where alone they could enjoy real freedom and happiness."

45. Dr. Samuel F. McGill to MS, May 16, 1854; May 7, 1856, FHL.

X: MARYLAND QUAKERS AND SLAVERY

1. Charles A. and Mary R. Beard, *The Rise of American Civilization* (New York, 1930), pp. 696-697.

2. *Ibid.*

3. Moses Sheppard (MS) subscribed to the Genius of Universal Emancipation. Benjamin Lundy, a member of the Baltimore Monthly Meeting at this time, was "a quiet, persistent, drab-clothed, meek, old man, one of the valiant little mice who nibble undismayed on the nets which enchain the strongest lions." S. B. Nelson, *History of Maryland* (Baltimore, 1898), pp. 88, 89. Garrison wrote, "I want much to help him [Lundy], for he had been all along for gradual emancipation; and as soon as I began to look into the matter I became convinced that immediate abolition was the doctrine to preach, and I scattered his subscribers like pigeons." Nelson, *History of Maryland,* p. 89.

4. Walter Merrill, *William Lloyd Garrison* (Cambridge, 1963), p. 35-38.

5. *Ibid.,* p. 36.

6. MS Papers of MS, FHL. Mr. Garrison's lawyer appealed the case, but the appeal was denied for lack of evidence.

7. *Ibid.*

8. MS to Nathan [Shoemaker] fragment, no date, FHL.

9. Thomas E. Drake, *Quakers and Slavery* (Cambridge, 1950), p. 141.

10. *A Voice from the South, Comprising Letters from Georgia to Massachusetts* (Baltimore, 1848).

11. Samuel Eliot Morison, *The Oxford History of the American People* (New York, 1965), p. 524.

12. William W. Sweet, *The Story of Religions in America* (New York, 1930), pp. 443, 448-49.

13. Drake, *Quakers and Slavery,* p. 133.

14. Ibid., p. 166.

15. *Ibid.,* pp. 165-166, 174-177.

16. *Ibid.,* p. 141.

17. MS Min Baltimore Yearly Meeting, 1835, FHL.

18. *Ibid.,* 1842, FHL.

19. *Ibid.* At this Yearly Meeting the minutes, for the first time, contained a list of all recorded ministers traveling with minutes from Yearly Meetings beyond Baltimore. There were

thirteen present from Philadelphia Yearly Meeting, including Lucretia Mott; one from New York Yearly Meeting; one from Indiana Yearly Meeting; and one from Upper Canada [Genesee Yearly Meeting]. The minute added, "We may carefully look to direction to that unerring Guide, which alone can point to a path of safety for us to walk in . . . avoiding the dangers which any hasty or injudicious steps might involve us in. Our test was . . . love to our fellowmen, a feeling of compassion for the poor oppressed slaves as well as a benevolent regard to those who held them in bondage. . . . We support the doctrine of the equal right of the African race with ourselves to the enjoyment of personal freedom. . . . Founded in injustice, and supported by violence, slavery cannot continue forever in a Christian community. . . . To the ardent laborer in the cause of the oppressed Africans, the progress of the concern may appear slow and tedious and there is danger that he may become impatient . . . we need to be patient and have charity least in our zeal for the Trust, we act indiscreetly. . . ."

20. *Ibid.*

21. *Review of an Address Issued by Baltimore Yearly Meeting of Friends by the Clarkson Anti-Slavery Association of Pennsgrove,* Pennsgrove Meeting House, November 26, 1842, FHL.

22. Benjamin F. Taylor to MS, November 6, 1845, FHL.

23. *Ibid.*

24. "Henry Clay in 1849 proposed gradual compensated emancipation financed by the sale of public land, and removing the freedman. These and other suggestions of the sort received only abuse in the South; Lincoln, as late as 1862, presented a gradual emancipation plan to the representatives of the loyal slave States, with the appropriation of $100 million, but they would have none of it." Morison, *History of the American People,* p. 509.

25. Nathan Shoemaker to MS, June 2, 1844, FHL.

26. MS to Dr. Samuel F. McGill, 1843, FHL.

27. Dr. Samuel F. McGill to MS, May 31, 1848, FHL.

28. John Jackson, *Considerations of the Impropriety of Friends Participating in the Administration of Political Government* (Philadelphia, 1840).

29. At the convention of 1832, which nominated Andrew Jackson for the presidency, the first truly national delegated

convention, the Democrats adopted the two-thirds rule which was to keep so many able men from becoming the leaders of the party. The Democratic platform of 1836, passed in the Hall of the Maryland Institute, declared, "Congress has no power under the Constitution to interfere with or control the domestic institutions of the several States; that such States are the sole judge of everything appertaining to their own affairs, not prohibited by the Constitution. . . ." *Proceedings of the National Democratic Convention Held in the City of Baltimore, 5th May, 1840* (Baltimore, 1840). In 1840 General Harrison was nominated after a great procession to the Canton Race Track, where Daniel Webster and Henry Clay addressed the delegates.

30. MS to Thomas Ellicott, December 12, 1845, FHL. As part of the Republic of Mexico, slavery was outlawed in Texas.

31. MS to Joshua Dugan, 1846, FHL.

32. MS to Thomas Ellicott, January 29, 1850, FHL.

XI: THE VITAL FIFTIES

1. Hamilton Owens, *Baltimore on the Chesapeake* (Garden City, 1941), p. 257.

2. MS Richard H. Townsend, Diary, vol. II, p. 498. Enoch Pratt Free Library, Baltimore.

3. Moses Sheppard (MS) to Thomas Ellicott, August 27, 1848, FHL.

4. MS Townsend, *ibid.,* p. 498.

5. Benjamin F. Taylor to MS, February 26, 1850, FHL.

6. MS to Thomas Ellicott, August 27, 1849, FHL.

7. *Ibid.,* August 27, 1848, FHL.

8. Benjamin F. Taylor to MS, March 1, 1848, FHL. At this time, in contrast to Taylor, Richard Townsend could write, "The troubles . . . were more among demagogues at the capital, than among the people: no sensible or sound man, in the length and breadth of the land, dreamed or feared any disunity, however the politicians in Washington might bandy words about it." MS Townsend, Diary, vol. II, p. 495.

9. *Ibid.,* pp. 501-502.

10. Samuel Eliot Morison, *The Oxford History of the American People* (New York, 1965), p. 590.

11. MS to Samuel McGill, February 16, 1848, FHL.

12. Thomas E. Drake, *Quakers and Slavery in America* (New Haven, 1950), pp. 185-189.

13. *Report of the Board of Managers of the Maryland State Colonization Society.* . . . (Baltimore, 1850), p. 27.

14. MS to Joshua Stewart, February 19, 1843, FHL.

15. MS to Anthony Wood, November 1845, FHL. English Quakers charged American Friends with racial bias. They insisted that although American Quakers desired abolition and treated individual Negroes kindly, they shared the prejudices of the country as a whole, and desired the removal of the men of color to Africa. Drake, *Quakers and Slavery,* p. 178.

16. *Op. cit.,* ref. 11.

17. MS to A. Simpson, January 24, 1849, FHL.

18. MS to Thomas Ellicott, January 24, 1849, FHL.

19. *Ibid.,* July 1, 1848, FHL.

20. MS to Anthony Wood, September 20, 1848, FHL.

21. MS to Thomas H. Gross, June 20, 1850, FHL. Sheppard gave $50 towards a sum of $500 to keep Thomas Gross from being sold South. (MS to Elizabeth Morris, October 29, 1850, FHL.) Gross wrote to Sheppard in March of 1850, "I must acknowledge the benefits [that] your kindness has conferred on me and my family. . . ." (FHL) In 1850, Sheppard wrote to Thomas Gross, "You have escaped from going to the cotton fields of Georgia, and I hope you will do well." With this letter Sheppard sent $21 worth of clothing and twelve tin plates. Meanwhile, Dr. Fletcher wrote Sheppard, "There never was a day that my mind was free from suspicion or from embarrassment, [duing] the days I spent in the United States. . . . I ever revert with pleasure to the time I had in your company." (Dempsey R. Fletcher to MS, September 16, 1850, FHL.

22. Samuel F. McGill to MS, May 31, 1848, FHL.

23. MS to Samuel F. McGill, 1848, FHL.

24. *Ibid.,* July 18, 1850, FHL. Dr. McGill expressed the desire that Moses Sheppard might someday visit him in Liberia. Sheppard replied, "You say you would be glad to see me under your roof. I would rather be there than in London or Paris. I do not expect ever to embark upon the Atlantic Ocean." (MS to Samuel F. McGill, January 18, 1850. FHL.)

25. *Ibid.,* MS to Dr. Samuel F. McGill, January 18, 1850.

26. *Ibid.,* January 18, 1850, FHL.

27. Samuel F. McGill to MS, April 23, 1851, FHL. Dr.

McGill found it necessary to put down an attack by the natives who lived east of Sheppard Lake.

28. *Ibid.*, April 18, 1852, FHL. McGill asked MS how he now thought slavery could be abolished. Sheppard replied, "that it could not be ended by force, only by raising the moral standard of the community. . . ." In answer to where the Quakers stood, he wrote, "that all Quakers were for the abolition of slavery, but the individuals differed as to the means by which it could be done. "The highest attribute of freedom is freedom of choice," he wrote, "each Quaker should follow his own conscience as to the method."

29. MS to Thomas Ellicott, June 30, 1845, FHL.

30. Joshua Dugan to MS, July 27, 1850, FHL. Joshua Dugan said further, "Nothing presents human nature in a more exalted light than the mighty energy which a man exhibits in improving conditions in this life."

31. MS to Joshua Dugan, November 25, 1844, FHL.

32. *Ibid.*, May 1, 1845, FHL.

33. MS to N. C. Brooks, MS MS's Letter Book 1, March 21, 1852, FHL.

34. MS to Charles Shipley, *ibid.*

35. MS to John McPherson, *ibid.*, March 25, 1853, FHL.

36. MS to William H. Rose, ibid.

37. MS to B. M. High, *ibid.*, 1851, FHL.

38. MS to Charles Evans, May 8, 1852, FHL.

39. MS to Oliver Evans, October 4, 1853, FHL.

40. MS to Benjamin Price, May 9, 1846; August 29, 1846, FHL.

41. *Ibid.*, September 5, 1846, FHL. On October 26th, Moses wrote to the principal, "Whatever is required for his use and comfort, get for him. . . ."

42. Benjamin C. Price to MS, January 10, 1847, JHL.

43. *Op. cit.*, ref. 39, March 11, 1849, FHL.

44. *Ibid.*, January 15, 1849, FHL.

45. Nathan S. Tyson to MS, September 24, 1849, FHL.

46. MS to Nathan Sheppard, Jr., December 13, 1851, FHL. MS said he once hired a man who was so well educated that he was good for nothing.

47. Nathan Sheppard, Jr., became a correspondent of the *New York World* and *Chicago Tribune and Journal,* and lectured in Universities in England and Scotland. Later he became

the pastor of the famous Tremont Temple in Boston. MS
Lavens M. Thomas, Jr., Moses Sheppard, 1775-1857, Humanitarian, 1941, pp. 60, 61. Trustees' Records, SEPH.

48. *Op. cit.*, ref. 39, October 4, 1853, FHL.

49. *Ibid.*, August 18, 1852, FHL.

50. MS to Samuel C. Sheppard, November 18, 1852, FHL.
The mortgage was for $4,000.

51. MS Gerard T. Hopkins, Reminiscences of MS, Trustees'
Records, SEPH. Also in Letter to Eliza Bayard, 1845. MS
Thomas, p. 66. For a period of years, the name of Sheppard led
the list of subscribers to the Association . . . for the Relief of
the Sick and Infirm. MS Book of Edward Jessop, Treasurer, FHL.

52. MS to Oliver Evans, Letter Book A, April 10, 1852,
FHL.

53. MS to Thomas Ellicott, January 29, 1850, FHL.

54. Thomas Sheppard died on December 5, 1853; Nancy
Sheppard died in August, 1856. There was a daughter Mary but
no mention is made of her except as a child.

55. *Op. cit.*, ref. 53, June 14, 1846, FHL.

56. *Ibid.*

57. *Ibid.*, February 25, 1847, FHL.

58. *Ibid.*, Sheppard had a debilitating attack of fever in the
summer of 1848, which kept him home from going to Meeting
for some weeks. He wrote to Thomas Ellicott, "I am fortunate
in sickness . . . my colored people are attentive as they can be,
and they appear to act from affection rather than duty, and my
friends exceed my merits in their kindness."

59. Isaac Tyson lived with MS for the rest of Moses' lifetime. Nathan Shoemaker to MS, March 24, 1848, FHL.

60. J. H. B. Latrobe to MS, April, 1855, FHL.

61. MS to Benjamin F. Taylor, June 1, 1848; September 18,
1848, FHL.

62. Benjamin F. Taylor to MS, nd, FHL.

63. *Op. cit.*, ref. 53, October 26, 1840, FHL.

64. Nathan Shoemaker to MS, September 10, 1849, FHL.

65. *Op. cit.*, ref. 53, May 4, 1848, FHL.

XII: A NEW CONCERN

1. MS, "To the Trustees of the Sheppard Asylum," Moses
Sheppard (MS), January 16, 1855, SEPH.

2. Francis F. Beirne, *The Amiable Baltimoreans* (New York, 1951), p. 45.

3. *Ibid.*

4. John H. B. Latrobe to MS, April 8, 1846, Maryland Historical Society, MS 1402.

5. *Ibid.*

6. MS Lavens M. Thomas, 2nd, MS, 1775-1857: Humanitarian, 1941, p. 70, SEPH.

7. *Ibid.*

8. MS to Thomas Ellicott, March 26, 1841, FHL.

9. Between 1847 and 1850, MS mentioned to Thomas Ellicott that several of their friends were afflicted with mental illness. Sam House in a letter of October 10, 1847; Rachel Dorsay and Rachel Colvin, July 19, 1849; Hugh Boyle in January 29, 1850, and Anthony Whitely; Nathan Evans, a relative, was taken to *Friends Hospital.*

10. *Op. cit.,* ref. 6, p. 80.

11. *Ibid.,* p. 81.

12. *Ibid.,* p. 77.

13. George W. Howard, *The Monumental City, Its Past History and Present Resources* (Baltimore, 1889), pp. 48, 49. MS Thomas, MS, pp. 73-74.

14. Charles Dickens, *American Notes for General Circulation* (London, 1842), vol. 1, pp. 221-223.

15. *Report of the Commission to Visit and Inspect Present Conditions in the Maryland Hospital,* February 19, 1839 (Baltimore, 1839). *Report of the Board of Visitors of the Maryland Hospital to the General Assembly, 1848-49* (Baltimore, 1849). MS Mildred E. Hilberg, Some Aspects of Public Welfare, Typed Thesis, Johns Hopkins Univ, 1926.

16. *Ibid.*

17. *History of Mt. Hope Retreat, 1840-1940* (Baltimore, 1940).

18. *Op. cit.,* ref. 15.

19. *Ibid.*

20. *Report of the Visitors to the Maryland Hospital, 1849.*

21. *Op. cit.,* ref. 17, William H. Stokes, MD, *Report of Mt. Hope Institute for the Year 1845* (Baltimore, 1845).

22. Henry M. Hurd, MD, ed., *The Institutional Care of the Insane in the United States and Canada* (Baltimore, 1916), vol. I, pp. 231-232.

23. Richard A. Clark, *Quakers and Psychiatry,* Friends Journal reprint, June 13, 1958, pp. 380-382.

24. *Report of the Pennsylvania Hospital for the Insane, 1846,* p. 7.

25. *Ibid., 1846,* p. 9.

26. *Ibid., 1846,* p. 10.

27. *Ibid.*

28. *Ibid., 1849,* p. 27.

29. *Ibid., 1846,* pp. 11, 12.

30. *Description of the Retreat, An Institution Near York for Insane Persons of the Society of Friends. . . . by Samuel Tuke* (Philadelphia, 1813) Reprint. Harold C. Hunt, *A Retired Habitation, A History of the Retreat York* (London, 1932), p. 5.

31. *Ibid.,* p. 110.

32. Clark, *Quakers and Psychiatry,* p. 363.

33. *Account of the Rise and Progress of The Asylum . . . for the Relief of Persons Deprived of the Use of Their Reason* (Philadelphia, 1814).

34. MS to Samuel F. McGill, November 20, 1842, FHL. Henry Payson was also a member of the Board.

35. *Ibid.,* MS Article by Henry Payson on MS's work while a member of the Penitentiary Board of Inspectors, June 9, 1824, FHL. Sheppard commented on this experience "Until punishment can be apportioned to crimes, reformation cannot be affected by punishment; moreover, we must know a priori whether correction, alias remedy, must be applied to body or soul."

36. Helen E. Marshall, *Dorothy Lynde Dix, Forgotten Samaritan* (Chapel Hill, 1937), pp. 76, 77. "She discovered overcrowding uncleanliness, and herding together of the innocent with the guilty and the sane with the insane, a condition of things which at that time characterized the prisons and almshouses not alone of Massachusetts, but throughout the world." *The Institutional Care of the Insane,* vol. 1, p. 105.

37. MS Thomas, MS, p. 90.

38. MS to Dr. Nathan Shoemaker, March 19, 1853, FHL. The exact wording, not strictly quoted by Laven M. Thomas was, "My attention has long been directed to the case of the insane: I expect what I may leave, will take that direction, and not to individuals."

39. The common belief of the members of the Society of Friends, stated in various ways in their Disciplines.

40. *The Baltimore Sun,* March 6, 1857.

XIII: THE DEVELOPING CONCERN

1. Moses Sheppard (MS) to Dr. Nathan Shoemaker, March 19, 1853, FHL.

2. J. Sanbourne Bochoven, MD, Moral treatment in American psychiatry, J Nerv Ment Dis *124:*(#2)15, August, 1956.

3. The figures for Worcester State Hospital in Massachusetts were impressive:

5-YEAR PERIOD	NUMBER ADMITTED	NUMBER DISCHARGED, RECOVERED	% DISCHARGED, RECOVERED	NUMBER DISCHARGED, IMPROVED	% DISCHARGED, IMPROVED
1833-37	300	211	70	39	8.3
1838-42	434	324	74.6	14	3.2
1843-47	742	474	63.9	34	4.6
1848-52	791	485	61.3	37	4.7

From the annual report of *The New York Hospital Westchester Division,* 1963, p. 83. The numbers reported from the old Bloomingdale Asylum, in New York, its predecessor, from 1821 to 1893 were: admitted 9,305, recovered 3,635, improved and much improved 2,436, not improved 1,565. The ratio of recoveries in State institutions declined decidedly at a later time when the fundamentals of moral treatment had to be discarded because of the overcrowding and lack of attending staff. Bockoven, *op. cit.,* ref. 2, p. 16.

4. MS Lavens M. Thomas, 2nd, MS, 1775-1857, Humanitarian, 1941, p. 83. SEPH.

5. *Ibid.,* p. 83.

6. *Ibid.,* pp. 84, 85.

7. *Ibid.,* pp. 84, 85.

8. *Ibid.,* p. 85.

9. MS to Dr. Nathan Shoemaker, March 19, 1853, FHL.

10. Memo of David M. Perine, Trustees Papers, SEPH, Thomas, MS, p. 95.

11. MS to Philip Poultney, May 20, 1853, FHL.

12. An Act to Incorporate the Trustees of the Sheppard Asylum, May 28, 1853, J. Pinkney, Secretary to the General

Assembly of Maryland. Henceforth called The Charter of the Sheppard Asylum.

13. *Ibid.*

14. *Ibid.*

15. *Ibid.*

16. *Ibid.*

17. *Ibid.*

18. *Ibid.*

19. *Ibid.*

20. MS Min BMM, July 9, 1814, FHL.

21. Henry F. Powell, *Tercentary History of Maryland* (Baltimore, 1925), vol. 14, pp. 67-69.

22. His son, E. Glenn Perine, was elected to succeed his father as a Trustee of the Sheppard Asylum in 1878, and served until 1899.

23. George W. Howard, *The Monumental City, Its Past and Present Resources* (Baltimore, 1899), pp. 532-534.

24. *Biographical Cyclopedia of Representative Men of Maryland and the District of Columbia* (Baltimore, 1879), p. 417.

25. Richard H. Townsend's Diary, which he kept meticulously over many decades of the 1800's, is an invaluable source of information for the economic and political life of Baltimore, especially related to the Society of Friends. It is found in the Maryland Room of the Enoch Pratt Free Library.

26. MS Townsend Diary, vol. II, p. 608.

27. MS Liber 1, Trustees of the Sheppard Asylum, June 23, 1853, p. 1. Trustee's Records, SEPH.

28. MS Liber 1, Trustees of the Sheppard Asylum, pp. 8, 9.

29. *An Historical Sketch of the First National Bank of Baltimore, 50th Anniversary, 1864-1914; op. cit.,* ref. 24, pp. 442-443. J. Saurin Norris married Henrietta, the daughter of Isaac Tyson.

30. *Ibid.,* pp. 498-499.

31. MS Thomas, MS, pp. 82, 147. In addition to reports from such establishments as *The Retreat* in York, England; *The Pennsylvania Hospital, The Friends Hospital, The McLean Asylum, The Hartford Retreat,* and *Worcester State Hospital,* MS had ground plans of several asylums.

32. MS Memo Richard H. Townsend, February 1, 1857, Trustee's Records, SEPH.

33. Thomas, *Moses Sheppard,* p. 97.

34. Dorothy L. Dix to MS, April 21, 1852, FHL.

35. Letter of Dr. Richard S. Steuart, *The Baltimore American*, November 1, 1853. Scrapbook of MS, FHL.

36. MS to Dr. R. S. Steuart, November 1, 1853, FHL.

37. MS Moses Sheppard to the Trustees, 1856 and 1857. Records of the Trustees, SEPH.

38. MS to Richard H. Townsend, September 22, 1856, FHL.

39. MS Reminiscences of Gerard H. Reese, Trustee's Records.

40. *Ibid.*

41. MS Papers of David M. Perine, Trustee's Records.

42. MS Reminiscences of Gerard H. Reese, January 1897, Trustee's Records.

43. *Op. cit.*, ref. 39.

44. *Op. cit.*, ref. 41, SEPH.

45. *Op. cit.*, ref. 42, SEPH.

46. J. Saurin Norris, MS Biographical Sketch of the Late MS, Trustee's Records, SEPH.

47. *Ibid.*

48. *Ibid.*

49. Dr. Richard S. Steuart to MS, June 26, 1853, FHL.

50. *Ibid.*

51. *Ibid.*

52. Dr. Thomas Kirkbride to Dr. Nathan Shoemaker, Moses Sheppard's Scrapbook, FHL.

XIV: THE CLOSING MONTHS

1. Edward N. Brush, MD, The Sheppard and Enoch Pratt Hospital, *The Institutional Care of the Insane in the United States and Canada* (Baltimore, 1916), vol. II, p. 559.

2. John M. Galt, MD, to MS, June 1, 1853, *The Institutional Care of the Insane*, vol. II, 660 insert.

3. Dr. Nathan Shoemaker to MS, July 18, 1853, FHL.

4. MS to John Bigelow, June 7, 1853, FHL.

5. MS to Benjamin F. Taylor, November 24, 1853, FHL.

6. Abijah Hall to MS, June 8, 1853, FHL.

7. C. R. Reese to MS, June 11, 1853, MS's scrapbook, FHL.

8. Henry Higgins to MS, scrapbook, FHL.

9. Harriet M. Keller to MS, June 20, 1853, FHL.

10. Marion R. Voochers to MS, June 25, 1853, scrapbook, FHL.

11. Aaron Davis to MS, June 24, 1853, scrapbook, FHL.

12. Mrs. A. West to MS, July 2, 1853, scrapbook, FHL.

13. Mrs. M. E. Downing to MS, November 19, 1856, FHL.

14. Solomon Franklin to MS, June 29, 1853, scrapbook, FHL.

15. Charlotte D. Steele to MS, July 4, 1853, FHL.

16. *Ibid.*

17. Samuel Wiley to MS, July 16, 1853, scrapbook, FHL.

18. Clarkson C. Sheppard to MS, November 2, 1853, FHL.

19. MS to Samuel Sheppard, December 10 and 14, 1853, FHL.

20. MS to Clarkson C. Sheppard, December 8, 1853, FHL.

21. Miss Carroll to MS, July 5, 1853, scrapbook, FHL.

22. John M. Dickey to MS, February 27, 1857; March 16, 1857, scrapbook, FHL.

23. Elmira Stowe to MS, September 18, 1853, scrapbook, FHL.

24. *Ibid.*, February 19, 1854, scrapbook, F.H.L.

25. John Jackson to Richard Townsend, no date, FHL.

26. John Jackson to MS, February 18, 1852, FHL.

27. MS to John Jackson, May 10, 1853 F.H.L.

28. *Ibid.*, January 28, 1852, FHL.

29. Dr. Samuel F. McGill to MS, May 26, 1853, FHL.

30. *Ibid.*, July 10, 1852, FHL. Moses Sheppard remembered other young people. Benjamin Taylor wrote, "My daughter is truly grateful for your kind Christmas present, she desires me to present her cordial and sincere thanks." January 30, 1855, FHL. Mrs. Russwurm thanked Sheppard for a silver thimble given to her daughter at Cape Palmas.

31. The list of gifts received in Liberia from Moses Sheppard did not diminish. For example: Fifteen dollars worth of clothing to Thomas H. Gross, July 15, 1851; seeds to Dr. Fletcher, and books, July 18, 1851, and January 7, 1852; clothing and garden seeds to John Stewart, April 28, 1852; two grind stones to William Cassell, April 31, 1852, and clothing in March 25, 1853 and August 1853; tools and books to Dr. McGill in July, 1852; sheeting to Thomas Gross, August, 1852; two grindstones to Allen Dorsey, November 20, 1852; two grindstones to A. F. John, September 10, 1853; a trunk full of books from Sheppard and Isaac Tyson for the Lyceum at Cape Palmas, January 30, 1854; chest of articles for Dr. McGill, June 30, 1854; a double bladed knife with silver handle inscribed "Moses Sheppard of Baltimore to Samuel F. McGill of Cape Palmas," January 28, 1854, FHL. The new Lieutenant Governor of

Maryland in Liberia thanked Sheppard for books received on government, and wrote, "I would be happy to receive others, as we are almost destitute, to lay the foundation of such a library as the Republic shall ultimately need. If not imposing too much, I beg you would procure them . . . from good friends in Baltimore . . . standard works of Law . . . for reference . . . or other books you think would enlighten our minds or illustrate the principles of self-government." November 1, 1856, FHL. The official added, "As you are, as I have been informed by the history of the Colony and others, a true and faithful friend of the Colony." Georgian Williams wrote to Moses Sheppard, "Thank you for your many acts of kindness during my sojourn in Baltimore previous to my departure for Liberia." Georgian Williams to MS, August 19, 1854, FHL.

32. MS to Anthony Wood, July 20, 1852, FHL.

33. MS to Isaac Tyson, July, 1853, FHL.

34. MS to Dr. Samuel F. McGill, January 24, 1854, FHL.

35. Address, John H. B. Latrobe before the House of Representatives, January 21, 1862. Repeated from an address given before the Massachusetts Colonization Society, May 25, 1853. In substance contained in a letter from Latrobe to Sheppard, February 10, 1851, FHL.

36. John H. B. Latrobe to MS, February 10, 1851, FHL.

37. MS Moses Sheppard, Colonization in Africa, FHL.

38. MS to Dr. Samuel F. McGill, 1854, FHL. Sheppard wrote, "Colonization is a very simple thing, it is an attempt to benefit a few now, in the hope that it may hereafter be beneficial to many, it is not necessarily connected with the slave question, it is preparing an asylum for the oppressed as Penn and the Pilgrims sought." MS to Dr. Samuel F. McGill, May, 1851, FHL. In answer to the question as to the next political step Maryland in Liberia should take, Sheppard wrote, "The highest attribute of freedom, is right of choice civil and political." [In Cape Palmas] the Negroes "are placed in a favorable position to test the long contested question of their ability to exercise that right. I know of no other spot on earth, on which the black man is, in every sense, free and civilized." Sheppard to Dr. Fletcher, March 28, 1853, FHL.

39. MS Indian Affairs Committee, October 14, 1855, FHL.

40. *Ibid.*, October 15, 1855, FHL.

41. Hamilton Owens, *Baltimore on the Chesapeake* (Garden City, New York, 1941), p. 261.

42. Samuel Eliot Morison, *The Oxford History of the American People* (New York, 1965), pp. 590-591.

43. Owens, *Baltimore,* pp. 166-270; Morison, *American People,* pp. 550-91. Massachusetts was the only other State carried in the election of 1856 by the Know-Nothing Party. One result of the riots in Baltimore was that in Baltimore the city police were placed under State control, where they have remained ever since.

44. MS Diary, Richard H. Townsend, vol. II, p. 725, Enoch Pratt Free Library.

45. *Op. cit.,* ref. 42, p. 575.

46. *Ibid.,* pp. 588-589.

47. Thomas E. Drake, *Quakers and Slavery in America* (New Haven, 1950), p. 190.

48. *Ibid.,* p. 192.

49. MS Min BYM, 1854, FHL.

50. *Op. cit.,* ref. 48. Edwin and Barclay Coppoc, Quaker boys from Iowa, went with John Brown to Harpers Ferry; Barclay escaped and Edwin was hanged with John Brown.

51. Carl Sandburg, *Abraham Lincoln* (New York, 1954), p. 119. Morison, *American People,* p. 595. "As the shadow of war crept over the land, paralysis gripped the Society of Friends. . . . No right opening appeared. . . . When the Civil War came, many young Quakers enlisted in the Northern armies. They went as individuals. . . . Nor did the Quaker boys who went to war suffer disownment automatically . . . as in the Revolutionary War, or 1812, and the Mexican War. . . . No Meeting could bring itself to be too strict with its young men, who compromised one Quaker principle in order to fight for another." *Op. cit.,* ref. 48, pp. 193, 197.

52. *Op. cit.,* ref. 29, April 25, 1853, FHL.

53. *Ibid.*

54. Dr. Hall brought the oil portrait of MS to Monrovia for Dr. McGill. McGill wrote, "When my eyes caught sight of your portrait in oil which had been taken from its case and stood in the room, thus bringing together the two individuals towards whom I have constantly felt the strongest attachment, events running through the last twenty years all passed rapidly

through my mind . . . produced feelings of intense gratitude."
Ibid., March 18, 1856, FHL.

55. Benjamin F. Taylor to MS, October 7, 1856, FHL. One
copy of the portrait went to the Pennsylvania Colonization
Society; one copy hangs in the SEPH. A copy of the charcoal
drawing of MS, the best likeness, is in the Hospital. When Dr.
Nathan Shoemaker received his copy he wrote, "I acknowledge
the reception of an excellent likeness of my esteemed friend,
Moses Sheppard, and fully appreciate the kind feeling which
prompted the present. I often gaze at it with pleasure, and can
almost imagine I am holding converse with him." Dr. Nathan
Shoemaker to Moses Sheppard, January 22, 1856, FHL.

56. *Op. cit.,* ref. 29, May 16, 1854, FHL.

57. *Ibid.*

58. *Ibid.,* May 6, 1856, FHL.

59. *Ibid.,* December 6, 1856, FHL.

60. Dr. Dempsey R. Fletcher to MS, March 2, 1856, FHL.

61. MS Trustees Minutes Sheppard Asylum, Lib. 1, p. 11,
December 22, 1856, SEPH.

62. Benjamin F. Taylor to Richard Townsend, November
15, 1856, FHL.

63. MS Nathan Sheppard's Notes, FHL. Also Thomas, Moses
Sheppard, 1775-1857, Humanitarian, pp. 118-119. Trustee's Records, SEPH.

64. *Ibid.*

65. *Ibid.*

66. *Ibid.*

67. *Ibid.*

68. Reminiscences of Isaac Tyson, Trustee's Papers, SEPH.

69. *Op. cit.,* ref. 44, pp. 732-735.

70. *Ibid.,* p. 735.

71. In 1843 a group of Baltimore business men including
several Quakers, among whom was MS, formed a corporation
to purchase the Robert Oliver Estate for a Cemetery. The location was on a knoll at what is now North Avenue (then Boundary
Avenue) and York Road. Moses Sheppard bought four lots for
four hundred dollars, and was buried in the center of the plot.
Sheppard never gave any information as to why he was not buried
in the Friends Cemetery on the Harford Road. MS to Thomas
Ellicott, May 10, 1843; November 19, 1843, FHL.; *op. cit.,* ref. 44,
p. 735; Thomas, *Moses Sheppard,* p. 119.

72. *Ibid.,* p. 732.

73. The editor of the *Baltimore Patriot* wrote of Sheppard's gift, "It is doubtful if any other branch of benevolence would have contributed so much towards the alleviation of human suffering. . . ." *Baltimore Patriot,* March 7, 1857.

74. The *Baltimore American* wrote of Moses Sheppard, "He brought to the city a strong natural understanding; great decision of character; untiring patience, and an indomitable will. One thing he was resolved on, and that was success in the sphere of action he had chosen for himself." *Baltimore American,* February 2, 1857.

75. *The Baltimore Sun,* March 6, 1857.

XV: EPILOGUE: SHADOWS CAST BEFORE

1. MS Min Trustees of the Sheppard Asylum, February 21, 1857, Lib. 1, pp. 13-15. Trustee's Records, SEPH.

2. Will of Moses Sheppard, Trustee's Records. The fourth section of the will directed, "I give and bequeath to my friend, Isaac Tyson, son of Elisha Tyson, deceased, One Thousand Dollars, and in addition thereto, I also hereby release and exonerate the said Isaac Tyson from all and every debt or claim, which he may owe or appear to owe me, at the time of my decease." David M. Perine and Richard H. Townsend were named as Executors of the Will.

3. Richard Townsend took over the care of the two servants, Eveline Scott and George Barton. He kept a careful record of monies spent for this purpose. The record for March, 1857, for example, was:

March	1	Market	$ .50	March 12	Market	$ .75
do	5	do	.75	do 16	do	.75
do	9	do	.50	do 19	do	.75
do	10	Milk	.69	do 23	do	.75
do	11	Bacon	6.27	do 26	do	.75
do		Market	.75	do 30	do	.75

Wages of $5.00 were paid to Eveline Scott for the month, and George Barton received $6.00. During the month a bill of $24.11 for groceries was also paid, as well as a gas bill of $2.70, coal for $3.35, and wood for $4.00. A chimney sweep received $.12.

299

4. MS Memorandum to the Trustees, January 16, 1855; October 10, 1856. Trustee's Records.

5. MS Min Trustees, December 24, 1857, Lib. 1, p. 17.

6. MS Report to the Governor, April 22, 1858, Book 1, pp. 11, 12. Trustee's Records.

7. *Op. cit.*, ref. 5, p. 22.

8. *Ibid.*, November 21, 1861, Lib. 1, p. 61.

9. MS Lavens M. Thomas, 2nd, MS, 1775-1857, Humanitarian, Trustee's Records, SEPH, p. 136. MS Memorandum, David M. Perine, Trustee's Records.

10. MS Diary, Richard H. Townsend, vol. II. Enoch Pratt Free Library, Baltimore; MS Min Trustees, November 8, 1858, Lib. 1, p. 41.

11. *Op. cit.*, ref. 5, May 18, 1858, Lib. 1, p. 31; Richard Townsend recorded in his Diary that forty-nine farms were offered for sale. Also *ibid.*, September 8, 1859, Lib. 1, p. 38.

12. Purchases of land by the Sheppard Asylum Trustees were as follows: From Rachel R. Brown, July, 1858, 340.5 acres; from Rebecca Bowen, November, 1858, 22.82 acres; from Edward Sweeney, September, 1859, 2.49 acres; from Edward Sweeney, March, 1851, 10.42 acres. In the 1900's an additional 87.745 acres were purchased by the Trustees. MS Land Area SEPH. Trustees Records.

13. *Op. cit.*, ref. 5, June 9, 1859, Lib. 1, pp. 48-50; December 30, 1859, Lib. 1, p. 51.

14. *Ibid.*, pp. 48-50.

15. *Ibid.*, July 6, 1858, Lib. 1, pp. 34-36; May 5, 1873, Lib. 1, p. 98. MS Report to the Governor, December 30, 1859, Book 1, p. 77.

16. *Ibid.*, May 2, 1859, Lib. 1, p. 46. A lake was also dug. MS Report to the Governor, December 30, 1859, Book 1, p. 77. In 1860, a total of 686, 287 bricks were baked in the kilns on the grounds. MS Report to the Governor, May, 1860, Book 1, p. 93.

17. MS Report to the Governor, May 6, 1861, Book 1, p. 59.

18. *Op. cit.*, ref. 5, May 6, 1861, p. 60.

19. *Op. cit.*, ref. 17, January 6, 1862, Book 1, p. 123.

20. "The first stone of the Sheppard Asylum, western division, was laid by Daniel Shesley (a workman for Isaac Crother), a stone mason, at the SW corner . . . on the 30th day

of June, 1862." On a page pasted into the Trustees book, Lib. 1, p. 1, is the statement that, "The first stone of the Eastern Division was laid by the same (then working on his own account), at the SE corner, May 8th, 1871. The first brick of the Western Division, was laid by Henry Bargar, then in the employ of his Uncle, Decter Bargar, on the 25th of July, 1862. The last brick on the Exterior Wall of the Sheppard Asylum (being the top of the chimney of the Eastern Division), was laid by the same man (the Superintendent of masonry), on the 17th day of September, 1879."

21. *Op. cit.,* ref. 17, January 1, 1864. In the Report of January, 1865, the Trustees said, "That in adhering to the policy heretofor pursued of not allowing expenditures materially to exceed the income, they have during the year just ended, not been enabled to prosecute the erection of buildings, to the same extent. . . ."

22. Thomas, *Moses Sheppard,* p. 137. Over thirty springs were located on the grounds, with a capacity of one million gallons. Bricks were baked at a cost of $1 per thousand. *Op. cit.,* ref. 5, September 11, 1866, p. 77.

23. *Op. cit,* ref. 17, January 3, 1870, Book 1, p. 200.

24. *Ibid.,* January 3, 1871, Book 1, p. 271.

25. *Ibid.,* January 7, 1878, Book 1, p. 318. On several occasions, as in the Report to the Governor of 1868, mention was made that the Trustees had spent more than their income, and would curtail work the following year.

26. David M. Perine wrote, "Being now in my eighty-second year . . . infirmities render me unable to attend to the duties of a Trustee [I tender] my resignation. Having been connected with this Institution from the beginning, having suggested the Charter to its benevolent Founder, I have felt and shall continue to feel, a deep interest in its prosperity and success, and with my best wishes, for each member of the Board . . . ." *Op. cit.,* ref. 5, May 6, 1878, Lib. 1, p. 112. David Perine's son, E. Glenn Perine, was elected to take his father's place on the Board.

27. The Board resolved, "that in the death of Richard H. Townsend . . . we mourn the loss of one of the original Corporation . . . selected by Moses Sheppard . . . who since the organization of the Board acted as Secretary. . . ." *Op. cit.,* ref. 5, April 11, 1879, Lib. 1, p. 119.

28. The Board wrote to the family, "An esteemed, active, and useful member of the trust committed to our care." *Ibid.*, September 4, 1897, Lib. 1, p. 122.

29. *Ibid.*, December 30, 1882, Lib. 1, p. 146.

30. *Op. cit.*, ref. 17, January 3, 1883, Book 2, p. 83. The stone house towards the eastern entrance of the grounds was named the Norris Cottage in honor of the second President. *Op. cit.*, ref. 5, December 27, 1894.

31. *Ibid.*, January 3, 1883, Book 2, p. 83.

32. *Op. cit.*, ref. 5, January 28, 1891, Lib. 1, p. 232. Dr. Brush, on commencing his work, was paid an honorarium of $3,000 per year, provided with suitable quarters for himself and family, with maintenance and servants. A horse and carriage was placed at his disposal. *Ibid.*, February 1, 1891, Lib. 1, p. 234. Dr. Brush served with great distinction until 1920.

33. *Op. cit.*, ref. 17, December 30, 1891, Book 2, p. 292.

34. Letter signed A.P.S. *Baltimore Sun,* February 24, 1888.

35. Thomas, *Moses Sheppard,* p. 138.

36. Physicians from the city and county visited the Asylum, and the Association of Medical Superintendents for the Insane came to the Sheppard for an inspection on April 28, 1891. The Trustees were forced to borrow $60,000 in 1891-92 to finish the current work on the buildings, and the first year's operation showed a loss of $701.91. *Op. cit.*, ref. 5, March 24, 1892, Lib. 1, p. 242. Reports to the Governor 1895, 1896, 1897.

37. *Op. cit.*, ref. 5, June 24, 1881, Lib. 1, pp. 139-40.

38. Francis F. Beirne, *The Amiable Baltimoreans* (New York, 1951), pp. 51-55.

39. Henry M. Hurd, MD, ed., *The Institutional Care of the Insane in the United States and Canada* (Baltimore, 1916), vol. II, p. 564.

40. *Ibid.*

41. The Estate was given "without limitation and unclogged by any trust," *op. cit.*, ref. 5, December 29, 1898, Lib. 1, p. 323. "To broaden the work of the Institution and to enable it to extend its benefits to a larger number of afflicted [people] of limited means than it could under the Sheppard estate alone. . . . The trust unfettered." Both interest and income could be expended, but the Trustees resolved to use only the income, as was done with the Sheppard estate. Further, the Trustees did

not feel it necessary to build a new building, but did plan to finish part of the existing structures not yet completed. "A considerable number of additional inmates, nearly one-third more, can be provided for and supported mainly from the income at low rates, or free, without great delay." *Ibid.*, December 17 and 28, 1896; November 30, 1898, and December 29, 1898. The estate was appraised at $1,192,151.13. Taxes were $5,060.38, court costs $121,460.58.

42. *Op. cit.*, ref. 5, February 11, 1897, Lib. 1, January 28, 1897.

43. E. Glenn Perine to Joseph Grape, Secretary, January 28, 1897; February 13, 1897, FHL.

44. *Baltimore Patriot,* March 7, 1857.

Index

Index

Index

311

Index

61, 62, 78, 152, 161, 194, 243, 268, 299

Tyson, Henrietta, 81

Tyson, Isaac, 33, 35, 46, 49, 50, 52, 78, 81, 112, 194, 195, 237, 246, 249, 289, 293, 295, 296, 298, 299

Tyson, Isaac, Jr., 41

Tyson, Nathan S., 189, 190, 288

Two-guns, Harry, 125, 127, 276

Union, dissolution of, 180, 286

Union Manufacturing Company, 38, 43

Unitarianism, 82

United Brethren Church, 82, 271

United States, territorial expansion, 41, 101; economy in 1850's, 178-179

University of Pennsylvania Medical School, 280

Van Buren, Martin, 114, 115, 173

Vaux, Charles, 253

Voice from the South, A, 284

Voochers, Marion, 294

Waggoner, Madeline S., 276

Walker, Kenneth O., 16

War of 1812, Quakers excused from serving in, 39; commerce after, 40; privateers, 40; Quaker

view of, 55, 57; Indians in, 58

Warden, Benjamin, 73

Washington College, 280

Washington, George, 96, 123, 273

Webster, Daniel, 162

Weld, Isaac, 264

West, A., 295

Wever, Casper, 274

Whan, T. A., 281

Wheeling, West Virginia, 110, 177, 274

Whig Party, 173-174, 181

White, Willoughby, 140, 278

Whittier, John Greenleaf, 169, 172, 269

Wilbur, John, 89

Wiley, Samuel, 295

Williams, Georgian, 296

Wirt, Catherine, 273

Wirt, William, 97, 273

Wood, Anthony, 183, 185, 287

Worcester State Hospital for the Insane, 210, 213, 292, 293

Worthington, John, 43, 266

York, Pennsylvania, 274

York Retreat, 207-208, 209, 210, 216, 291, 293

Young Chief, 126

Young Men's Colonization Society, 145, 149